THE ETHICS OF DESTRUCTION

This book is a volume in the series
Cornell Studies in Security Affairs
edited by Robert J. Art, Robert Jervis, *and* Stephen M. Walt.
A complete listing appears at the end of the book.

The Ethics of Destruction

Norms and Force in
International Relations

WARD THOMAS

CORNELL UNIVERSITY PRESS

ITHACA AND LONDON

First published 2001 by Cornell University Press

First printing, Cornell Paperbacks, 2001

Printed in the United States of America

Library of Congress Cataloging-in-Publication Data

Thomas, Ward, b. 1963
    The ethics of destruction : norms and force in international relations / Ward Thomas.
       p. cm.—(Cornell studies in security affairs)
    Includes bibliographical references and index.
    ISBN 0-8014-3819-5 (cloth : alk. paper)—ISBN 0-8014-8741-2 (pbk. : alk. paper)
       1. International relations—Moral and ethical aspects.   2. Political ethics.   I. Title.   II. Series.
    JZ1306 .T48 2000
    172'.4—dc21

                                                                    2001000054

Cornell University Press strives to use environmentally responsible suppliers and materials to the fullest extent possible in the publishing of its books. Such materials include vegetable-based, low-VOC inks, and acid-free papers that are recycled, totally chlorine-free, or partly composed of nonwood fibers. Books that bear the logo of the FSC (Forest Stewardship Council) use paper taken from forests that have been inspected and certified as meeting the highest standards for environmental and social responsibility. For further information, visit our website at www.cornellpress.cornell.edu.

Cloth printing   10   9   8   7   6   5   4   3   2   1
Paperback printing   10   9   8   7   6   5   4   3   2   1

FSC   FSC Trademark © 1996 Forest Stewardship Council A.C.
SW-COC-098

To my wife, Kari

Contents

Acknowledgments

Anyone who has written a book (or who has spent time around someone writing a book) knows that despite the countless hours of solitary work involved, it is in many important respects a collective effort. In writing this book I was assisted and influenced by many people. I was extremely fortunate to have the advice of Steven David of Johns Hopkins University. His firm but patient and sympathetic guidance through crises of both confidence and concept will always be appreciated. I also thank Eliot Cohen at Hopkins's School of Advanced International Studies. His encyclopedic knowledge of strategic studies was a source of wonder; as important was his insistence on careful and rigorous scholarship. I am grateful, too, to Kenneth Thompson, whose influence on my career as a scholar has been considerable and whose example remains inspiring.

I thank the many teachers, colleagues, and friends who read and commented on various parts of the book, including Thomas Berger, Martha Bishai, Nora Bensahel, Timothy Crawford, Michael Desch, John Dietrich, Andrew Erdmann, Siba Grovogui, Anthony Lang, James Marino, Tracy Melton, Susan Peterson, Ivan Toft, Monica Toft, Herb Wilgis, and two anonymous reviewers. Elizabeth Kier, Stephen Kocs, and Jonathan Mercer each read the entire manuscript and offered thoughtful and detailed suggestions; they also supplied valued words of encouragement. Among the many extraordinarily helpful people at Cornell University Press, Teresa Jesionowski and David Capello substantially improved the manuscript with their careful and diligent editing, while Roger Haydon provided insightful editorial judgment and patiently indulged endless questions about the publishing process.

I am grateful for the generous support provided at various stages of this project by the Department of Political Science and the Office of the Dean of the School of Arts and Sciences at Johns Hopkins University, the Institute for the Study of World Politics, the College of the Holy Cross, and the John M. Olin Institute for Strategic Studies, where in 1998–1999 I was a postdoctoral fellow. My time at the Olin Institute was

Acknowledgments

both intellectually and personally enriching, and I am indebted to Samuel Huntington and Steven Rosen for affording me the opportunity to spend the year there. I also thank participants in Olin's National Security Seminar, as well as the William and Mary Government Department Faculty Colloquium, at which I presented earlier versions of the project.

I also thank my students at Johns Hopkins and Holy Cross, especially in my Ethics and International Relations courses at Holy Cross. I have benefited immensely from spirited and thoughtful dialogue with these young men and women.

My deepest gratitude is to my family. My parents instilled in me a love of learning and sacrificed to allow me to pursue it. My sons, Jack and Patrick, have been a source of great joy and welcome perspective. Finally, I dedicate this book to my wife, Kari, with appreciation for her limitless patience, support, and inspiration.

WARD THOMAS

Worcester, Massachusetts

THE ETHICS OF DESTRUCTION

CHAPTER 1

Ethics, Norms, and the Study of International Relations

> Attached to force are certain self-imposed, imperceptible limitations hardly worth mentioning, known as international law and custom, but they scarcely weaken it. . . . To introduce the principle of moderation into the theory of war itself would always lead to logical absurdity.
>
> Carl von Clausewitz, *On War*

The central premise of this book is that Clausewitz was wrong: moderation is not alien to war, and the self-imposed limitations of international law and custom are not "imperceptible" but in fact are often crucial to determining how and when force is used in international relations. This argument is not novel; indeed, much of the work of international lawyers, ethicists, and theologians has been predicated on the idea that not only is restraint possible but it can be based on moral grounds. Nevertheless, this idea has typically been subordinated to the purportedly more sober and mature view that when it comes to the rough-and-tumble world of international politics, and especially in war, anything goes. The idea was most famously and pithily expressed by General William Tecumseh Sherman: "War is hell." The unspoken implication behind Sherman's maxim, of course, is that in war, as in hell, there is no order, only chaos; no mercy, only cruelty; no restraint, only suffering.

No one can deny that war is a humanitarian nightmare, with horrors incomprehensible to any who have not experienced them. Nevertheless, the "anything goes" view is demonstrably incorrect. It does not accurately reflect how most people think and talk about the use of force in international relations, and in all but the most extreme cases neither does it accurately describe the way national leaders actually use force. We cannot understand the actions of states in conflict with one another—whether in Kosovo or the Persian Gulf in the 1990s, or even Europe in the 1940s—unless we depart from this assumption. As the case studies in this book will show, the use of force in international relations is regularly affected by common understandings about what is ethically acceptable and unacceptable. Moreover, military professionals themselves are by no means exempt from such sensibilities; indeed, it is they who are most keenly aware of the role played by custom and convention in restraining the conduct of war. It is worth noting that Sherman himself, even as his troops laid waste to the South, indignantly condemned the Confederates' use of hidden land mines as "not war, but murder."[1]

There are several reasons why, in the analysis of international politics, ethical norms have not been given their due. One is the presence of puzzling anomalies: even when ostensibly moral considerations place limits on the use of force, the results do not always seem to make sense in moral terms. Many commentators have noted, for example, that norms against assassination and the personal targeting of foreign leaders and ruling elites often necessitate large-scale uses of force or crippling economic sanctions that have grievous effects upon large numbers of innocent people while the offending despots suffer little.[2] The laws of war in general present similar anomalies. While certain means of killing enemy soldiers in wartime are forbidden, equally ghastly means are time-honored. As both Richard Price and Jeffrey Legro have pointed out, there are strong norms against the use of poison gas and other chemical weapons but no similar restrictions on many other types of weapons that are arguably no more humane or militarily effective.[3] Neither the spe-

---

[1] William T. Sherman, *Memoirs of General William T. Sherman*, vol. 2 (New York: D. Appleton and Company, 1875), p. 194.

[2] See, e.g., Ralph Peters, "A Revolution in Military Ethics?" *Parameters* 26, no. 2 (Summer 1996): 102–8; Albert C. Pierce, "Just War Principles and Economic Sanctions," *Ethics and International Affairs* 10 (1996): 99–113; Robert F. Turner, "Killing Saddam: Would It Be a Crime?" *Washington Post*, October 7, 1990, pp. D1–2.

[3] Richard Price, "A Genealogy of the Chemical Weapons Taboo," *International Organization* 49, no. 1 (Winter 1995): 79; Jeffrey Legro, "Which Norms Matter? Revisiting the 'Failure' of Internationalism in World War II" (paper presented at the annual conference of the American Political Science Association, Chicago, August 31–September 3, 1995), p. 7.

cific content of certain norms nor the extent to which some are adhered to while others are violated, they point out, can be readily explained by reference to the moral precepts that underlie them. Such anomalies have led some to conclude that moral considerations themselves are relatively unimportant to norms governing the use of force, which are merely "habits that have come to pass for ethics."[4]

Another problem is found in the set of analytical tools available for examining how ethical norms work in international politics. Indeed, most theoretical approaches to norms only reinforce the confusion. Mainstream theories of international relations have a difficult time accounting for norms, particularly norms with ethical content, because their underlying theoretical assumptions simply do not accommodate them. Both neorealism and neoliberalism proceed from the premises of rationalism, in which egoistic actors instrumentally pursue interests taken to be stable and logically prior to interactions with other actors; and materialism, in which ideas, such as normative beliefs, are of only derivative importance compared to more concrete and tangible causes, such as the distribution of power in the international system. These theoretical premises not only define ethics out of the equation from the start but also tie theory to a stark and one-dimensional view of power. The result is a flawed understanding of both the role of normative factors in foreign policy and the ways in which power and interest shape the international system. A more nuanced and flexible approach is required in order to take norms seriously, as well as to fully understand the elusiveness of abstract moral judgments in the political sphere.

This book takes the position that moral principles are fundamentally important to understanding norms governing the use of force, although they are seldom applied in their unadulterated form. This is because norms are products of political processes and therefore cannot be divorced from considerations of power and interest, which often distort—but do not obliterate—moral principles. Nevertheless, norms are neither merely epiphenomenal reflections of power and interest nor aspirational statements of ideal behavior. Rather they can in their own right not only constrain states in how they pursue their interests but more fundamentally shape state interests themselves. Norms are both products of power and sources of power in the international system. Instead of viewing ethical norms and state interests as distinct and competing phenomena, therefore, I examine the manner in which each

[4] Peters, "A Revolution in Military Ethics?" p. 105.

3

shapes the formulation, development, and articulation of the other. In this way, I believe that it is possible to reconcile the existence of ethics and ethical norms with the goal of theorizing about international politics in structural terms.[5] In doing so, I hope to show that ethics are "embedded" in international relations in two senses: first, abstract moral principles are embedded in specific international norms governing the use of force; and second, these norms constitute part of the structure of the international system itself and thereby become embedded in state interests.

This chapter presents a brief survey of the problem of ethics and ethical norms in the study of international relations. It begins by examining the division in the discipline between international relations theory and international ethics and considers two types of attempts to bridge this gulf. I argue that although these efforts succeed as critiques of mainstream theory, they fail to challenge crucial theoretical assumptions that create the division in the first place. A second section follows in which I argue that norms restricting the use of force are useful points of departure for a study of ethics in international relations, and I consider several competing accounts of norms in the theoretical literature. Here, I examine some of the assumptions that render theories based on rationalist premises ill-suited to provide a satisfactory account of norms in the international system. Finally, I outline the components of a structural theory of ethical norms and discuss the concept of the international society. This notion, I argue, with its emphasis on shared normative understandings and common interests in rules and institutions, provides an indispensable framework for the systematic study of norms.

INTERNATIONAL RELATIONS THEORY AND INTERNATIONAL ETHICS

Ethics has not always been marginalized in the study of international relations. From at least as early as Thucydides through the Second World War, the problem of reconciling ethical principles with self-interested state behavior held a central place in international relations schol-

---

[5] Structure can be defined as "a set of constraining conditions which produce a gap between intention and outcome." David Sanders, "International Relations: Neo-realism and Neo-liberalism," in *A New Handbook of Political Science*, ed. Robert E. Goodin and Hans-Dieter Klingemann (New York: Oxford University Press, 1996), p. 430. In the context of international politics, therefore, structural theory is theory that ascribes primary significance to the structure of the international system as a determinant of outcomes.

arship. As Robert McElroy argues, however, two trends changed this focus in the decades following the war, particularly in the United States. The first was the ascendance of realist thought, with its emphasis on power and its dismissal of ethics as irrelevant to international politics. Realism's trenchant critique of the interwar focus on normative factors to the neglect of geopolitical realities set the tone for the debate over international ethics during the Cold War. The second trend was the influence of positivist thought on the social sciences, which led to the desire to produce analytically rigorous, "value-free" explanations of international politics.[6] These two trends were, moreover, mutually reinforcing. Positivist theories could only be built upon premises that greatly simplified state behavior—such as the realist assumption that states acted in a uniformly self-interested manner. The complementary nature of the two trends has, in effect, embedded the realist interpretation of state behavior in international relations theory. As a result, ethics has been, in McElroy's words, "banished to the periphery of the field,"[7] where it is presumably free to converse with history and philosophy without interfering in the business of building structural theories about what states actually do, as opposed to what they ought to do. Despite a revival of interest in international ethics since the end of the Cold War, a substantial gulf remains between dominant theories of international relations and those that seek to explore the ethical implications of state action.[8]

Various scholars have tried to bridge this disciplinary gap. The main point of contention has been the realist view, which is classically expressed by Hans Morgenthau: "The actions of states are determined not by moral principles and legal commitments but by considerations of interest and power. Moral principles and legal commitments may be invoked to justify a policy arrived at on other grounds . . . but they do not determine the choice among different courses of action."[9] Critiques

[6] Robert W. McElroy, *Morality and American Foreign Policy: The Role of Ethics in International Affairs* (Princeton: Princeton University Press, 1992), p. 3.

[7] Ibid.

[8] See, e.g., Charles W. Kegley, Jr., "The Neoidealist Moment in International Studies?: Realist Myths and the New International Realities," *International Studies Quarterly* 37 (1993): 131–46; and Steve Smith, "The Forty Years' Detour: The Resurgence of Normative Theory in International Relations," *Millennium* 21, no. 3 (1992): 489–502.

[9] Quoted in Robert J. Myers, "The Virtue of Moral Restraint," *International Journal* 43 (Spring 1988): 320.

of this view have generally followed one of two paths. The first, which could be called the "moralist" challenge, questions the empirical accuracy of realism, identifying examples of state behavior that cannot be explained solely by reference to self-interest but rather reflect the influence of moral concerns. David H. Lumsdaine, for example, argues that U.S. foreign aid policy serves humanitarian principles rather than strategic or material interests.[10] Similarly, David Welch challenges realism by asserting that national leaders often choose to go to war for normative reasons, including the desire to see justice done.[11] Robert McElroy likewise argues that leaders are often influenced by moral norms even if national interests dictate other policies.[12]

The second type of challenge, which could be called "theoretical," goes beyond empirical falsification to question the basic epistemological premises of realism and other mainstream theories. It holds that the analytical focus upon sovereign states in fact privileges and reifies a certain normative understanding of the proper mode of political organization to the exclusion of other possible modes that may entail different— and more expansive—notions of moral responsibility.[13] The result, it is claimed, is that the purportedly value-neutral conclusions of positivist international relations theory are in fact value-laden to their core, and that the practice of morality is arbitrarily "bounded" by state borders.[14] This theoretical challenge, then, contests the basic constitutive assumptions of state-centric theory, whereas the moralist challenge accepts these assumptions but denies that the anarchical structure of the international system constrains states to act only out of self-interest. Instead, it is argued, they are often motivated by more noble and altruistic impulses.

Both the moralist and the theoretical challenges provide powerful correctives to the systematic neglect of ethics in mainstream interna-

---

[10] David H. Lumsdaine, *Moral Vision in International Politics: The Foreign Aid Regime, 1949–1989* (Princeton: Princeton University Press, 1993).

[11] David A. Welch, *Justice and the Genesis of War* (Cambridge: Cambridge University Press, 1993).

[12] McElroy, *Morality and American Foreign Policy*, passim.

[13] See, e.g., Chris Brown, *International Relations Theory: New Normative Approaches* (New York: Columbia University Press, 1993); Robert H. Jackson, "Martin Wight, International Theory, and the Good Life," *Millennium* 19 (Summer 1990): 261–72; and Andrew Linklater, "The Problem of Community in International Relations," *Alternatives* 15 (Spring 1990): 135–53.

[14] Charles Beitz, "Bounded Morality: Justice and the State in World Politics," *International Organization* 33, no. 3 (Summer 1979): 405–24.

tional relations theory. Nevertheless, these gains are realized only at the cost of abandoning the benefits of structural theory. This is because one approach requires the assumption of state altruism, which makes theory-building difficult, while the other entirely redefines the parameters of the structure of the international system. Without dismissing the contributions of either approach, I propose to take a somewhat different tack. Taking structural theory on its own terms, I wish not only to identify ethical behavior in international politics but also to locate sources of such behavior within the structure of the international system itself, as well as in the state practices that are constrained and constituted by that structure.

International norms provide an ideal point of departure for such a project. Norms can be defined as "collective understandings of the proper behavior of actors."[15] A norm, therefore, contains elements of both *prescription*, characterizing certain behavior as "proper," and *description*, since arriving at "collective understandings" depends upon a certain amount of regularity of behavior among relevant actors. Norms that seek to restrict the use of force by states represent the intersection of explicitly normative concerns and more mainstream rationalist theories of conflict and cooperation. This is because they are international institutions aimed at directly influencing state action that also reflect moral judgments about appropriate and inappropriate means of conducting foreign policy.[16] As such, it would appear that focusing on norms would provide a valuable means of breaking down the disciplinary barriers between ethics and international relations theory. The recent proliferation of writings on norms and security, however, has only rarely made the ethical implications of norms its explicit focus.[17] More

[15] Legro, "Which Norms Matter?" p. 2.

[16] Robert Keohane defines institutions as "persistent and connected sets of rules (formal and informal) that prescribe behavioral roles, constrain activity, and shape expectations." *International Institutions and State Power: Essays in International Relations Theory* (Boulder: Westview Press, 1989), p. 3. Legro prefers a definition that omits reference to activity and expectations, rightly arguing that Keohane's definition assumes that institutions actually affect behavior, thereby preempting a significant debate in the literature. Jeffrey Legro, *Cooperation under Fire: Anglo-German Restraint during World War II* (Ithaca: Cornell University Press, 1995), p. 13 n. 30.

[17] Some exceptions are Martha Finnemore, *National Interests in International Society* (Ithaca: Cornell University Press, 1996), chap. 3; Richard Price, *The Chemical Weapons Taboo* (Ithaca: Cornell University Press, 1997); and Richard Price and Nina Tannenwald, "Norms and Deterrence: The Nuclear and Chemical Weapons Taboos," in *The Culture of National Security: Norms, Identities, and World Politics*, ed. Peter Katzenstein (New York: Columbia University Press, 1996), pp. 114–52. The ethical content of norms has been a

often, this work has sought to engage the rationalist literature on international institutions, which typically eschews an ethical orientation and concentrates instead on the instrumental importance of norms in creating and maintaining patterns of cooperation among states.[18] To understand why most work on international norms remains distinctly "non-normative," it will be helpful to review prevailing theoretical approaches.

NORMS IN INTERNATIONAL RELATIONS THEORY

The theory ascribing the least causal significance to norms is neorealism.[19] According to this familiar position, the actions of states are strongly constrained by the distribution of material power in the international system, and thus norms, where they exist, are merely the epiphenomenal reflections of that power structure. As such, they embody the interests of the strongest states in the system and will change as those interests change, or as the distribution of power within the system changes.[20] Rather than influencing policy, norms are at most convenient tools available to national leaders wishing to justify interest-driven behavior in moral terms. Compliance with norms, then, presents little puzzle at all for neorealism: strong states comply because norms prescribe action that they would take anyway; weak states comply if failure to do so would result in being subject to sanctions by strong states. In either case, it is power and interest doing the talking, not the norms themselves. Norms that limit the use of force present a "hard case" for critics of neorealist theory because they seek to constrain states under precisely the circumstances in which neorealism seems most apt—in

---

more common focus outside the realm of security studies. See, e.g., Audie Klotz, *Norms in International Relations: The Struggle against Apartheid* (Ithaca: Cornell University Press, 1995); Lumsdaine, *Moral Vision and International Politics;* and McElroy, *Morality and American Foreign Policy.*

[18] Among the important works in this tradition are Stephen D. Krasner, ed., *International Regimes* (Ithaca: Cornell University Press, 1983); Robert O. Keohane, *After Hegemony: Cooperation and Discord in the World Political Economy* (Princeton: Princeton University Press, 1984); and Keohane, *International Institutions and State Power.*

[19] I have chosen to deal here with neorealism, rather than realism more generally, for two reasons. First, neorealism proceeds from explicit and rigorously defined rationalist premises. Second, the range of positions associated with realism is so broad that it is prohibitively difficult to identify a definitive realist theory of norms.

[20] Kenneth Waltz, *Theory of International Politics* (Reading, Mass.: Addison-Wesley, 1979); John J. Mearsheimer, "The False Promise of International Institutions," *International Security* 19, no. 3 (Winter 1995): 5–49.

wartime or in defense of interests serious enough to warrant the use of force.[21] In such cases, according to neorealism, cooperation has failed, the stakes are high, and altruism, rare enough under ordinary conditions, could be self-destructive. Normative restraint under such circumstances constitutes a serious empirical anomaly for neorealism.

Neoliberal institutionalist theorists differ substantially from neorealists on the importance of norms in international politics. The crucial contention of neoliberal institutionalism, or neoliberalism, is that states gain more from cooperation than they do from discord. Therefore, it is in states' interests to create and maintain institutions, or "regimes," that facilitate cooperation on an ongoing basis. Because these regimes depend upon the predictability of interactions and reliable expectations about the behavior of others, states are required to sacrifice some freedom of action in order to maintain them. So even if greater short-term gain can be achieved by breaking regime rules in a particular circumstance, the long-term interest of the state in continued cooperation encourages compliance. An important difference between neorealism and neoliberalism, then, is the latter's more "sophisticated" and "complex" view of how interests are to be interpreted.[22] Norms are among the features of regimes that serve to regulate the behavior of actors so that mutually beneficial patterns of cooperation among them may continue. Examples include norms governing such trade practices as the setting of tariff rates or the dumping of underpriced products in foreign markets. Norms are, in this view, both products of and constraints upon state action, serving an essentially instrumental purpose.

Both of these accounts of norms suffer from some serious shortcomings. Neorealism, for example, cannot readily explain why norms exist at all—or why states, especially non-democratic states that are not answerable to public opinion, often go to great lengths to be seen as observing them. Moreover, neorealism seems to fly in the face of empirical evidence (such as that presented by Welch, Lumsdaine, and McElroy) that states are often influenced by moral concerns and not just narrowly defined self-interest, or that they often comply with norms even when it is not in their immediate interests to do so. Although it explains more than neorealism, the neoliberalist account of norms also remains incomplete. While providing a powerful explanation of the role of norms and

---

[21] Legro, "Which Norms Matter?" p. 1; Gary Goertz and Paul Diehl, "Toward a Theory of International Norms," *Journal of Conflict Resolution* 36 (1992): 635.

[22] Keohane, *After Hegemony*, pp. 63, 66.

regimes in solving coordination problems, it provides little guidance for understanding how norms influence behavior outside of cooperative contexts. This is a particular problem in dealing with norms on the use of force.[23] Furthermore, it does not account well for norms that reflect moral, as opposed to simply instrumental or functional, concerns.

Despite their differences, neorealism and neoliberalism are founded upon similar analytical premises. Both are state-centric structural theories: taking states as their basic units of theoretical analysis, they try to explain patterns of broadly convergent behavior by reference to the material structure of the international system. Moreover, both operate explicitly within the rational choice model.[24] Rational choice, or rationalist, theories make certain simplifying assumptions concerning human motivation in order to derive a "coherent and unified theoretical view of politics."[25] Several of these assumptions, however, create significant problems for the study of ethical norms. I will consider three of these assumptions in some detail.

Material Structures and Ideational Structures

Rationalist theories of international relations proceed from materialist premises, defining the structure of the international system in terms of the material capabilities of state actors. The distribution of these capabilities, it is argued, forms the basic causal framework by which the range of outcomes in the international system is determined.[26] Norms, as ideational phenomena, are left out of the structural picture. To materialists, "norms do not matter because they are mere words."[27] The problem is that this materialist orientation limits rationalist theories to too narrow a conception of power in international politics. The substance of

[23] Most neoliberal scholars generally concede that norms will be of much less consequence in security matters than in issue-areas defined by cooperation between states. See, e.g., David Baldwin, "Neoliberalism, Neorealism, and World Politics," in *Neorealism and Neoliberalism: The Contemporary Debate*, ed. Baldwin (New York: Columbia University Press, 1993); Keohane, *After Hegemony;* and Charles Lipson, "International Cooperation in Economic and Security Affairs," *World Politics* 37 (October 1984): 1–23.

[24] For detailed discussions of the rational choice premises of neorealism and neoliberalism, respectively, see Waltz, *Theory of International Politics,* passim; and Keohane, *After Hegemony,* chap. 5.

[25] Donald P. Green and Ian Shapiro, *Pathologies of Rational Choice Theory: A Critique of Applications in Political Science* (New Haven: Yale University Press, 1994), p. 1.

[26] Waltz, *Theory of International Politics,* pp. 92–96.

[27] Gary Goertz, *Contexts of International Politics* (Cambridge: Cambridge University Press, 1994), p. 237.

international politics is defined not only by material realities but by other factors as well, including intersubjectively held ideas and understandings about what constitutes appropriate behavior for states in the system. As Michael Barnett points out, each state is "embedded in an increasingly dense normative web that constrains its foreign policy in general and its use of force in particular."[28] Furthermore, as Barnett suggests, normative context is important not only in issue-areas commonly associated with humanitarianism and morality but in all facets of international politics, including the use of force. Military historian John Keegan has shown, for example, that the conduct of warfare itself is shot through with cultural and normative understandings that often take precedence over military effectiveness.[29] Similarly, Martin van Creveld argues that moral restrictions on war not only constrain states in the pursuit of their objectives but also serve to fundamentally define the nature of both warfare and the state system itself.[30]

What is important about the normative context of international politics,[31] however, is not only its role in constraining state power but also its potential as a source of power itself. States often influence outcomes in international politics by means other than military or economic might, and sometimes in a manner disproportionate to their material capabilities.[32] Clearly, therefore, state power is not strictly a function of material power any more than the power of important institutions in civil society is defined solely by their ability to physically coerce the citizenry. Instead, power relies upon a sense of legitimacy that, while seldom entirely independent of them, does not stem from material and coercive power alone. Indeed, normative and material factors are in constant

---

[28] Michael N. Barnett, "The United Nations and Global Security: The Norm Is Mightier than the Sword," *Ethics and International Affairs* 9 (1995):50.

[29] John Keegan, *A History of Warfare* (London: Hutchinson, 1993).

[30] Martin van Creveld, "The Persian Gulf Crisis of 1990–91 and the Future of Morally Constrained War," *Parameters* 22, no. 2 (Summer 1992): 37–38.

[31] This phrase, and the idea it represents, are featured prominently in Goertz, *Contexts of International Politics.*

[32] Barnett notes, for example, that Canada and the Scandinavian states "wield greater influence in world affairs than might be expected from their military power because of their close association with the values espoused by the international community and embodied in the United Nations." Barnett, "The United Nations and Global Security," pp. 49–50. See also Kenneth Forsberg, "Normative Principles and State Interests: Constructivism Illustrated" (paper presented at the meeting of the Northeast Political Science Association, Newark, N.J., November 3–5, 1995).

interaction in any political system, each shaping and limiting the other.[33] Consequently, the ability to influence outcomes in the international system is determined not only by military and economic strength but also by the power to shape the norms that govern dealings among states. Former U.S. Director of Central Intelligence Robert Gates argues, for example, that the much-maligned human rights policy of the Carter administration in fact helped to create norms that significantly undermined Soviet legitimacy in Eastern Europe and Afghanistan.[34] This type of influence is harder to measure in concrete terms such as tanks or GNP, but it is no less real. By limiting their focus only to material factors, rationalist theories neglect the ideational components of power and therefore provide an incomplete account of how power is manifested in the international system.[35]

Positivism, Norms, and Interests

A second feature of rationalist theory that creates problems for the study of norms is its adherence to a strict positivist methodological model. In order to generate broadly applicable theoretical propositions, rationalist social scientists emulate the methodology of the physical sciences, isolating causal forces (independent variables) in order to determine their effects on outcomes in the system. Of course, it is impossible to strictly control variables in the social sciences: many factors may influence the behavior of groups or individuals, and one cannot strip away extraneous influences as one might in a laboratory experiment. Consequently, the isolation of the independent variable in the social sciences is a simplifying assumption only. In rationalist international relations theory, the structure of the international system is an independent variable, while the behavior of states is a dependent variable. While it may be acknowledged that actors can and do shape or constitute structures in the real world, this empirical fact is held out of theory in the interests of parsimony and the isolation of causal relationships.[36] Power, for

[33] Francis Boyle notes that Morgenthau himself used to teach that "power endowed with legitimacy" was far more effective than naked power alone. Francis A. Boyle, "International Law and the Use of Force: Beyond Regime Theory," in *Ideas and Ideals: Essays on Politics in Honor of Stanley Hoffmann,* ed. Linda B. Miller and Michael J. Smith, (Boulder: Westview Press, 1993), p. 378.

[34] Robert M. Gates, *From the Shadows: The Ultimate Insider's Story of Five Presidents and How They Won the Cold War* (New York: Simon and Schuster, 1996), pp. 95–96.

[35] For an excellent explication of this point, see Finnemore, *National Interests in International Society,* chap. 1.

[36] Keohane, *After Hegemony,* pp. 30, 78.

example, is part of the independent variable; a cause, but not an effect. Similarly, rationalism takes the interests of states as either independent variables or fixed parameters in the causal equation, typically treating them as constant, unitary, and unproblematic.

Norms do not fit easily into this rigid scheme because they are complex phenomena. Insofar as they are shaped by the preferences of strong states, they can be reflections of both interests and the distribution of power and therefore seen as "effects" of the international structure. Because they also serve as important constraints on state action and sources of power, however, they are part of that structure itself and therefore act as "causes" as well. Moreover, as I will argue, norms can be internalized by states in such a way as to fundamentally change state interests. What is most interesting about international norms, in fact, is their recursive interaction with the interests of states and their complex relationship to power in the international system. Norms can be both dependent and independent variables, and to fully understand their impact in international politics it is necessary to take account of both sides of the equation.

Egoism, Altruism, and Ethics

Perhaps the most fundamental premise of rationalism is that actors (states, in international relations) are "rational egoists"—when confronted with options, actors choose the course of action that they think will maximize their own utility, without regard for the utility of others. The assumption of egoism means that actors look out for themselves, and are concerned with the good of others only to the extent that it affects their own interests.[37] This assumption arguably is required by the deductive logic of structural theory itself, and as such I have no quarrel with it. If behavior is to be deduced from structural constraints, actors must be assumed to be thinking in terms of their own interests; any other assumption would make the task of theory-building prohibitively complicated. As a result, a sharp theoretical line must be drawn between "egoism" and "altruism"—the latter term referring to concern for others for their own sake, not just as a by-product of concern for one's self. For the purposes of this inquiry, the important issue is how ethics fits into this dichotomy. Problems arise not from the assumption of egoism itself but from the derivative assumption that egoism is incompatible with ethical action, which is assumed to derive only from altruistic motives. As

[37] Ibid., p. 14.

Robert Keohane puts it, actions based upon moral principles can be considered "rational" in terms of fit between means and ends, but they violate the assumption of egoism in that the ends sought are defined by reference to the good of others, not one's own good.[38] According to this formulation, ethical action is that which, by definition, is not in one's interest to do. The result is a rigid theoretical dichotomy between ethics and self-interest, with ethical imperatives not only clearly distinct from, but antithetically opposed to, the interests of state actors.

I contend that this demarcation between interests and ethics is drawn too distinctly, and severely handicaps rationalist theories in understanding the influence of normative factors on foreign policy. The problems inherent in this view of ethics become apparent when one considers the issue of collective utility, or "common good." When an actor acts on behalf of the common good, she may sacrifice some measure of her own utility in order to enhance the collective utility of a larger whole of which she is a part. While she may on balance believe that she herself ultimately will be better off for having done so, she certainly believes that the whole to which she belongs will be better off. Such an action could reasonably be considered to be ethically praiseworthy, in that it is motivated not by reference only to one's own good but also by a sense of concern for the good of others. The prospect of some benefit accruing to the actor does not necessarily negate the action's ethical merit.[39] Actions for the common good present a classification problem for rationalist theory, however. Because of its stark dichotomy between egoism and altruism, rationalist theory is forced either to deny the ethical value of such actions or to ignore the fact that benefit to the common good entails some benefit for the actor as well.[40] What is not envisioned is the

---

[38] Ibid., pp. 74–75.

[39] For example, giving to charity remains praiseworthy notwithstanding the tax deduction one may claim for it.

[40] Keohane takes the latter course. He associates actions for the common good with ethics because he sees them as inconsistent with the assumption of egoism. *After Hegemony*, p. 75. This position can be partially attributed to the nature of Keohane's project in *After Hegemony*. Devising a rationalist explanation of regimes and norm compliance without "smuggling in" idealist assumptions requires Keohane to draw a clear line between egoism and the idealist notion that states can be motivated by a "common good." Keohane is therefore forced to assume that egoism stops and "ethics" starts at the point where the actor can reasonably expect to derive no benefit whatsoever from the action. It is not enough to show that the actor is sacrificing something of value or suffering some harm, because this sacrifice or harm may be recompensed or mitigated—even if not fully—by a benefit of some other sort. This, after all, is how Keohane characterizes compliance with regime rules, which he emphatically does not wish to ascribe to ethical impulses. The prob-

possibility that an action may be both ethical and also in the interests of the actor, however broadly these interests are defined. This has two important consequences. First, it imposes an unrealistic and unduly demanding criterion of moral assessment, holding states to a moral standard that in our everyday judgments we do not even apply to individuals in civil society. Second, because ethics and interests are seen as competing forces, ethical questions are, in effect, defined out of rationalist theory from the outset. Consequently, any actions based on moral grounds must be treated as anomalous acts of self-denial, external to structural theory. Ethical norms, therefore, are viewed as "variables" that "intervene" between exogenous state interests and action.[41] In effect, then, international politics becomes divided into geopolitical and normative spheres, one concerned with interest and power and the other with ethical goals[42]—a division that is only reinforced by the materialist orientation of rationalism. It is this narrow view of rational egoism, as much as any other assumption, that fundamentally handicaps rationalist theory in dealing with ethical norms in the international system.

The Moralist and Sociological Challenges

Critics have mounted two primary challenges to the rationalist approaches to norms. One is represented by what I have referred to as the "moralist" position, which holds that certain norms originate not in any self-interested calculus on the part of states but rather in a code of moral conduct that is prior to and independent of state interaction. The moral precepts comprising this code give rise to norms of behavior that are applicable to states as well as to individuals, even if states are more likely to violate them in practice. Compliance with these norms, then, comes from the commitment of national leaders or their constituencies to the moral precepts underlying the norms, not from an attempt to realize material gains for the state. Indeed, the moral impulse is unrelated to (and in the neorealist view, contrary to) the logic of national

---

lem is that there are very few actions imaginable from which the actor receives absolutely no benefit. Reserving ethical status only for such cases excludes most actions typically regarded as ethically praiseworthy.

[41] See, e.g., Stephen D. Krasner, "Structural Causes and Regime Consequences: Regimes as Intervening Variables," in Krasner, *International Regimes*.

[42] Robert W. Cox writes that the theme of "power versus morality" is an "obligatory theme of debate" and "a systemic conditioning of American thought" in international relations theory. "Social Forces, States, and World Orders: Beyond International Relations Theory," in *Neorealism and Its Critics*, ed. Robert O. Keohane (New York: Columbia University Press, 1986), p. 240.

interest. Again, the arguments of Lumsdaine, Welch, and McElroy provide examples of how moral principles can supersede material state interests as determinants of action.

It is clear that the moralist account requires a departure from the assumption that states always behave egoistically, looking out only for their own interests. Rather than attempting to redefine the notions of egoism or self-interest, however, moralist accounts accept the rationalist equation of ethics with self-abnegating altruism, thereby leaving in place the rigid dichotomy between ethics and interests. McElroy, for example, cites the defining characteristic of moral action as "consideration of the effects of the actor's action on others, *not from the point of view of the actor's own interests, but from the point of view of the others' interests.*"[43] To the extent that most moralist work on norms engages the theoretical literature, it therefore generally accepts the "intervening variable" formulation, attacking the link between interests and action rather than the manner in which interests themselves are defined. So not only is moralism not a structuralist explanation in the way that neorealism and neoliberalism are, it requires assumptions that make structuralist explanations of ethical behavior more or less impossible.

A different type of response to the shortcomings of rationalism has been mounted by scholars applying insights from the field of sociology to the study of international politics. This approach, which proponents have termed "sociological institutionalism," takes rationalism to task for its neglect of ideational factors and its failure to examine how national interests come to be.[44] First, sociological institutionalism insists on viewing the environment for state action in cultural and institutional, instead of simply material, terms. This entails taking into consideration the significance of a broad range of ideas, not just narrowly construed "rationality," in determining outcomes in international politics. Second, these ideas are seen as influencing policy not merely by affecting the incentives facing states but more fundamentally by shaping the interests and identities of states themselves. This perspective points to a close affinity between sociological institutionalism and the analytical strategy of con-

---

[43] McElroy, *Morality and American Foreign Policy*, p. 31 (emphasis added). Consequently, McElroy's account of the influence of norms on U.S. foreign policy relies heavily on the actions of "moral politicians" motivated by personal conscience. See, e.g., pp. 40–43, 57–87.

[44] See Ron Jepperson, Alexander Wendt, and Peter Katzenstein, "Norms, Identity, and Culture in National Security," in *The Culture of National Security*, pp. 33–75.

structivism.[45] Constructivists refuse to accept that the theoretical assumptions behind "national interests" are unproblematic, seeking instead to trace the processes by which these interests are constructed and reconstructed in interaction with both international and domestic political environments. An important corollary is that interests, identities, and environments affect one another recursively; unlike in rationalist theories, the "causal pathways" between structure and action are not seen as one-way streets.[46]

Sociological institutionalism, then, takes a more multifaceted and less instrumental view of the role of norms in international relations. Norms are seen as ubiquitous features of international politics, important not only in the context of cooperation among states but in all areas of endeavor, including matters of national security.[47] To ask why states comply with norms that are contrary to short-term interests, according to this position, is to take a view of interests that is altogether too narrow, and not simply in terms of time frame. States comply with norms for many reasons, among them being that norms define what and who they are, what they want, and how they view international politics. Compliance is therefore seen not only in terms of narrowly defined incentives but also in terms of shared normative understandings that provide matrices of meaning for national or supranational cultures. These understandings, moreover, cannot be theoretically divorced from the

---

[45] Literature on constructivism has proliferated in recent years. For seminal explanations of the constructivist project, see David Dessler, "What's at Stake in the Agent-Structure Debate?" *International Organization* 43 (Summer 1989): 441–73; and Alexander Wendt, "The Agent-Structure Problem in International Relations Theory," *International Organization* 41, no. 3 (Summer 1987): 335–70.

[46] The idea of "causal pathways" is David Dessler's, cited in Judith Goldstein and Robert O. Keohane, "Ideas and Foreign Policy: A Framework for Analysis," in *Ideas and Foreign Policy*, ed. Goldstein and Keohane, (Ithaca: Cornell University Press, 1993). An extensive debate has arisen about whether the logic of neoliberal institutionalism itself implies the recursive construction of interests and identities of states. See, e.g., Michael Lipson, "Nonlinearity, Constructivism, and International Relations: Or, Changing the Rules by Playing the Game" (paper presented at the annual conference of the American Political Science Association, Chicago, August 31– September 1, 1995); Robert O. Keohane, "International Institutions: Two Approaches," *International Studies Quarterly* 32, no. 4 (December 1988): 379–96; and Friedrich Kratochwil and John G. Ruggie, "International Organization: The State of the Art on the Art of the State," *International Organization* 40, no. 4 (1986): 753–75. Although my argument will touch upon some aspects of this debate, an extensive examination of the epistemological points at issue is beyond the scope of this project.

[47] See, e.g., Katzenstein, *The Culture of National Security*.

structure of international politics, as that structure itself comprises—indeed relies upon—many such understandings. This approach therefore goes behind the narrow view of interests posited by rationalist theory to examine how interests come to be.[48]

Sociological institutionalism clearly offers a richer and more textured approach to norms than can be accommodated by rationalist theory. Even so, it is not without limitations of its own. First, it is so broad in its focus that it cannot really be said to provide a unifying theory of norms.[49] Because it recognizes that norms exist at all levels of social and political interaction, it can fall prey to what has been called the "embarrassment of norms" problem: in any given situation an abundance of norms may be involved, sometimes in conflict with one another.[50] Sociological institutionalism itself provides little guidance in such cases to explain why some norms prove more effective than others. Second, while empirical studies based on sociological insights have done a good job of showing how norms can explain outcomes in ways that rationalist theories cannot, this work seldom examines where the norms in question come from, focusing instead on their effects. As Kowert and Legro observe, while many sociological institutionalists "take existing international relations theory to task for treating the construction of political actors and their preferences as exogenous, [they] tend to treat their own core concepts as exogenously given."[51] In this sense, work in the sociological mode has seldom followed through on one of its central

---

[48] Of course, there are limits to how far this type of approach can be pursued in empirical analysis. One can imagine an infinite regress of cultural causes and effects. For this reason, even empirical studies based on sociological institutionalist assumptions must often take some interests as fixed, if only for the purpose of establishing causal relationships. Paul Kowert and Jeffrey Legro, "Norms, Identities, and Their Limits: A Theoretical Reprise," in *The Culture of National Security*, ed. Katzenstein, pp. 488–90. Sociological institutionalism and neoliberalism may converge in application, therefore, as the latter must incorporate some auxiliary assumptions to give meaning to the otherwise vacuous notion of interests, while the former must start from somewhere. Similar points are made in Keohane, *After Hegemony*, p. 75; and Jepperson, Wendt, and Katzenstein, "Norms, Identity, and Culture in National Security," pp. 67–68.

[49] Jepperson, Wendt, and Katzenstein acknowledge this point, claiming that sociological institutionalism is not a theory as such, but an "orienting framework." "Norms, Identity, and Culture in National Security," p. 36. See also Finnemore, *National Interests in International Society*, p. 16; and Deborah Avant, "The New Institutional Economics and Norms of Warfare" (paper presented at the annual meeting of the International Studies Association, 1994), p. 28.

[50] Kowert and Legro, "Norms, Identity, and Their Limits," pp. 486–88.

[51] Ibid., p. 469.

points—the recursive and mutually constitutive relationship between norms and state interests. Finally, the sociological approach often neglects the importance of power in the processes it describes. To be fair, this perhaps reflects more a reaction to neorealism's narrow focus on material power than the logic of sociological institutionalism itself. Nevertheless power, too, is present in all social relations, and it is reasonable to expect the process of social construction (whether of interests, norms, or other institutional structures) to reflect this fact. Attention to the role of power and interest in the creation and operation of norms, moreover, may help provide structure that sociological institutionalism itself lacks.

THEORETICAL ASSUMPTIONS

One goal of this book is to show that the role of normative factors in international relations can be understood without sacrificing the benefits of structural theory. This requires the use of theoretical assumptions consistent with a structural analysis. I therefore accept the state-centrism of rationalist theory, along with the assumption that states in the international system act in accordance with their interests as they perceive them, matching available means to desired ends in an essentially rational way given the relevant context. Note that the latter assumption does not constitute an acceptance of rationalism outright but admits only that state actors pursue goals in a purposive manner.[52] I also accept the assumption that states behave egoistically, but I reject the rigid dichotomy between self-interest and ethics already described. Breaking down this dichotomy permits examination of the ways in which self-interest can interact with ethical imperatives, as well as how ethical norms can be of strategic use in the pursuit of national interests.

Accommodating ideational and normative phenomena within the concept of international structure requires a flexible and expansive

---

[52] This "ends-means" notion of rationality is nonetheless sometimes described as a variant of rational choice theory. In Ferejohn's terms, this constitutes "thin" rationalism, as opposed to "thick" rationalism, which assumes interests to be fixed and uniform. Green and Shapiro, *Pathologies of Rational Choice Theory*, pp. 17–18. The significance of this classification is unclear, however. Without the thick rationalist assumptions about interests, thin rationalist assumptions are unremarkable; even infants and lunatics act purposively, given how they perceive their interests. Indeed, it is hard to imagine what a social theory that did not assume at least thin rationality of actors would look like. Consequently, I reject the assertion that adopting the assumption of so-called thin rationality binds me to rational choice theory in any meaningful sense.

notion of state interests. I therefore follow sociological institutionalism in rejecting both the materialism of rationalist theory and its insistence that state interests be treated as fixed and exogenous to interaction with structure. Because I am interested in the content and effects of norms on a systemic level, however, I adopt a somewhat different focus than some sociological institutionalists, concentrating upon international norms rather than norms whose influence is confined to one or a few national societies or cultures. By "international" norm I mean one that, although its normative foundations may not be universally shared, nevertheless commands a broad range of support in international society and makes implicit demands on states' foreign policies across national, regional, and cultural boundaries. Although subnational, national, or regional norms may strongly influence foreign policy, I will be concerned with them primarily to the extent that their influence evolves to become closer to global in scope—as, for example, with rules for the limitation of armed conflict that originated in Western Europe in the just war tradition of the Catholic Church, but which today form the core of the customary international law of war.

Finally, I emphasize the mutually constitutive and recursive nature of the relationship among norms, interests, and power, recognizing that all three can be both causes and effects in the international system. Although this analytical strategy has come to be identified as constructivism, the idea of tracing the processes by which material and ideational forces influence and constrain one another long predates recent methodological debates, and can be described most simply as a historical approach to theory building.[53]

"STRUCTURAL ETHICS" AND INTERNATIONAL SOCIETY

Overcoming the division of international politics into geopolitical and normative spheres calls for developing a model of "structural ethics." Such a model would theoretically as well as empirically reconcile the importance of power and the egoistic nature of states with ethical action, such as commitment to a collective good or adherence to norms with moral content. What is required, in other words, is to explain how self-seeking states can have a stake in the welfare of a larger entity. Such an explanation can be found in the venerable Grotian idea of the inter-

---

[53] Richard Price calls this a "genealogical" approach, identifying it with Friedrich Nietzsche. "A Genealogy of the Chemical Weapons Taboo," pp. 84–89. Again, this contrasts with the explicitly ahistorical approach to theory-building employed by rationalism.

national society. This concept, a staple of international relations scholarship before the Second World War, has in the past few decades been neglected by the mainstream of the discipline in the United States, which has been dominated by rational choice theories. It has recently been most closely associated with scholars of the "English School," such as Hedley Bull, Martin Wight, and Charles Manning.[54]

Work in this tradition treads much of the same ground as neoliberal regime theory. In the words of Andrew Hurrell, both are interested in exploring "the relationship between law and norms on the one hand and power and interests on the other."[55] Both the similarities and the crux of the critical differences between the two approaches are apparent in the definition of international society offered by Bull and Adam Watson: "a group of states (or, more generally, a group of independent political communities) which not merely form a system, in the sense that the behavior of each is a necessary factor in the calculations of the others, but have also established by dialogue and consent common rules and institutions for the conduct of their relations, and recognise their common interest in maintaining these arrangements."[56] The distinction between "society" and "system" here embodies the idea, central to the notion of international society, that the interaction of states can produce a whole that is greater than the sum of its parts. International society, therefore, fits Durkheim's conception of society as an institution that is not merely the aggregation of its members but a "specific reality which has its own characteristics."[57] As such, it can be a causal force in its own right, exerting an independent influence upon the actions of its constituent members. According to this view, states comprising a society are neither atomistic nor simply "positional" actors but participants in a

---

[54] Hedley Bull, *The Anarchical Society* (New York: Columbia University Press, 1977); Martin Wight, *Systems of States* (Leicester: Leicester University Press, 1977); Martin Wight, "Western Values in International Relations," in *Diplomatic Investigations*, ed. Herbert Butterfield and Martin Wight (London: Allen and Unwin, 1966); and C. A. W. Manning, *The Nature of International Society* (London: Macmillan and the London School of Economics, 1975).

[55] Andrew Hurrell, "International Society and the Study of Regimes: A Reflective Approach," in *Regime Theory and International Relations*, ed. Volker Rittberger (Oxford: Oxford University Press, 1993).

[56] Hedley Bull and Adam Watson, eds., *The Expansion of International Society* (Oxford: Clarendon Press, 1984), p. 1.

[57] Quoted in John Gerard Ruggie, "Continuity and Transformation in the World Polity: Toward a Neorealist Synthesis," in *Neorealism and Its Critics*, ed. Robert Keohane (New York: Columbia University Press, 1986), p. 131.

larger social project defined by common interests, institutions, and a shared normative framework.[58] Significantly, however, the existence of an international society does not depend upon altruism—states are expected to act in their own interests, although these are conceived broadly enough to accommodate interests held in common with other states. The idea of international society therefore offers a valuable perspective for exploring the prescriptive power of norms, and more generally the possibility of structural sources of ethical state behavior. When a state's interests are understood to include the maintenance of the "common rules and institutions" that constitute international society, compliance with a broad variety of norms commonly understood as ethical can be explained by reference to the structure of the system itself.

W. David Clinton has used Tocqueville's idea of the "principle of self-interest rightly understood" to capture the nature of prescriptive power inherent in what he calls "the international community." As Clinton explains, this principle does not require altruistic devotion to the common good but rather seeks to inculcate in society members two ideas: "(1) that diverting some of their resources to maintaining the system that gave them the freedom to pursue their own interests was itself in the long run in their interests; and (2) that the preservation of the system depended to some extent on their willingness to moderate the demands of their private interests and to compromise their claims with those of others."[59] A society based upon this principle, according to Tocqueville, is distinguished neither by exceptional virtue nor crass selfishness, but by moderation:

> The principle of self-interest rightly understood produces no great acts of self-sacrifice, but it suggests daily small acts of self-denial. By itself it cannot suffice to make a man virtuous; but it disciplines a number of persons in habits of regularity, temperance, moderation, foresight, self-command; and if it does not lead men straight to virtue by the will, it gradually draws them in that direction by their habits. If the principle of interest rightly understood were to sway the whole moral world, extraordinary virtues would doubtless be more rare; but I think

---

[58] See Joseph M. Grieco, "Anarchy and the Limits of Cooperation: A Realist Critique of the Newest Liberal Institutionalism," in *Neorealism and Neoliberalism* ed. Baldwin.

[59] W. David Clinton, "The National Interest: Normative Foundations," *The Review of Politics* 48 no. 4 (1986): 514.

that gross depravity would then also be less common. The principle of interest rightly understood perhaps prevents men from rising far above the level of mankind, but a great number of other men, who were falling far below it, are caught and restrained by it.[60]

It is essentially this principle that Adam Watson, too, sees as the rationale for states' participation in international society. Wishing to distinguish this conception of interest from the *"raison d'etat"* of realist thought, Watson uses the term *"raison de systeme,"* which he pithily defines as "the belief that it pays to make the system work."[61] The idea of *raison de systeme* is important to understanding in empirical terms how norms influence the behavior of states in the international system, but I wish to suggest that it also has significant ethical implications. It shows how ostensibly egoistic states will take into account the vitality of rules and institutions that also serve the interests not only of other specific states, such as military allies or trading partners, but of a general collective entity embodying a type of common good. The notion of international society upon which this idea is based is therefore crucial to fully understanding norms, because it encompasses both structural theoretical explanation and ethical content, serving as a bridge between the geopolitical and normative spheres of international politics.

One reason the international society and its idea of common interests in institutions fell out of favor with many international relations scholars was its association with the "harmony of interests" position that was central to the work of the idealists of the early twentieth century—and was the focus of some of the most trenchant criticism of that school by realists such as E. H. Carr.[62] Important distinctions, however, must be drawn between these positions. First, the international society perspective recognizes that states possess vital interests that may conflict with those of other states or of international society as a whole. Other interests always exist that may trump even very strong interests in norms and institutions. As a result, norms must be seen as operating on a sliding scale, or

---

[60] Alexis de Tocqueville, *Democracy in America*, vol. 2 (New York: Vintage Classics, 1990), p. 123.

[61] Adam Watson, *The Evolution of International Society* (London: Routledge & Kegan Paul, 1992), p. 14.

[62] E. H. Carr, *The Twenty Years' Crisis, 1919–1939* (New York: Harper and Row, 1964). See especially chapter 4.

on what Michael Walzer has eloquently termed a "map of human crises" wherein normative requirements, whatever their connection to self-interest, may have to yield to the exigencies of national security in dire circumstances.[63] But while norms are by no means determinative, the same must be said of any interest a state may have. For example, two interests commonly referred to as among the "vital interests" of the United States are the Monroe Doctrine's injunction against foreign powers establishing a strong presence in the Western Hemisphere and the Cold War–era commitment to containing the spread of communism, especially in areas of strategic importance to the United States. Still, these two interests *combined* never sufficed to compel the United States to launch an outright invasion of either Castro's Cuba or Sandinista Nicaragua, even though it would likely have succeeded militarily in either case. The reasons for this are undoubtedly complex, but the bottom line is that the strategic or material interests at stake, however vital, were not worth risking harm to other interests.

A second distinction between international society theorists and idealists involves the fundamental nature of their respective projects. Interwar idealism took an essentially prescriptive approach, seeking to guide states and their citizens to an awareness of the common bonds among them and the possibilities of a peaceful future.[64] The international society project is less utopian and more empirical, describing and explaining patterns of international relations as they exist and have existed. Moreover, its focus is decidedly more state-centric than the cosmopolitan outlook of idealism. While some within the English School address the possibilities of a more cosmopolitan future, their stance remains fundamentally Grotian, not Kantian. As Hedley Bull emphasizes, while the "society of all mankind" may be "morally prior" to the society of states, "it could not be seriously argued . . . that the society of all mankind is already a going concern."[65] Because of this focus, work in the international society tradition never loses sight of the role of power and interest in international politics. The international system is still seen as anarchical, lacking a centralized authority to enforce rules and coordinate cooperation. International society is, in sum, a political as well as a

---

[63] Michael Walzer, *Just and Unjust Wars*, rev. ed. (New York: Basic Books, 1992), p. 253.

[64] Michael J. Smith, *Realist Thought from Weber to Kissinger* (Baton Rouge: Louisiana State University Press, 1986), chap. 3.

[65] Bull, *The Anarchical Society*, pp. 22–23.

legal and social system, and as such it is characterized by competition and conflict.[66]

Using the idea of international society as a foundation, in the following chapter I set forth the theoretical framework for a study of norms. I begin with an examination of how norms emerge from the interaction of moral and political influences and the different ways in which they can constrain actors in the international system. I then discuss the relationship between ethical norms and international law. I conclude the chapter by considering various methodological challenges presented by the study of international norms and discussing how to confront them.

The themes introduced in chapters 1 and 2 are developed in two empirical case studies of norms addressing the use of force in international politics. Chapter 3, the first of the two case studies, addresses the norm against the assassination of foreign leaders. I propose that the norm against assassination, and its morally ambiguous consequences, is best explained by its "power maintenance" function in the international system. I trace the rise of this norm in the international system, demonstrating that while the norm is based on fundamental moral principles its development was decisively influenced by geopolitical factors. Specifically, powerful states benefited from a norm that defined acceptable political violence on terms most favorable to the means at their disposal—war in the traditional sense of clashing armies in the field, rather than plots against individual leaders.

Chapters 4 and 5 address the norm against the aerial bombing of

---

[66] Hurrell, "International Society and the Study of Regimes," p. 61. Although most work in this tradition has been more historical than overtly theoretical in focus, it is possible to explain the emergence of an international society deductively, without appealing to historically contingent circumstances. See, e.g., Barry Buzan, "From International System to International Society: Structural Realism and Regime Theory Meet the English School," *International Organization* 47, no. 3 (Summer 1993): 327–52; and Hurrell, "International Society and the Study of Regimes." This work shares much in common with constructivist accounts showing how states in anarchy can, contrary to neorealism, move beyond elementary self-help measures such as the balance of power. See, e.g., Alexander Wendt, "Collective Identity Formation and the International State," *American Political Science Review* 88, No. 2 (June 1994): 384–96; and Alexander Wendt, "Anarchy Is What States Make of It: The Social Construction of Power Politics," *International Organization* 46, No. 2 (Spring 1992): 391–425.

noncombatants in wartime. This oft-told tale is typically regarded as one of unmitigated failure, with the dramatic disintegration of the norm during World War II held out as evidence of the impotence of norms in general when faced with the exigencies of war. The conventional interpretation, however, tells only part of the story. First, it does not account for the fact that other norms proved far more durable in circumstances at least as extenuating. Second, most accounts do not follow the story long enough, as the norm has enjoyed a revival since 1945. In Chapter 4 I examine the antecedents of the norm against bombing civilians and its development up to and during World War II. I argue that the failure of the norm in World War II was largely a consequence of the exceptional fragility of the pre-war norm, which fit poorly into the prevailing normative, technological, and geopolitical structure of international politics. In Chapter 5 I trace the revival of the norm in the latter half of the twentieth century, ascribing it to the emergence of a different set of normative, technological, and geopolitical factors. In this regard, I consider the possibility that the norm has evolved from a tenuous, convention-dependent injunction viewed ambivalently by strong states to a stronger power-maintenance norm that serves the interests of great powers vis-à-vis other states in the international system.

I conclude in Chapter 6 by returning to the relationship between ethics and international relations theory. Here I clarify the sense in which norms shaped by self-interest can nevertheless be considered ethically significant and explore the limits of purely altruistic ethics in international politics. I argue that such possibilities are greatly restricted by the institutional situation of national leaders and the duties inherent in this leadership. These duties imply that moral preference be given to fellow citizens over foreigners and suggest limits on the range of choices available to a leader morally accountable to a national constituency. Although this institutional situation is related to the anarchical nature of the international system, it is not, as neorealists claim, the material fact of anarchy per se that limits international altruism but rather the ideational (and normative) significance that state actors attach to this fact. Therefore, it is the "statesman's" understandings of structural circumstances that serve to define the normative content of anarchy—understandings that may be significantly constrained but are never strictly determined. This institutional situation makes the application of common criteria of interpersonal moral judgment problematic in the international context, but it does not preclude the possibility of an ethics based upon reciprocity and mutual restraint.

CHAPTER 2

Principle Meets Power
Groundwork for an
Analysis of Ethical Norms

Everybody I see about me seems bent on teaching his contemporaries, by precept and example, that what is useful is never wrong. Will nobody undertake to make them understand how what is right may be useful?
Alexis de Tocqueville, *Democracy in America*

In order to establish a foundation for analysis, a fundamental distinction must first be made between *moral principles* and *ethical norms.* I take "moral principle" to mean a proposition or tenet that expresses an abstract judgment about right or wrong. Such a principle must necessarily be expressed in very general terms. While it can serve as a guide to action, the essence of a moral principle is the judgment, not the command, which is only implicit. "Human life is intrinsically valuable" is a highly abstract moral principle; "it is morally wrong to kill without justification" and "it is morally wrong to kill the innocent" are somewhat less abstract corollaries, closer to the realm of action than the first statement.

In Chapter 1 norms were defined as collective understandings of the proper behavior of actors. Although I am primarily interested in ethical norms, not all norms have ethical content. Norms embedded in many social conventions, for example, are instrumental or perhaps ritualistic, not ethical, in nature. Ethical norms, by contrast, are specifically concerned with moral notions of right and wrong and therefore prescribe or prohibit behavior that is subject to moral praise or blame.[1] An ethical norm, then, can be understood as being at least implicitly based upon or referring to a moral principle of one description or another. These definitions raise two points. First, a moral principle may be held by any number of people, but a norm necessarily entails a broader, more intersubjective level of understanding. While a single individual could subscribe to a principle, a norm subscribed to by only one person or a few people would not be a norm at all. Second, while moral principles guide action only by implication, ethical norms do so more explicitly and therefore can be expressed in less abstract terms, such as "states in the international system should not use assassination as an instrument of foreign policy."

It is difficult to account for the existence of certain norms without reference to some prior and independent moral principle. Norms protecting human rights, for example, reflect fundamental beliefs concerning the proper treatment of individuals and would not exist but for those beliefs. This does not mean, however, that power and interest play no part in the way these norms develop or how they influence state policy. Cathal Nolan, for example, has linked the rise of a viable human rights regime in the years after World War II to the ability of the United States to set the agenda for postwar international politics.[2] Other examples are norms aimed at protecting human life, including particularly those rules of war associated with the just war doctrine of *jus in bello*.[3] While such norms undoubtedly will be stronger if they are associated with the interests of a strong state (or states) in the international system, they also reflect deep-seated moral principles. The content of such norms cannot be explained by power and interest alone.

---

[1] The distinction between the terms "moral" and "ethical" can be an elusive one, and the terms are often used interchangeably. Here I take ethics to mean either that branch of philosophy concerned with moral right and wrong or the application of abstract moral judgments to the realm of action. Hence, my use of the term "ethical" to describe norms reflects their status as guides to action, while I reserve "moral" for more abstract principles or judgments.

[2] Cathal J. Nolan, *Principled Diplomacy: Security and Rights in U.S. Foreign Policy* (Westport, Conn.: Greenwood Press, 1993).

[3] Hans J. Morgenthau explains the laws of war in this way. *Politics Among Nations: The Struggle for Power and Peace*, 4th ed. (New York: McGraw-Hill, 1967), chap. 15. Bull, on the other hand, groups some laws of war among those rules originating solely in the interests of powerful states and only later taking on moral status. *The Anarchical Society*, p. 67. Bull's focus, however, is less on laws relating to *jus in bello* than *jus ad bellum*.

Often, however, a considerable gap exists between moral principles and their real-world manifestations, which as noted can lead to curious anomalies. Consider, for example, Winston Churchill's famous account of an exchange with Stalin at the Tehran Conference:

> The German General Staff, he said, must be liquidated. The whole force of Hitler's mighty armies depended upon about fifty thousand officers and technicians. If these were rounded up and shot at the end of the war, German military strength would be extirpated. On this I thought it right to say: "The British Parliament and public will never tolerate mass executions. Even if in war passion they allowed them to begin, they would turn violently against those responsible after the first butchery had taken place. The Soviets must be under no delusion on this point."
>
> Stalin, however, perhaps only in mischief, pursued the subject. "Fifty thousand," he said, "must be shot." I was deeply angered. "I would rather," I said, "be taken out into the garden here and now and be shot myself than sully my own and my country's honor by such infamy."[4]

Next consider that scarcely two months later Churchill authorized the firebombing raid on Dresden, in which an estimated sixty thousand civilians died and perhaps a million more were left homeless.[5] The latter event is mentioned only in passing in Churchill's memoirs, and then with no sense of moral anxiety or regret.[6] While it is true that the raid on Dresden, and Churchill's role in it, remains controversial, the contrast between his outrage in Tehran and his acquiescence to Dresden is less a reflection on Churchill than on the apparently arbitrary moral effects of norms on the propriety of certain types of killing. Mass executions, even of those bearing a large measure of responsibility for the war, were unthinkable, whereas the norm against the aerial bombing of noncombatants was an early, if unfortunate, casualty of the exigencies of war. Similar inconsistencies exist not only in determining which norms are obeyed and which are violated but sometimes in the content of the

---

[4] Winston S. Churchill, *Closing the Ring* (Cambridge: Houghton Mifflin, 1951), pp. 373–74.

[5] Max Hastings, *Bomber Command* (New York: The Dial Press, 1979), p. 341; McElroy, *Morality and American Foreign Policy*, p. 148.

[6] Winston S. Churchill, *Triumph and Tragedy* (Cambridge: Houghton Mifflin, 1953), pp. 540–41.

norms themselves. As noted earlier, the relatively strong norm against assassinating foreign leaders can be explained neither by the scope of the violence involved nor by the presumed innocence of the victims.

What, then, accounts for these anomalies? The answer lies in the way in which moral principles take the form of ethical norms. For any principle to be operationalized as a norm it must move from the abstract realm of morality to the concrete realm of political action. In so doing it becomes subject to the calculations of states that, as realism reminds us, pursue their interests in a competitive environment. In the process the underlying moral imperative is often distorted or diluted. Moreover, because they are collective understandings and not abstract principles (that is, intersubjective rather than subjective phenomena), ethical norms derive their strength from the degree of consensus they enjoy and the level of commitment they engender. It is therefore impossible to discuss ethical norms without at least implicit reference to a power structure that constructs and maintains them. For this reason, Hedley Bull argues that rules regulating conduct in international society, including norms prohibiting certain uses of force, will reflect the interests of strong states:

> It is of course the case that all actual systems of social rules are imbued with the special interests and values of those who make them. Since the influence exerted by members of a society in the process of making the rules is likely always to be unequal, any historical system of rules will be found to serve the interests of the ruling or dominant elements of society more adequately than it serves the interests of the others. . . . Thus the particular kinds of limitations that are imposed on resort to violence . . . will bear the stamp of those dominant elements. But that there should be limits of some kind on resort to violence . . . is not a special interest of some members of a society but a general interest of all of them.[7]

While moral desiderata are crucial to the existence of norms restricting force, then, the specific content and effectiveness of these norms may only imperfectly reflect these concerns. This is because norms, as global political structures, are not only socially constructed but also *geopolitically constructed*. Norms, therefore, are not simply alternatives to power as explanations of state behavior. Rather they rely upon and reflect real power, as well as the interests of those who wield it.

[7] Bull, *The Anarchical Society*, p. 55.

An example of the importance of interest and power in the development of norms can be found in Michael Howard's account of the rules regarding commerce raiding at sea.[8] A debate arose in the seventeenth century over whether attacks on merchant ships constituted a proper means of warfare, despite the danger of harm to civilians. Condemning this practice were jurists from the continent, led by the Dutch, who, as Howard points out, relied upon the freedom of trade in order to carry on their fight for independence. Britain's growing power, however, relied heavily on commerce raiding and blockades; and, as might be expected, British jurists espoused an interpretation of the rules of noncombatancy that would define the economic activity of civilians as a legitimate naval target. It is important to note that the debate was technically a juridical and normative matter, not a problem of diplomacy, insofar as it is possible to separate the two. At stake was the application of principles that were grounded on fundamental moral judgments. Moreover the debate played out not in diplomatic conferences between state agents but in treatises written by scholars, who sought to translate the dictates of natural law into a code of conduct among nations. Still, the interests of the states with a major stake in the question tended to be reflected in the content of the juridical and normative arguments. Significantly, as British power grew, it was the British argument that ultimately won out.

This analysis suggests two hypotheses regarding ethical norms restricting the use of force. The first is that such norms are grounded upon a priori moral principles and to some degree reflect those principles, even if imperfectly. The second hypothesis endorses Bull's observation: because norms are geopolitically constructed, their specific content and application will tend to reflect the broad interests of powerful states in international society over time. The desire to prevent inhumane killing, for example, must be filtered through the interests of states whose power over others rests in part upon their relative advantage in the proficiency at certain means of killing. It would surprise us to find, therefore, a state with substantial superiority in a particular type of militarily effective weapon agreeing to calls to ban the weapon on the grounds that it is inhumane. On the other hand, one might expect states without

---

[8] Michael Howard, "Temperamenta Belli: Can War be Controlled?" in *Restraints on War: Studies in the Limitation of Armed conflict,* ed. Michael Howard (Oxford: Oxford University, Press, 1979), pp. 8–10.

the weapon to call for such a ban.[9] If the "have" state were also in a position of influence in international society, as would likely be the case, a norm restricting the weapon would be less likely to arise. Conversely, if a restriction serves to reinforce the dominant position of a strong state or group of states in international society, it is more likely to be the basis for a strong norm. This leads to two corollaries to the latter hypothesis: first, weapons or practices that have the potential to close the gap between strong and weak states in international society are more likely to be restricted than those that reinforce the relative advantage of strong states; and second, the more directly a norm reflects the interests of strong states, the stronger the norm will be—strong norms being defined as those that compel high degrees of compliance or threaten substantial sanctions for their violation. Taken together, these corollaries reflect what I will call the *power-maintenance* function of some prohibitory norms.

This account can be distinguished from the starker neorealist position in several ways. First, the "dominant elements in society" that Bull refers to are not necessarily those that possess the greatest military or economic capabilities. As noted earlier, some states may exercise influence out of proportion to their material strength, while others may find themselves on the fringes of international society despite considerable military might. (China and Iraq fit this description to varying degrees.) Second, even these "dominant elements" are usually not able to construct norms in exactly the way they would like, both because their power has limits and because, as intersubjective ideas that rest on notions of proper and improper behavior, norms are not easily manipulable.[10] Therefore, norms are not epiphenomenal reflections of the interests of strong states, as neorealists claim, but reflect these interests rather less distinctly. Third, once norms do take shape, they can serve as constraints

---

[9] An example was a proposal made at the 1974–77 Geneva Conference on the laws of war by the West African nation of Togo. Its delegation proposed that if war broke out between a state with an air force and a state without an air force, the state with the air force should be forbidden to use it. Not surprisingly, Togo and like-minded states were unable to garner support for the provision among more powerful states. W. Hays Parks notes that the Geneva Conference in general "witnessed a constant effort by the less-developed nations to offset the military and technological advantage of the developed nations by rules cloaked in humanitarian law." W. Hays Parks, "Conventional Aerial Bombing and the Law of War," *Proceedings of the U.S. Naval Institute* 108 No. 5 (May 1982): 106.

[10] Elizabeth Kier and Jonathan Mercer, "Setting Precedents in Anarchy: Military Intervention and Weapons of Mass Destruction," *International Security* 20, no. 4 (Spring 1996): 77–106.

upon the behavior of even strong states, rather than merely acting as moralistic window-dressing supporting self-serving actions.

It is also important to bear in mind that the process of norm construction is a historical one. In other words, norms are not continually re-created from scratch; rather, at any stage in history states operate within a preexisting normative context that is both the product of past processes and the starting point for future ones. While the geopolitical processes that shape norms are ongoing, at any given time norms exist that will govern state behavior, perhaps even as they change in content or application. It is therefore important to think in terms of both the construction of norms and the ways in which norms can influence behavior. The latter raises what Keohane terms "the puzzle of compliance." The puzzle is "why governments, seeking to promote their own interests, ever comply with rules . . . when they view these rules as in conflict with . . . their 'myopic self-interest.' "[11] When norms simply reinforce short-term material or strategic interests, after all, it is hard to say that they are influential. The argument of this chapter, however, points to several other reasons for states to comply with norms.

As noted above, when the distribution of power in international society is more or less directly reflected in the content of a norm, the norm can be said to serve a power-maintenance role. Powerful states would have an important incentive to comply with such norms even if their short-term material interests might be served by violating them. States with less of a stake in the status quo, on the other hand, might have an incentive to oppose such restrictions and try to subvert, rather than reinforce, the prevailing power structure. A prominent example is the nuclear nonproliferation regime. Some non-nuclear states have argued (with some justification) that the regime denies them the same right to provide for their security afforded to nuclear states, therefore forever consigning them to the ranks of second-rate powers.

Because no state has the ability to create norms by fiat, not all norms in international society reflect the interests of the powerful so directly. Other norms may exist because the moral principles underlying them are so compelling, or because they used to reflect great power interests but no longer do so with developments in technology, shifts in power among states, or other changes. Because of the diffuse interest that strong states have in the continued vitality of international society as a whole, however, we should not expect them to violate these norms at will

[11] Keohane, *After Hegemony,* p. 99.

in light of the broad societal importance of norms per se. This reflects the *raison de systeme* and the role of "common rules and institutions" in making the system work. Neither, however, should we expect these norms to be as strongly held or as vigorously guarded as those that reinforce the prevailing distribution of power. Norms of this nature may be more fragile, taking the form of what Hume refers to as conventions. In terms similar to Tocqueville's "interest rightly understood," Hume describes conventions as being based on

> a general sense of common interest; which sense all the members of a society express to one another, and which induces them to regulate their conduct by certain rules. I observe that it will be to my interest to leave another in the possession of his goods, *provided* he will act in the same manner with regard to me. He is sensible of a like interest in the regulation of his conduct. When this common sense of interest is mutually expressed and is known to both, it produces a suitable resolution and behaviour. And this may properly enough be called a convention or agreement betwixt us, though without the interposition of a promise; since the actions of each of us have a reference to those of the other, and are performed upon the supposition that something is to be performed on the other part . . . and it is only on the expectation of this that our moderation and abstinence are founded.[12]

Convention-dependent norms, then, rely heavily on precedent and patterns of reciprocal adherence. At this point, a third hypothesis may be added: the less directly a norm reflects the interests of powerful states in international society, the more likely its effectiveness will depend upon reciprocity. The contingent nature of obligations under convention-dependent norms, in a sense, suits the anarchical nature of international society; because no central authority exists to punish violations, aggrieved states may protect their interests by resort to self-help, even if it means disregarding the norm. It also demonstrates, however, how the practices surrounding norms can diverge significantly from their moral underpinnings. Some norms, such as those prohibiting the bombing of noncombatants, purport to protect the lives of the innocent by placing restrictions on striking certain targets in wartime. The moral basis for this injunction does not change with the violation of the norm by a warring party; that nation's "innocent" are no more "guilty" as a result of the

---

[12] Quoted in Henry D. Aiken, ed., *Hume's Moral and Political Philosophy* (New York: Hafner Press, 1948), pp. 59–60 (emphasis in original).

actions taken by their leaders. In practice, however, the aggrieved state is often permitted—by the doctrine of reprisal or by the terms of the institutionalized prohibition itself—to undertake similar action in return. To prohibit it from doing so would, the logic goes, place it at the mercy of the original offender, who could act with impunity.[13] The ethical obligation, which was absolute in its deontological form, is instead now convention-dependent, in that it can be relieved or at least relaxed by the prior transgressions of others.[14]

Of course, concerns with maintaining the prevailing distribution of power or preserving the normative apparatus of international society do not exhaust the possible incentives for norm compliance. In fact, some norms may exercise considerable influence even if they neither command genuine ethical commitment from a state actor nor reflect that state's broad institutional interests. Instead, simply by virtue of their existence and their central role in international society, norms may take on a presumptive legitimacy that gives them prescriptive power in dealings among states. Precisely because many other states *do* have interests in norms, there is always the prospect that violators may be placed under sanctions. Roughly speaking, sanctions are of two types. The first could be described as "active" sanctions. These include measures such as intervention, embargoes, and reciprocal noncompliance, as well as less coercive steps such as the recall of ambassadors or the denial of favorable trading terms. For most states, the possibility of sanctions will provide a strong disincentive to violate norms, even after hostilities have already commenced. In the Persian Gulf War, for example, Saddam Hussein's Iraq was deterred from the use of chemical weapons (although not from other norm violations) by the concern that violating the taboo on such weapons would cause the coalition to prosecute the war with far less restraint than it would otherwise. This example demonstrates that sanctions depend upon both power and interest; in the war with Iran, Iraq had violated the same taboo with relative impunity.

The second category of sanctions, which could be described as "passive," arises from the normative basis for international society and the importance of legitimacy for the effective exercise of state power. Disregard for the norms of international society may eventually undermine

---

[13] Walzer, *Just and Unjust Wars*, chap. 13.

[14] For an argument that the norm of noncombatant immunity takes the form of a convention-dependent obligation, see George Mavrodes, "Conventions and the Morality of War," *Philosophy and Public Affairs* 4 (Winter 1975): 117–31. This issue is addressed in some detail in Chapter 4, infra.

the strength of those norms but more immediately is likely to undermine the legitimacy of the norm-breaker. This damage to a state's "moral status" may have tangible effects, from boycotts and protests organized by nonstate actors (who can also create pressures upon states that may lead to more active sanctions, as in the case of apartheid-era South Africa)[15] to a diminished ability to influence action in intergovernmental bodies such as the United Nations. Neither superpowers nor states on the periphery of international society can afford to ignore the moral status problem. It is striking, for example, how even states pursuing aggressive foreign policies seek to justify their actions to avoid being cast as outlaws or "pariah" states, and how great powers jockey vigorously for the "moral high ground" in their dealings. The global scale of modern international society makes it impossible for any state to opt out of the system. Dense and complex interactions with other states are inevitable, and disregard for norms in one issue-area may adversely affect these relationships. The prospect of damage to a state's moral status, therefore, creates a considerable structural disincentive to norm violation that must be weighed against the immediate advantages gained. This discussion of sanctions suggests a fourth hypothesis: there are costs associated with violating norms, ranging from reciprocal action to damage to a state's moral status in international society.

Again, what is at stake here may have little to do with any sincere moral commitment to the norm in question. The point is that the presumptive legitimacy of norms in international society creates its own incentives for compliance, and states violating norms incur costs for doing so. From a structural standpoint, for example, it matters relatively little whether the ruling white minority in South Africa ever "saw the light" regarding apartheid, or whether it simply determined that growing international pressure made its position politically untenable. By the same token, it is highly unlikely that Saddam Hussein suffered any moral qualms about the use of chemical weapons in the Gulf War, especially since he had already used them against Iran. Still, the existence of a discrete norm against their use presented a threshold at a certain level of force (or, in the parlance of limited war theory, a "firebreak") that could only be crossed at the risk of incurring costs deemed unacceptable.[16] While sincere moral scruples may have been irrelevant in both cases, the

[15] For the role of norms and nonstate actors in pressuring the South African government to end apartheid, see Klotz, *Norms in International Relations*.

[16] See, e.g., Price and Tannenwald, "Norms and Deterrence."

norms in question were nevertheless both ultimately based upon moral principles, and their violation was widely viewed by the international community as raising moral issues. These examples show that the conventional dichotomy between ethics and interests often obscures the way in which norms can shape outcomes in the international system. This point can perhaps be better understood by reference to James March and Johan Olsen's distinction between the "logic of consequentiality" and the "logic of appropriateness."[17] The former is concerned with finding the course of action that yields the best consequences; it requires an actor to conduct the sort of economistic calculus envisioned by rationalist theory. The latter, on the other hand, asks what course of action is most appropriate for a particular type of actor in a particular type of situation. It is this logic that is typically associated with norm compliance. My point here is that *when a norm is widely held, there is considerable convergence between the logic of appropriateness and the logic of consequentiality.* Indeed, the logic of appropriateness *structures* the logic of consequentiality, because failure to act appropriately creates consequences in its own right and therefore affects the utilitarian calculations facing rational actors. Consequently, norm-based behavior and interest-based behavior are by no means mutually exclusive.[18]

BEYOND RATIONALISM: NORMS AS GENERATIVE STRUCTURES

A central argument of this book is that norms are not simply statements about the propriety of certain actions but are also, in Durkheim's words, "social facts" that themselves influence action. To this point the discussion of the influence of norms has proceeded in terms roughly consistent with rationalist methodology. Norms have been described as creating incentives and imposing costs upon state actors. In this sense, norms can be referred to in rationalist terms as "constraints" on state action, or as "intervening variables" interposed between interests (which are still assumed to be fixed) and foreign policy outcomes.[19] Because of

---

[17] James G. March and Johan P. Olsen, *Rediscovering Institutions: The Organizational Basis of Politics* (New York: Free Press, 1989), especially chap. 2.

[18] See, e.g., Martha Finnemore and Kathryn Sikkink, "International Norm Dynamics and Political Change," *International Organization* 52, no. 4 (Autumn 1998): 887–917; and Kevin Hartigan, "Matching Humanitarian Norms with Cold, Hard Interests: The Making of Refugee Policies in Mexico and Honduras, 1980–1989," *International Organization* 46, no. 3 (Summer 1992): 709–30.

[19] Krasner, "Structural Causes and Regime Consequences."

the ubiquity of norms and the costs associated with violating them, however, it is reasonable to expect that states would incorporate these incentives and disincentives into their decision-making processes on something more than an ad hoc basis. In other words, the desirability of conforming to norms may become a more or less fixed assumption. Once a norm becomes internalized in this way, it is not simply one among a number of considerations that must be factored into the calculus of foreign policy decision-making. It instead becomes one of the foundational assumptions upon which that calculus is premised.

Norms may become internalized to varying degrees. Most dramatically, a very strongly held norm, or one whose violation would entail prohibitive costs, might become internalized to such a high degree that its presence as a premise in policy-making is practically subconscious. The result is that certain courses of action never "make it onto the screen" of options under consideration. Norms forbidding slavery and dueling have been pointed to as examples of norms that have been deeply internalized.[20] Similarly, Janice Thomson notes that certain practices of diplomacy are so taken for granted that serious departure from them has become unthinkable.[21] More controversially, John Mueller argues that an appreciation of the costs of warfare in the modern world has led most industrial states to so strongly internalize the norm against using force to settle differences that war between such states has become "subrationally unthinkable."[22] The more deeply internalized a norm is, the more insulated it will be from social and geopolitical processes, and therefore the less likely it is to change or to be "reconstructed."

Norms that are highly valued but not unconditionally taken for granted are internalized to a lesser degree. Norms against the use of nuclear weapons, for example, are understandably strong, but their violation remains within the realm of policy options in extremely extenuating circumstances.[23] The norms against assassination and the aerial bombing of noncombatants in general might also be seen as falling into this category, although the former is almost certainly more internalized than the latter.

---

[20] John E. Mueller, *Retreat From Doomsday: The Obsolescence of Major War* (New York: Basic Books, 1990), pp. 9–12.

[21] Janice A. Thomson, "Norms in International Relations: A Conceptual Analysis," *International Journal of Group Tensions* 23 (1993): 73.

[22] Mueller, *Retreat From Doomsday*, pp. 11, 240–44.

[23] On norms relating to the use of nuclear weapons, see Price and Tannenwald, "Norms and Deterrence."

Finally, norms can be internalized in policy-making institutions to a much lower degree. The desire to avoid violating a norm might make certain policy options presumptively less desirable than others, but they are still among the options considered in exceptional circumstances. The frequency with which the norm against military intervention has been violated suggests that it is internalized only to a limited degree. Still, such norms do create presumptions in the policy-making calculus; they are not simply lumped in with more contingent factors as ad hoc variables. As such, they provide a reason to give pause before pursuing certain courses of action—acting as what can perhaps be characterized as "ethical speed bumps."

A fine example of the internalization of norms is provided by Jeffrey Legro's analysis of norms restraining the use of force in World War II.[24] Legro uses the idea of organizational culture to explain patterns of norm compliance and violation. Contrary to what realist theory would predict, the combatants in World War II did not violate these norms wholesale. Whether a state abided by a norm, Legro maintains, was most significantly determined by the extent to which the norm in question was compatible with the operational orientations of the state's military organizations—or, in other words, the extent to which the norm was internalized by these organizations. For example, Legro argues that British violation of norms against bombing noncombatants can be linked to the fact that the RAF was organized around the doctrine of morale bombing, and its organizational culture strongly reflected faith in its efficacy.[25] The norm against chemical warfare, however, was honored by the major belligerents regardless of how effective it might have proven. This was in large part because none of the armies had incorporated the use of these weapons into its doctrine, and all felt ambivalent or hostile toward using them.[26]

The internalization of norms can, paradoxically, make it more difficult to appreciate their impact on foreign policy. This is because when a norm is internalized, moral or instrumental judgments underlying the norm can recede so far into the background as to become invisible in decision-making processes. The judgments underlying the internalized norm may, moreover, be incompatible with those reflected by other norms with strong ethical content. The rejection of one ethical norm,

---

[24] Legro, *Cooperation under Fire.*
[25] Ibid., pp. 129–41.
[26] Ibid., chap. 4.

therefore, does not necessarily imply the insignificance of any moral concerns, since decision-making assumptions may already reflect moral judgments that are hidden from view. Focusing narrowly on the process by which specific policy choices are made, therefore, may understate the importance of moral judgments, and ethical norms, in foreign policy in general. This is a limitation in particular of the organizational culture approach, especially if organizational culture is treated primarily as an independent variable. For example, to fully explore the role of morality in the practice of strategic bombing in World War II, it would be necessary to closely examine other factors contributing to the RAF's embrace of bombing doctrine in the interwar era, including the impact of the belief that bombing would provide a humane and effective alternative to the morally repugnant carnage of trench warfare.[27] In a full account of the norms picture, therefore, organizational culture itself is something that needs to be explained, since norms can play a role in its construction as well as being influenced by it.

The concept of internalization forms a crucial part of the norms picture, demonstrating how necessary it is to move beyond rationalist methodology in order to fully understand how norms work. Instead of simply providing morally based alternatives to self-interested action, ethical norms and the moral principles that underlie them are in fact often "embedded" within the very institutions that determine state policy.[28] As constructivists point out, when norms become embedded in this way, they not only influence the determination of which policies best serve state interests but more fundamentally help to shape those interests themselves, as well as the identities that give rise to them.[29] They are, in other words, not merely constraints in the rationalist sense but generative structures in a constructivist framework. The logic of norm internalization, therefore, provides a link between rationalist analysis of the incentives and costs associated with norms and the sociological institutionalist focus on the mutually constitutive relationship between norms and interests. It also underscores the importance of norms to the ideational structure that lends meaning to the material structure of international politics.[30]

[27] See Chapter 4, infra.

[28] On how different types of ideas can become embedded in institutions, see Goldstein and Keohane, "Ideas and Foreign Policy: A Framework for Analysis," pp. 12–13.

[29] Thomson, "Norms in International Relations," p. 72. Also see Wendt, "Constructing International Politics"; and Katzenstein, *The Culture of National Security*, especially chap. 2.

[30] I am grateful to Susan Peterson for bringing this point to my attention.

INTERNATIONAL NORMS AND INTERNATIONAL LAW

Obviously, any discussion of norms in international society also raises the question of the role of international law. Because some international relations scholars use the terms "norms," "rules," "laws," and so on more or less interchangeably, the issues at stake in the study of norms are often treated coextensively with those involved with international law. Because I take a different approach in this study, it will be worthwhile to pause here in order to specify the distinction between norms and law. To some extent, this distinction can be a slippery one, in part because considerable areas of overlap exist between the two concepts. First, norms are not necessarily any more or less specific than laws. There may be general, overarching norms that are not terribly well-defined, but there may also be quite specific norms in areas where the law is less specific or even silent. While it might be tempting to simply say that laws are formal rules, whereas norms reflect what states actually do, the matter is not so clear. First, much international law is customary law and therefore reflects norms through usages and customs—reflecting, in other words, what states actually do (at least when they are on reasonably good behavior). As Martha Finnemore writes, "Customary international law exists only when states share an understanding that compliance with some rule of behavior is necessary and appropriate. Customary international law exists only where there is a norm."[31] So, for example, the laws of war for most of the time that it has been possible to talk about "laws of war" have been customary, changing over time to reflect widespread changes in practice.

Nevertheless, there are often considerable areas of divergence between norms and law. First, while customary law remains at the core of international law, an increasingly large proportion of the body of international law is not customary. This reflects a trend over the last century or more toward greater codification of international law, the product of treaties and the charters of international organizations. Sometimes these documents reflect established practice (and therefore a preexisting norm), but at other times the reverse is true: provisions of international law that may *not* be based on existing practice can give rise to expectations about legitimate behavior and may thereby bring practice into line with the law. This is, after all, one way in which states are able to "construct" the environment in which they interact. Second, even with

---

[31] Finnemore, *National Interests in International Society,* p. 139.

customary law, a period of time must usually elapse between a change in practice and the recognition of that change in the content of the customary law. This lag time shows not only that norms and laws can be quite distinct but also that it is the norms that are more determinative of state behavior. An illustration of this sort of lag between changes in practice and international law is presented in the trial at Nuremberg of Karl Dönitz, Grand Admiral of the German Navy and head of U-boat command.[32] The long-standing law with regard to naval warfare dictated that an enemy merchant ship could be sunk only if it was impossible to bring the ship into port, and even then only after the safety of passengers and crew was provided for. This rule proved impracticable for submarine warfare, however, since there was no room on board to accommodate captured merchant seamen, and in surfacing to give warning of an attack the lightly armed submarine would become vulnerable to ramming by the merchant vessel. Consequently, German U-boats, along with submarines of other belligerent nations, adopted a "sink on sight" policy, attacking without warning. Although this was technically a clear violation of the preexisting law of naval warfare, the Nuremberg tribunal declined to charge Dönitz on these grounds. Michael Walzer notes:

> The Judges apparently decided that the distinction between merchant ships and warships no longer made much sense. . . . The invention of the submarine had made [the "sink on sight" policy] "necessary." The old rules were morally if not legally suspended because supply by sea—a military enterprise whose participants had always been liable to attack—had ceased now to be subject to nonviolent interdiction.[33]

Moreover, Dönitz was acquitted of the charge of ordering U-boats to deny assistance to survivors of their attacks. His defense was strengthened by the testimony of U.S. Fleet Admiral Chester Nimitz, who observed that U.S. submarines also "did not rescue enemy survivors if by so doing the vessels were exposed to unnecessary or additional risk."[34]

The Dönitz case illustrates how technological and tactical innovation can make existing provisions in international law more or less obsolete. By the end of the Second World War, the law against "sink on sight" attacks was clearly (if a pun will be excused) dead in the water. And although the Nuremberg panel insisted that the rule requiring the res-

[32] This story is recounted in Walzer, *Just and Unjust Wars*, pp. 147–51.
[33] Ibid., pp. 148–49.
[34] Quoted in ibid., p. 150.

cue of survivors should remain intact, the fact that none of the belligerents actually observed the rule made it, in Walzer's words, "unenforceable."[35] In one case, international law changed to conform to prevailing practice; in the other, the law remained technically the same, but a new norm reflecting changes in practice made adherence to the law problematic.

Of course, it is not always the case that norms are more permissive than international law. Sometimes, in fact, the opposite is true. As we shall see, for example, norms against the personal targeting of leaders during wartime proscribe actions that international law would allow. Hugo Grotius wrote, quoting Euripides, "What the law does not forbid, then let shame forbid."[36] As I have argued, an analogue of shame—in the form of international condemnation and sanction for the violation of valued norms—remains a powerful influence on state behavior. In any case, for our purposes the fundamental point is that international norms and international laws are not always the same, and laws are neither necessary nor sufficient conditions for normative restraint. Often norms are inconsistent with international law. In these cases, I argue, state actors are more likely to be governed by the norm.

METHODOLOGICAL CHALLENGES

Although this book deals with issues that are inherently normative, the questions it sets out to answer—those concerning the formation and effects of norms—are empirical. In other words, I do not seek to pass ethical judgment in the cases I examine, instead taking the normative significance of certain actions or proscriptions more or less as matters of fact, apparent to national decision makers as such. For the purposes of understanding the norms at issue in Churchill's exchange with Stalin at Tehran, for example, what is important is that Churchill himself clearly saw mass executions as presenting ethical problems, not whether an observer would agree with his moral assessment. While my approach requires some measure of interpretation concerning the manner in which norms may diverge from underlying moral principles, the focus of the study is nevertheless fundamentally empirical and historical in both substance and tone.

[35] Ibid.

[36] Quoted in Guenter Lewy, *America in Vietnam* (Oxford: Oxford University Press, 1978), p. 270.

There are two major methodological challenges posed by the study of norms.[37] The first is determining when a norm exists. Because norms are *inter*subjective, not merely subjective, phenomena, this problem is less daunting than is often supposed. Again, ideational structures like norms may be less tangible than material phenomena, but they are not necessarily any less real. For example, the fact that both time and money are artificial constructs that rely on intersubjective understandings does not mean that the statement "the national minimum wage is X dollars per hour" is a matter of opinion. Facts based on shared understandings about ideas are still facts, and factual conclusions can be reached concerning their existence. Therefore, a review of such primary sources as the texts of international instruments, diplomatic archives, diaries of conference delegates and state policy makers, and personal interviews should yield reasonably clear evidence about the existence of and bases for the norms in question. The second, stickier, problem is determining the causal effects of norms. Although it is relatively clear, for example, when a norm has failed, the opacity of motivations makes it difficult to be sure when a norm has succeeded. (Although it can be noted that this problem has not dissuaded a generation of theorists of nuclear deterrence.) The challenge is compounded by the very interrelationship between norms and interests I am setting out to demonstrate. Because they are mutually generative, it is difficult to designate either as an independent or a dependent variable to test for causal effects; both phenomena are both sorts of variable at different times.

Nevertheless, there are at least two methods for gaining insight into the effects of norms. The first is careful and extensive examination of the historical record to try to trace specific decision-making processes that resulted in norm adherence.[38] The second is to employ counterfactual reasoning in these cases. This involves trying to discern as nearly as possible what constituted a state's material interests in specific circumstances, thereby creating a null hypothesis against which to judge actual policy. Neither method is likely to satisfy narrowly positivistic social scientists who wish to exclude matters of interpretation and intersubjectivity from the analysis of international politics. Still, if norms are to be

[37] For thoughtful evaluations of the methodological challenges inherent in studying norms, see Legro, "Which Norms Matter?" pp. 2–4; and Kowert and Legro, "Norms, Identities, and Their Limits."

[38] This method of "process tracing" is described by Jeffrey Legro as "intended to investigate and explain the decision process by which various initial conditions are translated into outcomes." *Cooperation under Fire*, p. 33 n. 93.

taken seriously it is impossible to avoid questions of motivation and interpretation, for it is on these levels that norms—or any structural constraints, for that matter—ultimately operate.[39] As Goldstein and Keohane point out, "After all, we do not observe beliefs directly; we observe only claims about beliefs and actions presumably based upon beliefs. Thus our descriptions of beliefs require inferences, which need insofar as possible to be tested."[40] The methodology of this study thus reflects two fundamental assumptions: that interpretation and inference are necessary and proper elements of the study of international relations; and that this approach is consistent with a strong commitment to empirical research and testing.

[39] This point is further developed in chapter 6, infra.
[40] Goldstein and Keohane, "Ideas and Foreign Policy: A Framework for Analysis," p. 27.

CHAPTER 3

International Assassination
"An Infamous and Execrable Practice"

Killing a man is murder unless you do it to the sound of trumpets.

Voltaire

In July of 1991 the *Los Angeles Times* reported that intelligence officials from Britain, France, Israel, and the United States had held a series of secret meetings between the previous August and the beginning of the Persian Gulf War in January. A major topic of discussion was the possibility of assassinating Iraqi leader Saddam Hussein. British agents operating within Iraq, the story stated, had devised a workable plan for the assassination, which was subsequently approved by the British government. Ultimately, however, President George Bush of the United States, along with the Israeli government, vetoed the plan.[1]

One can imagine that Bush was tempted by the prospect of getting rid of Saddam on these terms. Iraq's invasion of Kuwait in August had shown Saddam to be an aggressive threat to order in the strategically crucial Persian Gulf region. The United States was in the midst of a mas-

---

[1] Yossi Melman, "Why the Plot to Kill Hussein Failed," *Los Angeles Times,* July 21, 1991, pp. M1–2.

sive and costly buildup of troops in Saudi Arabia and faced the prospect of significant loss of life if it proved necessary to restore Kuwaiti sovereignty by force—a course that also presented tremendous political risks for Bush personally. Eliminating Saddam promised to obviate these problems; indeed, on the day after the invasion of Kuwait, Bush ordered the CIA to launch a covert campaign to destabilize the Iraqi regime and remove Saddam from power.[2] Domestically, public opinion viewed Saddam as a dangerous and irrational tyrant who was personally responsible for the Kuwait crisis. Finally, the assassination plot offered the advantage of being a multilateral operation, providing Bush some degree of cover from political fallout. In the final analysis, however, "Bush, who needed the support of a reluctant Congress for his war plans, realized a formal request to reverse the executive order [banning U.S. involvement in assassinations] and assassinate Hussein would infuriate Congress, triggering unprecedented condemnation domestically if it was ever disclosed. It also threatened to break Bush's carefully constructed international coalition."[3]

Whether they would agree with the decision or not, few observers of international politics could fail to understand Bush's trepidation about involvement in political assassination. There is a long-standing consensus in the international community that the murder of national leaders is a grossly inappropriate means of conducting foreign policy. Upon reflection, however, Bush's reaction raises some interesting questions. How, exactly, may his reservations be described? They were almost certainly not "strategic" reservations. Indeed, since killing Saddam might solve a huge strategic problem at low cost in terms of both human life and treasure, a rationalist analysis of the situation would seem to recommend assassination as a prudent step. It also somehow seems incongruous to refer to them as "moral" qualms. Saddam's death would have been viewed with considerable relief if not exuberance. As Bush would later say, "No one will weep for him when he's gone."[4] A clear, if unstated, objective of the air campaign that eventually ensued was to hasten Saddam's demise, a goal that was widely supported by the American public. Moreover, any moral objections to killing Saddam could be answered by pointing to his culpability in the current crisis and the thou-

[2] Bob Woodward, *The Commanders* (New York: Simon and Schuster, 1991), pp. 237, 282.
[3] Melman, "Why the Plot to Kill Hussein Failed," p. M2.
[4] George Bush, Press Conference, January 25, 1991, *Public Papers of the Presidents of the United States: George Bush, 1991*, vol. 1 (Washington: D.C. Government Printing Office, 1992), p. 68.

sands of innocent lives that would be spared if war were averted. On another level, however, the problem *was* fundamentally a moral one. The pernicious effects that Bush feared could not be explained without reference to the sense of moral outrage that would ensue over U.S. complicity in political assassination. At some level, of course, Bush's misgivings were clearly "political," in that he feared that the reaction to U.S. involvement would destroy his coalition and cripple him domestically. But this begs the question: what is it about assassination that would engender such a response?

It is clear that there exists, as one commentator puts it, "an internationally recognized rule prohibiting assassination."[5] Although this rule is well-established in international law, its significance in international politics arguably has less to do with technical legal proscriptions than with a more general and visceral aversion to assassination as an instrument of foreign policy, particularly when the intended victims are national leaders. There is, in other words, a strong international norm that excludes assassination from the menu of foreign policy options, even when important interests are at stake. As former presidential adviser George Stephanopoulos writes, "Of all the words you just can't say in the modern White House . . . none is more taboo than 'assassination.' "[6]

In the United States the issue came to prominence during the 1975–76 Church committee and Pike committee congressional investigations into U.S. intelligence abuses, which included involvement in plots to assassinate foreign heads of state in the 1950s and 1960s. In response to these embarrassing revelations, and to preempt legislation pending in Congress, in 1977 President Gerald Ford issued Executive Order 11905 prohibiting U.S. involvement in assassination.[7] This order, which has been renewed by every American president since, arguably broke no new legal ground, for assassination was already prohibited under both treaty and customary international law.[8] The executive order

---

[5] Francis A. Boyle, "Letter: Law of the Land," *New York Times*, February 9, 1991, p. A26.

[6] George Stephanopoulos, "Why We Should Kill Saddam," *Newsweek*, December 1, 1997, p. 34.

[7] W. Hays Parks, "Memorandum of Law: Executive Order 12333 and Assassination," *The Army Lawyer* (December 1989):4–9.

[8] Most fundamentally, international assassination constitutes both an unlawful use of force and intervention in the internal affairs of sovereign states, both of which are forbidden under the charters of the United Nations and the Organization of American States. The 1937 Convention for the Prevention and Repression of Terrorism and the New York Convention of 1973 codified the illegality of the assassination of foreign leaders, their families, and other "protected persons." Finally, a long line of customary international law,

and the Senate investigation, however, were prompted less by legal than by normative concerns. It was difficult to find anyone who was willing to defend the use of assassination as a foreign policy tool. The Church committee's report repeatedly stressed that assassination was unacceptable, and witnesses appearing before the committee, including former directors of Central Intelligence who had overseen the plots, "uniformly condemned assassination . . . as immoral."[9] The point, it seemed, was beyond debate.

Still, the presumptive immorality of assassination, as Michael Walzer notes, "only partially represents our common moral judgments. For we judge the assassin by his victim, and when the victim is Hitler-like in character, we are likely to praise the assassin's work."[10] This is particularly true if, by the taking of one life, many others are spared. Major Ralph Peters, writing in the journal of the U.S. Army War College, describes this as an "ethical disconnect":

> While it was acceptable to bomb those divisions of hapless conscripts, it was unthinkable to announce and carry out a threat to kill Saddam Hussein, although he bore overwhelming guilt for the entire war and its atrocities. We justify this moral and practical muddle by stating that we do not sanction assassination in general, and certainly not the assassination of foreign heads of state. Yet where is the ethical logic in this? Why is it acceptable to slaughter—and I use that word advisedly—the commanded masses but not to mortally punish the guiltiest individual, the commander, a man stained with the blood of his own people as well as that of his neighbors?[11]

Although the norm against assassination has been the subject of remarkably little scholarly attention,[12] it raises several compelling ques-

---

dating back to the seventeenth- and eighteenth-century writings of Grotius and Vattel and running through the incorporation of the restrictions of the Hague Convention of 1907 by the Nuremberg Tribunal, forbids assassination in time of war. Bert Brandenburg, "Note: The Legality of Assassination as an Aspect of Foreign Policy," *Virginia Journal of International Law* 27, no. 3 (1987): 661–62; Michael N. Schmitt, "State-Sponsored Assassination in International and Domestic Law, *Yale Journal of International Law* 17 (1992): 609–85; Parks, "Memorandum of Law."

[9] Select Senate Committee to Study Governmental Operations with Respect to Intelligence Activities, *Alleged Assassination Plots involving Foreign Leaders* (Washington, D.C.: Government Printing Office, 1975), p. 259.

[10] Walzer, *Just and Unjust Wars,* p. 199.

[11] Peters, "A Revolution in Military Ethics?" p. 104.

[12] More attention has been given to this issue by international lawyers, largely in response to calls for the assassination of Saddam Hussein in 1990 and 1991. See, e.g.,

tions. Where did the norm come from? How does it influence state actors? What accounts for its apparent precedence over other ethical injunctions, such as the principle of proportionality in the conduct of warfare? In this chapter I seek to answer these questions. I begin by tracing the rise of the norm in international politics, demonstrating that although the norm is grounded in fundamental moral principles its development was decisively influenced by the structure of the international system. In effect, by limiting legitimate modes of violence between states to war or large-scale intervention, the prohibition on assassination reinforces the position of great powers relative to other states and nonstate actors, thereby serving a power-maintenance function in the international system. This helps to explain the relative strength and durability of the norm despite its occasionally anomalous moral implications. I close by examining the status of the norm in contemporary international politics, taking up the question of whether the norm is in decline.

ASSASSINATION IN HISTORICAL PERSPECTIVE

The norm against the assassination of foreign leaders is a relatively recent construction.[13] Before the mid-seventeenth century, as Hans

---

Louis Rene Beres, "Assassinating Saddam: A Post-War View from International Law," *Denver Journal of International Law and Policy* 19, no. 3 (1991): 613–23; Louis Rene Beres, "The Permissiblity of State-Sponsored Assassination during Peace and War," *Temple International and Comparative Law Journal* 5 (1991): 231–49; Schmitt, "State-Sponsored Assassination in International and Domestic Law"; Patricia Zengel, "Assassination and the Law of Armed Conflict," *Mercer Law Review* 43 (1991): 615–44; and Boyd M. Johnson III, "Executive Order 12,333: The Permissibility of an American Assassination of a Foreign Leader," *Cornell International Law Journal* 25 (1992): 401–35.

[13] In this chapter I will be concerned with the norm against a government using the assassination of foreign heads of state or other very high-ranking officials as a tool of foreign policy. I define the norm in terms of foreign leaders, as opposed to foreign nationals more generally, because the idea of insulating national *leaders* from political violence was central to the development of the norm against international assassination and remains central to the strength of the norm in contemporary international politics. Of course, this focus excludes tyrannicides, as well as killings in aid of national liberation movements and the killing of officials of an occupying government by citizens of the occupied territory. Although there may be an "international" dimension to such killings, partisans and resistance groups do not face the same systemic pressures that confront sovereign governments, and it is the effect of such pressures that are of primary interest to us here. Norms operate differently for different types of actors, whether the content of the norm is the same or not. For example, Nachman Ben-Yehuda has shown that the frequency of "assassination events" by Jews in the Middle East dropped sharply soon after Israeli independence in

Morgenthau writes, "international politics was considered exclusively as a technique, without moral significance, for the purpose of maintaining and gaining power, [and] such methods [as assassination] were used without moral scruples and as a matter of course."[14] A late-nineteenth-century commentator on international law noted that "assassinations for public purposes seem to have been regarded with approval in ancient and medieval times."[15] Indeed, seventeenth-century jurist Alberico Gentili recounted a litany of cases that made it clear that the murder of enemy leaders was an exceedingly common method of pursuing foreign policy among the ancients.[16] Of course, the taking of a life presented obvious moral problems, but these did not give rise to a full-fledged international norm—a collective understanding that assassination in the conduct of foreign policy was improper—until considerably later.

The notable exception in the ancient world was Rome, where a norm emerged stigmatizing the assassination of foreign enemies. Martin Wight writes that "the Roman general Fabricius . . . disdainfully rejected a proposal for poisoning the invader Pyrrhus which was put to him by a deserter from Pyrrhus' camp, and handed the man over to Pyrrhus. Cicero comments that if we consult that vulgar conception of expediency, this one deserter would have put an end to a wasting invasion, but it would have been at the price of lasting disgrace."[17] Many authors, particularly the treatise writers of the sixteenth through eighteenth centuries, commented on the Romans' highly developed sense of honor in this regard. Gentili noted that the Roman emperor Tiberius and the Senate declined an offer to poison Arminius, "the most cruel and treacherous of their enemies," and Balthazar Ayala wrote that "the conduct of Quintus Servilius Caepio was much reprobated in that he made

---

1948, suggesting that assassination is a more popular tool of those fighting for sovereignty than of those exercising it. This drop-off is all the more striking when one considers that many of Israel's leaders in the years after 1948 were the same individuals who had been involved in assassination during the fight for independence. Nachman Ben-Yehuda, *Political Assassinations by Jews: A Rhetorical Device for Justice* (Albany: State University of New York Press, 1993), chap. 11.

[14] Hans J. Morgenthau, *Politics among Nations: The Struggle for Power and Peace*, 4th ed. (New York: McGraw-Hill, 1967), p. 225.

[15] Thomas J. Lawrence, *The Principles of International Law*, 7th ed. (Boston: D.C. Heath, 1923), sec. 208.

[16] Alberico Gentili, *De Iure Belli Libri Tres* (1612), reprinted in *The Classics of International Law*, trans. John C. Rolfe (Oxford: Clarendon Press, 1933), p. 166.

[17] Martin Wight, "Western Values in International Relations," p. 125.

away with Viriatus by fraud and snares and domestic assassins, so that he was said to have trafficked for a victory rather than to have gained one."[18] As Ayala's comment suggests, the Roman attitude toward assassination in foreign affairs derived not simply from a heightened moral sense but was tied to a military ethic that valued the pursuit of policy goals by the clash of arms rather than intrigue. Thus Ayala noted that the Romans "disdained all such frauds and deceptions and had no wish to conquer save by sheer valor and downright force—what they used to call Roman methods."[19] There is, however, a clear geopolitical subtext to these expressions of valor. The Romans possessed the most powerful army in the world and therefore uniquely stood to benefit from a normative structure that delegitimized subterfuge and exalted the military virtues of "sheer valor and downright force." That these were seen as heroic qualities was at least partly a social construction that reflected the status of Rome as the dominant power of the ancient world.[20] Strikingly, Romans displayed less ethical aversion to assassination in a domestic context. The death of Julius Caesar in the Senate was only one in a numbing chain of political murders justified by their perpetrators as tyrannicides.[21] It is certainly ironic that Cicero, who spoke eloquently of the precedence of valor over treachery in warfare, also offered one of history's most influential defenses of tyrannicide.[22] In any case, the Romans were exceptional among their contemporaries in eschewing international assassination so systematically.[23]

Throughout the medieval period there were occasional expressions of misgivings about assassination, sometimes reinforced by the knightly code of chivalry, which like the Roman ethic emphasized military virtues and face-to-face combat.[24] Although the chivalric code exercised a mod-

---

[18] Gentili, *De Iure Belli Libri Tres*, p. 156; and Balthazar Ayala, *De Jure et Officiis Bellicis et Disciplina Militari Libri III* (1582), reprinted in *The Classics of International Law*, trans. John P. Bate (Washington, D.C.: Carnegie Institution of Washington, 1912), p. 87.

[19] Ayala, *De Jure et Officiis Bellicis*, p. 85.

[20] In other civilizations and cultures, for example, assassination itself was often depicted as heroic. See, for example, Franklin L. Ford, *Political Murder: From Tyrannicide to Terrorism* (Cambridge, Mass.: Harvard University Press, 1985), esp. chaps. 1–5.

[21] Ibid., chap. 3.

[22] Gentili, *De Iure Belli*, p. 157.

[23] Ford, *Political Murder*, chap. 3.

[24] As James Turner Johnson argues, the code of chivalry was itself largely a social construction: its content reflected the self-interest and protection of prerogatives of the knightly class. Johnson, *Just War Tradition and the Restraint of War* (Princeton, N.J.: Princeton University Press, 1981), pp. 41–49, 131–50.

erating influence on the conduct of war through the medieval period and into the Renaissance, it failed to dampen the practice of assassination. The city-states of Italy were particularly notorious. According to Morgenthau: "The Republic of Venice, from 1415 to 1525, planned or attempted about two hundred assassinations for purposes of its foreign policy," and even chronicled these efforts in its official records.[25] Venice's ruling Council openly solicited proposals for the murder of domestic and foreign enemies, which led to business arrangements with aspiring assassins who ran the gamut from clergymen to, as historian Horatio Brown puts it, "the very scum of society."[26] Among the former was the enterprising Brother John of Ragusa, who in 1513 offered to "work wonders in killing any one [the Council] chose" according to a sliding price scale: "For the Grand Turk, 500 ducats; for the King of Spain (exclusive of traveling expenses), 150 ducats; for the Duke of Milan, 60 ducats; for the Marquis of Mantua, 50 ducats; for His Holiness, only 100 ducats. As a rule, the longer the journey and the more valuable the life, the higher would be the price."[27] So routine was assassination among the dealings of the state that official records often addressed it with the bureaucratic matter-of-factness evident in the expense report of an archbishop who was to poison an enemy:

> But for this purpose he requires a poison, which he charges himself to have made by a capable poison master if the money be supplied him; and, further, inasmuch as the said archbishop, from Easter last to the present time, has, out of his own pocket, been paying the inn charges of the said [accomplices] John of Este, John Barberio, and Baldaserre de Odoni, who is now in prison in Ferrara, following them all over the place in order to carry out his intent, in the course of which he has spent one hundred and eighty ducats of his own money. Be it resolved, that for making the poison, for necessary expenses, and for buying a horse for said archbishop—for his own is dead—the sum of fifty ducats out of our treasury be given to the archbishop and his companion.

The resolution passed by a vote of ten to five.[28]

To be sure, there remained some recognition that murder was, in the

[25] Morgenthau, *Politics among Nations*, p. 225.
[26] Horatio F. Brown, *Studies in the History of Venice* (New York: E. P. Dutton, 1907), p. 237.
[27] Ibid., pp. 236–37.
[28] Ibid., pp. 235–36.

abstract, morally wrong. Offers put to the Council often contained perfunctory language acknowledging that the drastic measures proposed were only being considered because of the great risk posed to the state by its enemies. As Brown explains: "Although the doctrine was thus formulated as a tenable thesis in political ethics, and assassination was sanctioned as a legitimate weapon in the hands of government, it is impossible to read the documents relating to the question without feeling that men had a bad conscience on the matter."[29] Still, given the frequency with which the Venetians and other Italian officials resorted to assassination, it is hard to conclude that their consciences presented much of an obstacle.

Nor was this phenomenon confined to Italy. Both the practice of international assassination and its acceptance as a valid means of conducting the affairs of state were widespread throughout Europe during the Renaissance.[30] It was a Spanish plot against Bartholomew Alvian, leader of the Venetian army, that prompted Francesco Guiccardini to note the contrast between the norms of sixteenth-century Europe and those of ancient Rome: "So different are the customs of the soldiery of today from those of antiquity, when such plots were even revealed by enemy to enemy."[31] This state of affairs was exacerbated by the Reformation, which not only created new lines of fracture in European politics but stirred religious passions, turning enemies into heretics and wars into crusades. Philip II of Spain, who played a major role in the Catholic Counter-Reformation, was an enthusiastic advocate of the assassination of Protestant leaders, placing a price on the head of William of Orange, the leader of Holland (who was in fact murdered in 1584), and sponsoring several plots to kill Queen Elizabeth I of England.[32] During the 1570s and 1580s alone, Elizabeth was the subject of at least twenty assassination plots supported by foreign powers, and herself employed assassins in Ireland.[33]

Even the Catholic Church, which as the supreme spiritual and moral authority in Europe had been central to the development of many of the

---

[29] Ibid., pp. 224, 243.

[30] Ibid., pp. 219, 231.

[31] Quoted in Gentili, *De Iure Belli*, p. 167.

[32] Ford, *Political Murder*, pp. 155–62; and Geoffrey Parker, *The Grand Strategy of Philip II* (New Haven: Yale University Press, 1998), pp. 134–35, 171.

[33] Geoffrey Parker, "Early Modern Europe," in *The Laws of War: Constraints on Warfare in the Western World*, ed. Michael Howard, George J. Andreopoulos, and Mark R. Shulman (New Haven: Yale University Press, 1994), p. 41.

rules that sought to humanize war, exercised no such restraining force in the case of assassination. This was for two reasons. First, a line of theological defenses of tyrannicide dating back to Thomas Aquinas and running through influential tracts such as that by the Spanish Jesuit Juan de Mariana were easily adopted as justification for political murder in general, especially during the Reformation.[34] Second, the popes, who had long taken an active role in European politics, had no less than other leaders made liberal use of assassination as a tool of policy.[35] During the Counter-Reformation some of the most vitriolic calls for the murder of Protestant leaders came from the Vatican. Pius V, in a papal bull in 1570, excommunicated Elizabeth, "the bastard daughter of Henry VIII and Anne Boleyn," and called for her to be deposed. Ten years later, a Vatican official went further: "Since that guilty woman . . . is the cause of so much injury to the Catholic faith and loss of so many million souls, there is no doubt that whoever sends her out of the world with pious intention of doing God service not only does not sin but gains merit." And in 1584, upon learning of the assassination of William of Orange, Pope Gregory XIII ordered a religious observance in celebration of the event.[36]

So prevalent was assassination in Europe that the practice gained acceptance in the treatises that would serve as the foundation for the nascent field of international law.[37] In 1516 Thomas More extolled the use of assassination both as a useful tool of statecraft and as a means of sparing ordinary citizens the hardships of wars for which their leaders were responsible.[38] Horatio Brown quotes from the treatise of an anonymous Italian author of the mid-sixteenth century that is remarkable for its similarity to many modern defenses of assassination. The subject of the treatise is "Of the Right that Princes have to compass the Lives of Their Enemies' Allies":

[34] Ford, *Political Murder*, pp. 123–25, 156–57; Alan Marshall, *Intelligence and Espionage in the Reign of Charles II, 1660–1685* (Cambridge: Cambridge University Press, 1994), chap. 8.
[35] Brown, *Studies in the History of Venice*, chap. 6; Ford, *Political Murder*, chaps. 7–8.
[36] Ford, *Political Murder*, pp. 162, 156.
[37] Early treatises, particularly in the sixteenth century, were not explicitly legal tracts but rather amalgams of history, political theory, and moral casuistry aimed not only at generating principles of conduct among nations but also at providing rules of prudence for leaders.
[38] Beres, "The Permissibility of State-Sponsored Assassination during Peace and War," p. 249; Gentili, *De Iure Belli*, p. 167.

In all strictness of sound policy you may and can debilitate your enemy in any way you choose, even by the treacherous murder of his allies. . . . This way of depriving him of friends and adherents is both most opportune and obligatory. . . . Nor should any methods you may adopt toward such an end seem strange and iniquitous, for open war does not exclude methods quite as vicious. I will even venture to declare that conspiracy may be the least impious method you can use. . . . For, pressed to its last issue, a conspiracy only results in the slaughter of one man who, as principal or ally, has had a share in the origin or in the progress of the war; while the mass of persons who perish in the incidents of a campaign are for the most part entirely innocent.

So, the treatise concluded, "conspiracy, as a wise and intelligent prince would know quite well, [is] both possible and legal for reasons of state."[39] What is striking about this passage is that assassination is defended not only as consistent with prevailing practice and custom but also as a morally superior course of action in terms of its consequences.

AN "INFAMOUS AND EXECRABLE" PRACTICE

In the early seventeenth century, attitudes toward assassination began to change dramatically. Historians and political philosophers began to condemn assassination, even of tyrants and religious enemies.[40] Moreover, this change was reflected in both the rhetoric and actions of the era's political and military leaders, leading to a marked decline in the number of assassinations and a distaste for the act that bordered on contempt. A mere generation after the open plotting of Philip II, Spain denounced as "an atrocious calumny" rumors that it had been involved in the assassination of French Huguenot King Henry IV.[41] Franklin Ford notes that, given the brutal nature of the Thirty Years' War, it is remarkable that so few of its major figures were "slain by stealth."[42] Both Hapsburg Emperor Ferdinand II and Philip IV of Spain, for example,

---

[39] Quoted in Brown, *Studies in the History of Venice*, pp. 225–29.

[40] Ford, *Political Murder*, pp. 181–84, 198.

[41] Emmerich de Vattel, *Le droit des gens; ou, principes de la loi naturelle, appliques a la conduite et aux affaires des nations et des souverains* (1758), reprinted in *The Classics of International Law*, trans. Charles G. Fenwick (Washington, D.C.: Carnegie Institution of Washington, 1916), p. 288.

[42] Ford, *Political Murder*, p. 185.

declined offers to assassinate Gustav Adolf of Sweden, even as his Protestant armies won repeated victories. And although assassination remained a common feature of domestic European political life in the 1600s, foreign powers were rarely involved. Although the English widely asserted at the time of the 1696 attempt on the life of King William that France's Louis XIV and the pope had conspired in the plot, there is no evidence that this was the case.[43] In fact, the exiled James II, whom the would-be assassins sought to restore to the throne, was unaware of the plot and reportedly became "furious" when the possibility of assassinating William was raised.[44]

The norm against international assassination grew stronger as the violence of the religious wars receded, and by the eighteenth century it was firmly entrenched in international society. In his 1758 treatise on international law, Emmerich de Vattel wrote: "I give, then, the name of assassination to treacherous murder . . . and such an attempt, I say, is infamous and execrable, both in him who executes it and in him who commands it. . . . The sovereign who makes use of such execrable means should be regarded as an enemy of the human race, and all Nations are called upon, in the interests of the common safety of mankind, to join forces and unite to punish him."[45] There was, moreover, a sense that assassination was an anachronism, a relic of an earlier, less enlightened age. Thomas Jefferson wrote in a 1789 letter to James Madison: "Assassination, poison, perjury. . . . All of these were legitimate principles in the dark ages which intervened between ancient and modern civilizations, but exploded and held in just horror in the eighteenth century."[46] Indeed, it is difficult to find evidence of assassination being used in the conduct of foreign policy in the eighteenth and nineteenth centuries. By the middle of the eighteenth century, the cabinet in which the Council of Venice kept the stores of poison for use against its enemies had fallen into such confusion and disrepair from generations of neglect that "of several neither the nature nor the dose was known."[47] In 1806, when British foreign secretary Charles Fox was approached with a plan to assassinate Napoleon, Fox not only rejected the offer but arrested the

---

[43] Jane Garrett, *The Triumphs of Providence: The Assassination Plot, 1696* (Cambridge: Cambridge University Press, 1980).

[44] Ibid.

[45] Vattel, *Le droit des gens*, p. 289.

[46] Quoted in Stephen F. Knott, *Secret and Sanctioned: Covert Operations and the American Presidency* (New York: Oxford University Press, 1996), p. 171.

[47] Brown, *Studies in the History of Venice*, p. 254.

would-be assassin and informed the French foreign minister of the plot.[48] Even as political violence increased in both the international and domestic spheres, the murder of foreign leaders remained out of bounds. A 1911 treatise that surveyed all nineteenth-century practice on the matter noted only one instance of the government of a "civilised nation" violating the norm—China, which placed a price on the heads of three enemy generals in its war with Japan.[49] Governments viewed international assassination with such sensitivity that in 1881 an English writer was sent to prison simply for commenting approvingly on the assassination of the Russian czar by his own countrymen.[50]

The prohibition on assassination was also included in the law of war that began to be codified in the late 1800s. Prior to that time, the law of war had been almost entirely a matter of custom, guided to an extent by the interpretations in the treatises but more commonly by an unwritten set of expectations based on prevailing practice. The first attempts at codification were manuals promulgated by governments to regulate the conduct of their own armies. Among the most influential was the U.S. Army's Lieber Code of 1863, which echoed the prevailing view when it stated: "Civilized nations look with horror upon offers or rewards for the assassination of enemies as relapses into barbarism."[51] This customary prohibition on assassination as "treacherous killing" was adopted at the Hague Convention in 1907 as the definitive statement of the law of war on the matter, and it has survived in more or less the same form in subsequent international agreements and conventions.[52]

Even the paroxysms of violence that shook the international system in the first half of the twentieth century failed to overcome the aversion to assassination as a foreign policy tool. Although the Soviet NKVD, and later the KGB, employed assassination on a wide scale against enemies abroad, few victims were foreign nationals, and there is little evidence that foreign officials were ever targeted.[53] One of the few instances in the first half of the twentieth century in which the involvement of a foreign

---

[48] Wight, "Western Values in International Relations," p. 125.

[49] J. M. Spaight, *War Rights on Land* (London: MacMillan, 1911), p. 86.

[50] David Rapoport, *Assassination and Terrorism* (Toronto: Canadian Broadcasting Corp., 1971), p. 4.

[51] Zengel, "Assassination and the Law of Armed Conflict," pp. 622.

[52] Ibid., pp. 621–31; Brandenburg, "The Legality of Assassination as an Aspect of Foreign Policy," pp. 659–60.

[53] Ilya Dzhirkvelov, *Secret Servant: My Life with the KGB and the Soviet Elite* (New York: Harper and Row, 1987); and Stephen Schwartz, "Intellectuals and Assassins—Annals of Stalin's Killerati," *New York Times Book Review*, January 24, 1988, pp. 3, 30–31.

government in the assassination of a national leader appears to have been likely—the 1934 murder of Austrian chancellor Engelbert Dollfuss—was believed to have been ordered by German chancellor Adolf Hitler, and was condemned as an extreme example of Hitler's disregard for the norms of international society.[54] Even Hitler, however, although he had no compunction about the murder of domestic opponents on a shocking scale, made little use of assassination in an international context.[55] Nor, most surprisingly, was Hitler himself a frequent target of foreign plots. In 1938, for example, the British military attaché in Berlin, Lt. Gen. Noel Mason MacFarlane, proposed to his government a plan for assassinating Hitler, thereby possibly averting the European war that seemed imminent. The British government, however, rejected the idea on the grounds that it was "unsportsmanlike."[56] Moreover, despite the gravity of the threat that Hitler posed to British interests, MacFarlane advanced the plan "without the slightest hope that it would be accepted" by his superiors.[57] He knew that his proposal was, quite simply, against the rules that govern state behavior. This attitude changed only gradually during World War II itself. Despite the desperate situation faced by Britain in the early years of the war, it was not until June 1944 that the British Special Operations Executive (SOE) undertook "a deliberate and continuous effort to try and liquidate Hitler."[58] Even then, there remained "a grave divergence of views" on the matter within the government and the SOE, and the plan was never implemented.[59]

ANALYSIS OF THE RISE OF THE NORM

Because international ethical norms are geopolitically constructed, they typically comprise two strands: one based upon a priori moral principles, and the other grounded in more historically contingent cultural and geopolitical factors. Until the early seventeenth century, the first strand of a norm against assassination—the principle that treacherous

---

[54] Ford, *Political Murder*, p. 267; and Joseph Bornstein, *The Politics of Murder* (New York: William Sloane, 1950), chap. 5.

[55] Ford, *Political Murder*, p. 269.

[56] "Plan to Kill Hitler Was 'Unsporting,'" *Times* (London), August 5, 1969, p. 5.

[57] Ewen Butler, "'I Talked of Plan to Kill Hitler'," *Times* (London), August 6, 1969, p. 1.

[58] "Hunting Hitler," *Sunday Times* (London), July 26, 1998, sec. 5, pp. 1–2.

[59] Ibid., p. 2; and Daniel Johnson, "Why Did We Hesitate to Kill Hitler?" *Times* (London), July 24, 1998.

murder is morally wrong—existed but had seldom been sufficient to significantly constrain foreign policy. In the early 1600s, however, a second strand was added: the association of assassination with disorder and systemic chaos. Specifically, conditions emerged that contributed to the idea that national leaders should be insulated from political violence. To understand the basis for these concerns, one must recall that the norm emerged at a time of enormous upheaval in European life. Religious divisions bred chaos and mistrust both within and among nations, eventually exploding into the Thirty Years' War, which consumed the continent in violence from 1618 to 1648. Stephen Toulmin has argued that the crisis of the early seventeenth century was so complete that it led to the rejection of prevalent modes of thought and a "quest for certainty" that demanded rationality in the intellectual arena and stability in the political arena.[60] The pivotal event in this crisis, Toulmin asserts, was the 1610 assassination of King Henry IV of France, who had championed religious accommodation. Although it was not the result of an international plot, Henry's death at the hands of a Catholic zealot had far-reaching implications for a fractured Europe, triggering the slide into general religious warfare.[61]

Although Henry's murder was perhaps the single most significant event in the emergence of the norm against assassination, the norm also reflected changes in the broader context of the European system. Among these were changes not only in the distribution of power in European society but also in the way in which that power was exercised. The most important political manifestation of the "quest for certainty" that Toulmin describes was the rise of the institution of sovereign statehood. The date commonly given for the beginning of the era of modern sovereign territorial states is 1648, the year in which the Peace of Westphalia ended the Thirty Years' War. The emergence of the modern states system was, however, less a discrete event than a gradual change in institutions and ideas that began well before 1648 and was not completed until some time afterward.[62] Along with sovereign statehood came two interrelated phenomena, one predominantly material and the other predominantly ideational—both of which contributed to the

[60] Stephen Toulmin, *Cosmopolis: The Hidden Agenda of Modernity* (New York: Free Press, 1990), see especially chap. 2. I am indebted to Ivan Toft for bringing Toulmin's argument to my attention.

[61] Ibid., pp. 47–53.

[62] See, for example, Stephen D. Krasner, "Westphalia and All That," in *Ideas and Foreign Policy*, pp. 235–64.

norm against assassination. The material development was the rise of the mass army. As Charles Tilly and others have argued, the mass army was both a cause and an effect of the organizational form of the state.[63] States with large armies could expand territorially, which made their power even greater. This expansion, along with the considerable cost of raising and maintaining the army, required the ability to extract resources from a large territorial base, which in turn required a dramatic increase in the size and power of the centralized state apparatus. States unable to play this game tended to disappear, victims of the states that could. As a result, smaller, weaker political entities (including the papacy, from whose influence states were breaking free) could not compete with large states, and conflicts between large states were decided by the clash of huge masses of men.[64] An effective norm against assassination further increased the already formidable advantage of large states by placing their leaders effectively off-limits from personal attack, thereby dictating that the use of force in international relations be conducted on terms most favorable to them.[65]

The ideational phenomenon that accompanied the rise of sovereign states was what Martin van Creveld describes as "the fiction that wars are waged by states, not men. The fiction has it that the members of the government have no personal interest in the matter and are merely acting on behalf of their states."[66] Rousseau offered this explication of the idea: "Individual combats, duels, encounters are not acts that constitute a state. . . . War is not, therefore, a relation between man and man, but

[63] Charles Tilly, "Reflections on the History of European State-Making," in *The Formation of National States in Western Europe*, ed. Tilly (Princeton: Princeton University Press, 1975); and Brian Downing, "Constitutionalism, Warfare, and Change in Early Modern Europe," *Theory and Society* 17, no. 1 (January 1988): 7–56.

[64] On the growth of armies from the late sixteenth century to the early eighteenth century, see Martin L. Van Creveld, *Supplying War: Logistics from Wallenstein to Patton* (Cambridge: Cambridge University Press, 1979), pp. 5–6.

[65] This situation was further compounded by the changes in tactics and command necessitated by the size of armies, which made it less common for a commander to lead his troops in battle. As a result, leaders themselves were at less risk of being killed in conventional combat. On the tactical and organizational aspects of the "military revolution" of the early seventeenth century, see Gunther Rothenberg, "Maurice of Nassau, Gustavus Adolphus, Raimondo Montecuccoli, and the 'Military Revolution' of the Seventeenth Century," in *Makers of Modern Strategy*, ed. Peter Paret (Princeton: Princeton University Press, 1986), pp. 32–63.

[66] Martin L. van Creveld, "The Persian Gulf Crisis of 1990–91 and the Future of Morally Constrained War," p. 31.

between State and State, in which private individuals are enemies only by accident, not as men, nor even as citizens, but as soldiers."[67] In other words, in international politics individuals should be seen as agents rather than principals, even if they happen to be kings or generals. One commentator describes it as "the premise that making war was the proper activity of sovereigns for which they ought not be required to sacrifice their personal safety."[68]

This "fiction," as van Creveld refers to it, is a distinctly modern idea that played a critical role in constructing the theoretical structure of sovereign statehood. While this idea reflected emerging institutional realities, it also hastened them along, disassociating wars from the personal ambitions of rulers while reinforcing the inchoate notion of states as meaningful political structures. Consequently, "the idea of the state as an abstract organization caused an increasingly sharp line to be drawn between the rulers' private persons and their public functions. The latter represented legitimate targets; the former were supposed to remain inviolate."[69] Legitimate targets assumed the use of legitimate means, however; using treachery crossed the line from war to assassination. Moreover, this aspect of the ideational structure of sovereign statehood interacted synergistically with mass armies: it reinforced the normative idea that clashes between large masses of men—rather than intrigue—was the proper way for conflicts to be settled. Consider, for example, the fate of the proposals for the assassination of Sweden's Gustav Adolph put to Ferdinand II and Philip IV. Ferdinand responded by expressing a preference for resolving the matter in battle, "openly and with the sword," rather than by intrigue.[70] Similarly, Philip objected that assassination "would be unworthy of a great and just king. . . . For, it being left to God to punish His enemies, and there remaining to us appropriate and legitimate means to resist and humiliate them according to what prudence and just intention will advise, God will favor [such means], and conscience and reputation will continue to be protected."[71] These objections show that by 1632 a collective understanding was emerging that

---

[67] Jean-Jacques Rousseau, *On the Social Contract*, ed. Roger D. Masters, trans. Judith R. Masters (New York: St. Martin's, 1978), p. 50.

[68] Zengel, "Assassination and the Law of Armed Conflict," p. 621.

[69] van Creveld, "The Persian Gulf Crisis of 1990–91 and the Future of Morally Constrained War," p. 32.

[70] Ford, *Political Murder*, p. 187.

[71] Quoted in ibid., pp. 187–88.

the "appropriate and legitimate" means of dealing with foreign antagonists was to send armies, rather than assassins, against them. Philip's reference to the damage to reputation that might result from involvement in such a plan provides a particularly striking contrast to both the actions and the rhetoric of his grandfather, Philip II, who had been so willing to undertake plots against the Protestant leaders of his day.

A crucial role in the development of the norm against assassination was played by early international lawyers, who in the late 1500s and early 1600s sought for the first time to systematically define the rights and responsibilities of nations in their dealings with one another. Indeed, one can discern a clear progression in the works of the early jurists on the issue of assassination in the conduct of war. Francisco de Vitoria, whose *De Jure Belli* is sometimes described as the first text of international law, did not mention the subject at all, despite devoting considerable attention to other matters concerning the just conduct of war.[72] Balthazar Ayala, writing half a century later, was the first prominent jurist to condemn the use of assassination in foreign policy, arguing that moral considerations of honor, valor, and good faith should take precedence over expediency and self-interest.[73] Although his critique of assassination served as a point of departure for future writers, Ayala was swimming against the current of his times: his treatise was published at the beginning of a decade, the 1580s, that would witness a spate of international plots.

The publication of Alberico Gentili's *De Iure Belli Libri Tres* in 1598 marked a departure from previous approaches. Like Ayala, Gentili condemned assassination on moral grounds, calling it a "shameful" and "wicked" practice, arguing that objectives in war should be achieved by valorous means.[74] Gentili, however, also made use of a distinctly different, subtler line of argument. Apart from being unjust, he wrote, assassination led to consequences that were harmful to the interests of nations that resorted to it. This appeal to self-interest had two dimensions. The first dealt with short-term consequences: the murder of an enemy leader would arouse the ire of his successor and his subjects, setting them on a path of revenge and vindication. Therefore, Gentili suggested, a leader deciding on such a course of action should consider the same action being visited upon himself.[75] The second dimension extended the idea

---

[72] Francisco de Vitoria, *De Jure Belli* (1532), reprinted in *The Classics of International Law*, trans. John P. Bate (Washington, D.C.: Carnegie Institution of Washington, 1917), sec. 34.

[73] Ayala, *De Jure et Officiis Bellicis*, pp. 84–87.

[74] Gentili, *De Iure Belli*, pp. 166–72.

[75] Ibid., pp. 167, 169.

of unintended consequences into the long term by considering the effects of assassination as a generalized practice carried out by all nations. These effects, Gentili argued, are to diminish the safety and security of everyday life and to contribute to disorder in society.[76] It was, however, a specific type of disorder that concerned Gentili, a fact that becomes clear when his comments on assassination are read in conjunction with his treatment of "secret attacks" on enemy leaders. Breaking with earlier authorities, he condemned such attacks: "Public hostility becomes a private matter when the life of one man is attempted in this way. For if such a thing happens on the battlefield, in forays from the camp, then no blame attaches to the enemy, who could not distinguish the leader of the foe from a common soldier. And yet I know that the enemy withheld their hands from the kings of the Lacedaemonians in battle through reverence for them."[77] This passage represents a crucial shift in focus from the *means* used to kill an enemy to the *identity* of the enemy to be killed. Gentili was concerned with protecting leaders themselves, regardless of how honorable or direct the means used to attack them. This shift in emphasis distinguishes Gentili from the simple moralist objections of commentators like Ayala. In fact, from a purely moral standpoint, the passages concerning the personal safety of leaders do not follow logically from concerns with assassination *unless* the essence of the problem is not simply the use of dishonorable means but also the potential for political disorder and instability.

These concerns come to the fore in the work of the most famous of the early jurists, Hugo Grotius.[78] In his writings on the law of war, Grotius granted greater latitude for killing than many of his contemporaries—allowing, for example, the execution of captives and soldiers wishing to surrender.[79] Nevertheless, he strictly forbade assassination, or killing "by treachery," even while holding that other treacherous acts were permissible.[80] Grotius was less concerned with either treachery or killing per se than with treacherous killing specifically. He explained this apparent anomaly in terms evocative of Gentili. A rule against assassination would not only contribute to order, he argued, but would also

---

[76] Ibid., p. 169.

[77] Ibid., p. 170.

[78] Grotius's definitive work, *De Jure Belli ac Pacis Libri Tres* (Three books on the law of war and peace), was first published in 1625.

[79] Hugo Grotius, *De Jure Belli ac Pacis Libri Tres*, rev. ed. (1646), reprinted in *The Classics of International Law*, trans. Francis W. Kelsey (Oxford: Clarendon, 1925), pp. 649–50.

[80] Ibid., pp. 655–56.

"prevent the dangers to persons of particular eminence from becoming excessive."[81] An attendant consequence, as with Gentili, was the reassertion of the normative idea that killing was proper only on the battlefield.

The fact that the shift in emphasis found within the legal treatises coincided with changes in attitudes and practices shows that jurists like Gentili and Grotius were not simply engaged in detached intellectual exercises. Instead, they were both responding to and influencing developments in the social and geopolitical structure of Europe. The moral principles of magnanimity and valor underlying the restriction on assassination were not uniformly applied, therefore, but were filtered through practical political concerns emerging at the time. Gentili and Grotius worried that if assassination were permitted, the safety of leaders would be compromised, with pernicious effects. The restriction, although ostensibly forbidding a certain mode of killing, had the practical effect of making certain individuals—leaders—harder to kill, because the killing would have to be done in the context of conventional military action. Although Gentili's work predated Henry IV's assassination, it is likely that the event figured heavily in the thinking of Grotius, who at the time of the publication of *De Jure Belli ac Pacis* was in the employ of Henry's son, Louis XIII, to whom he dedicated the work.[82] Seen in this perspective, Grotius's emphasis on both the personal safety of rulers and stability in the international order becomes clearer. Indeed, Toulmin cites Grotius's work as an early and influential exemplar of the "quest for certainty" that would define the modern era.[83]

Another indication that the norm against assassination reflected the sensibilities of the modern states system is the centrality to both of the idea of *reciprocity*. We have seen how Gentili's explanation of the rule against assassination relied not only on the idea that actions taken by states against their enemies might later be taken against them, but also on a broader notion of the same idea: that the consequences of an action are not limited to immediate results but include its more generalized effects on rules governing a system of states. Geoffrey Parker has argued that this idea of reciprocity was an important foundation for the rules of war in Europe in that it allowed states to appreciate the "advantages of mutual restraint." Ultimately, Parker writes, these rules

---

[81] Ibid., p. 656.

[82] In his dedication Grotius praised Louis as a monarch "set . . . against the trend of an age which is rushing headlong to destruction." *De Jure Belli ac Pacis Libri Tres*, p. 3.

[83] Toulmin, *Cosmopolis*, p. 76.

"reduced the danger and chaos of conflict for all combatants because creating a contractual etiquette of belligerence provided each party with a vital framework of expectations concerning the conduct of others."[84] Parker also argues that this sense of reciprocity really did not coalesce in Europe until between about 1550 and 1700.[85] The fact that this time frame roughly corresponds with the emergence of the sovereign states system is no coincidence. As Parker suggests, the acceptance of reciprocity represented a different mode of thinking about interstate relations that had important implications. Indeed, the concept of reciprocity seems to be crucial to the idea of the sovereign equality of states that is at the very core of the Westphalian system, along with the attendant principle that all states have certain rights which must be respected if orderly relations among them are to be preserved.

A complex combination of material and ideational factors, therefore, contributed to the rise of the norm against assassinating foreign leaders. On one hand, the norm reflected the institutional interests of powerful actors in the international system. On the other hand, the norm itself served a legitimizing function, reinforcing institutional changes by providing them with a normative foundation based on natural law principles of justice and honor. The norm addressed new political concerns, connecting moral judgments to emerging interests in a way that had not been done previously. Because of the propitious fit among principles, interests, and institutions, these judgments soon evolved into a common understanding, among states and supported by states, that certain types of actions were improper. Over time, national elites and institutions internalized this understanding to such a degree that a strong presumption against assassination developed. There was, in other words, little inclination to ponder the ethical propriety of assassination, or to engage in a cost-benefit analysis, because the attitude toward assassination was *less a calculation than a reflex.* The result was a visceral aversion to assassination that largely obscured the norm's relationship to the structure of the international system.

ALTERNATIVE EXPLANATIONS

Although I have emphasized the importance of the interaction of various historical forces in the rise of the norm against assassination, other

---

[84] Parker, "Early Modern Europe," p. 42.
[85] Ibid.

commentators have explained the norm by reference to more discrete and specific factors ranging from moral ideals of honor and chivalry to more pragmatic considerations of political expediency. Before examining the status of the norm in contemporary international politics, I will consider four of these alternative explanations.

The Norm as a Vestige of Chivalry

The first holds that the norm is a reflection of the emphasis on chivalry found in the laws of war. Proponents of this view point to the condemnation of "treachery" and "perfidy" in international conventions and military manuals as evidence of a sense of honor that constrains the use of force, including assassination. This explanation maintains that the norm is best understood in terms of what I have referred to as "first strand," or moral, concerns, as anachronistic as they may seem.[86] As a description of the way in which the norm influences actors, particularly military professionals, this is probably accurate. As an account of the origins of the norm, however, it is less convincing.

First, there are obvious problems with timing. As I have argued, chivalry had little effect on assassination even when it was still taken seriously; by the late 1500s, its influence had waned in other areas as well. Moreover, this explanation begs the question. Why are some morally problematic practices forbidden while others are allowed? Why did some practices survive from the age of chivalry while others did not? Consider, for example, the chivalric practice of single combat, which allowed disputes between nations to be resolved by a *mano a mano* battle between enemy leaders. Although this would spare the lives of many soldiers who would otherwise perish in battle, the idea strikes a modern observer as absurdly anachronistic. The decisive question, instead, was which norms fit most readily into prevailing political and social frameworks. With the rise of sovereign states, the prohibition of assassination was such a norm; single combat was not.[87]

---

[86] This interpretation is common in legal scholarship on the law of war and, interestingly, in works written by military professionals. See, for example, Schmitt, "State-Sponsored Assassination"; Peters, "A Revolution in Military Ethics?"; and Lt. Comdr. Bruce Ross, "The Case for Targeting Leadership in War," *Naval War College Review* 46, no. 1 (Winter 1993): 74–93.

[87] On the decline of single combat, see Theodor Meron, *Henry's Wars and Shakespeare's Laws: Perspectives on the Law of War in the Later Middle Ages* (Oxford: Clarendon, 1993), p. 131.

The Norm as a Reflection of International Gentility

A related, but more historically grounded, explanation points to the decline of political violence that followed the religious wars of the 1500s and 1600s. This period, the argument goes, was an exceptionally brutal one, marked by virulent religious strife that spilled over not only into the conduct of war but into all affairs of state.[88] The end of the religious wars, however, gave way to a gentler era in international relations in which restraints on war were more common, and a general sentiment of civility prevailed. The norm against assassination, some argue, was part of this larger change in the manners of international politics; a product of less violent times and more genteel social mores.[89]

This explanation suffers from several problems. The most obvious is that, as I have shown, the emergence of the norm predated the end of brutal religious conflict by several decades. Furthermore, other practices at least as violent and inhumane, such as the refusal of clemency to civilians in towns under siege, continued not only for the duration of the Thirty Years' War but well beyond, even into the relatively refined eighteenth century.[90] Finally, this explanation cannot account for the vitality of the norm over several centuries. Since the mid-1600s there have been at least two periods during which much of the international system has been consumed by extremely destructive wars—the Napoleonic era and the world wars of the twentieth century. In neither case, however, did the norm against assassination dissolve in the face of the surrounding brutality, even when the elimination of one individual promised to relieve the problem.

The Norm as a Concession to Reality

A third explanation suggests that the norm against assassination arose simply because states no longer found it worth the effort to try to kill troublesome foreign leaders. Two factors are sometimes identified as rendering assassination an ineffective tool of foreign policy. First, it is

[88] Geoffrey Parker notes that the age "abounded in brutality." Parker, "Early Modern Europe," p. 47. Similarly, in his introduction to Vattel's work, Albert de Lapradelle explains the difference between what he sees as Grotius's "severe and even barbarous" laws of war and the "humanized" version espoused by Vattel by noting that "between the lifetimes of the two men manners became less harsh." Vattel, *Le droit des gens*, p. xlviii.

[89] See, for example, Rapaport, *Assassination and Terrorism*, pp. 4–6; and Morgenthau, *Politics among Nations*, p. 226.

[90] See, for example, Harold E. Selesky, "Colonial America," and Gunther Rothenberg, "The Age of Napoleon," in *The Laws of War*, ed. Howard, Andreopoulos, and Shulman.

difficult to carry out: leaders are typically so well-protected that an assassination attempt would require a large expenditure of resources with a disproportionately small chance of success. The second purported problem is that the death of a single individual rarely has a significant impact on state policy. According to this logic, even if an attempt succeeded, it would be unlikely to bring about the desired changes. In historical terms this is often tied to the shift from dynastic rule to representative government and the corresponding increase in the stability of governing institutions. Martin van Creveld, dating the rise of the norm to the second half of the sixteenth century, reasons: "This, too, was the age when the principle of legitimate rule was becoming widely recognized. With continuity assured, killing, imprisoning, or otherwise molesting those responsible for the conduct of war at the top no longer served a useful purpose."[91]

This explanation, too, is problematic. First, it is not true that assassination attempts rarely succeed. The litany of assassinations in a domestic context—carried out by individuals with far fewer resources than any sovereign state would possess—belies the notion that assassination is prohibitively difficult to carry out. One striking aspect of the rise of the norm, after all, is that assassination continued to be a regular feature of domestic politics long after its use as a foreign policy tool receded. In terms of the inefficacy of assassination as a means of political change, two points can be made. The first is an appeal to counterfactual reasoning. It is difficult to imagine that the course of history would not have changed had Hitler indeed been killed in 1938. The same can be said of Gustav, Frederick, Napoleon, or Churchill at pivotal moments of their respective careers. Ultimately such questions are unanswerable, but it would take a committed structuralist to insist that exceptional individuals matter little in history, which is what the explanation from inefficacy amounts to. The second point, again, relates to timing: the shift from dynastic to representative rule, and the stability of political institutions that accompanied it, occurred too late to explain a norm that arose in the early 1600s. In fact, in most of Europe the seventeenth and early eighteenth centuries marked the heyday of absolutism, with power highly centralized in the person of the monarch. In such an environment, individual rulers would have presented meaningful targets indeed.

[91] Martin L. van Creveld, *The Transformation of War* (New York: Free Press, 1991), pp. 199–200.

70

The Norm as a Manifestation of Public Opinion

A fourth alternative explanation ascribes the aversion to assassination to the impact of domestic public opinion. It is sometimes asserted, for example, that the United States is exceptionally averse to assassination because it does not conform to American values of justice and fairness. This was the position taken in 1976 by the Church committee, which investigated the CIA's involvement in assassination plots. The committee found fault with assassination because it "violates moral precepts fundamental to our way of life . . . [and] traditional American notions of fair play."[92] According to this view, although there may be convergence of opinion among some states on the issue, fundamentally the norm is not an international norm at all, but operates on the state level.

Because of the relative novelty of opinion polling, it is impossible to assess the status of public opinion over the history of the norm. However, the norm was in place long before governments considered themselves responsible to the will of the general public. In addition, more recent evidence suggests that public opinion is not an important source of constraint on international assassination. First, the norm constrains non-democratic states, which have little concern for domestic public opinion, as well as democratic states. Although there have been states willing to break the norm, these have as often been democratic as non-democratic regimes. Second, even in democratic states aversion to assassination seems to derive from sources other than public opinion, which is often permissive when it comes to killing foreign leaders. Those espousing the exceptionalism of the United States in this regard, for example, often note that it is the only state that has enacted—in the form of an executive order—a clear declaratory policy renouncing assassination.[93] Yet polls have shown the American public to be receptive to the use of assassination in many cases.[94] Even the revelations of the

---

[92] Select Senate Committee to Study Governmental Operations with Respect to Intelligence Activities, *Alleged Assassination Plots Involving Foreign Leaders*, pp. 257, 259.

[93] See, for example, David Newman and Tyll Van Geel, "Executive Order 12,333: The Risks of a Clear Declaration of Intent," *Harvard Journal of Law and Public Policy* 12, no. 2 (Spring 1989): 433–47; and Newman and Bruce Bueno de Mesquita, "Repeal Order 12333, Legalize 007," *New York Times*, January 26, 1989, p. A23.

[94] Prior to the 1986 raid on Tripoli, for example, 61 percent agreed that the United States should "covertly assassinate known terrorist leaders." During the Persian Gulf War, a poll revealed that 65 percent of the American public favored "the covert assassination of Hussein to end the war quickly"; only 35 percent thought such an attempt would be wrong even if it succeeded. In 1993, after Saddam's role in the plot to assassinate former President George Bush had been revealed, 53 percent favored killing Saddam, while only 37

Church committee, which prompted the executive ban on assassinations, failed to trigger a strong public response.[95] Although the apparent lack of commitment to the norm among the general public may suggest that it does not appeal as strongly to moral intuition as it once did, it is unlikely that national leaders take their cue on this issue from their own constituencies. In fact, putting the question to public opinion in a sense misunderstands the nature of international norms, for which the most relevant audience is not domestic society but the "society of states."[96]

NORMATIVE CONSTRAINTS VS. LEGAL CONSTRAINTS

Although the prohibition on assassination is well-established in international law, the content of the norm is not fully reflected by relevant legal provisions. While international law does a good job of capturing the "first strand" of the norm against assassination—the moral concern with just and honorable means—it neglects the more geopolitically contingent "second strand." As a result, the norm diverges from international law in two important ways. First, while most prohibitions on assassination in international law apply with equal force to all foreigners, the norm applies more powerfully to heads of state and other top officials than it does to ordinary citizens. The reason for this, as we have seen, is the second-strand association of assassination with political disorder, a concern that only arises to any significant degree when the potential victims are individuals with considerable political significance. Not only is it difficult to explain this limitation on purely moral grounds, but the special protection afforded national leaders by the norm actually increases the ethical disconnect by safeguarding the very individuals who are most

---

percent opposed it. Brian Jenkins, "Assassination: Should We Stay the Good Guys?" *Los Angeles Times*, November 16, 1986, p. A2; Allan C. Miller, "The Risk in Targeting Saddam," *Los Angeles Times*, February 23, 1991, p. A1; and "Americans Favor Killing Saddam Hussein," *Los Angeles Times*, June 29, 1993, p. A6.

[95] Leslie H. Gelb, "Spy Inquiries, Begun amid Public Outrage, End in Indifference," *New York Times*, May 12, 1976, p. L20; and Nicholas M. Horrock, "The Meaning of Congressional Intelligence Inquiries," *New York Times*, April 30, 1976, p. A20.

[96] For example, in urging the Church committee not to publicize the details of its investigation, President Ford argued that "public release of these official materials and information will do grievous damage to our country. It would likely be exploited by foreign nations and groups hostile to the United States in a manner designed to do maximum damage to the reputation and foreign policy of the United States. It would seriously impair our ability to exercise a positive leading role in world affairs." "Ford Said to Fear Baring of CIA Role in Assassinations Abroad," *New York Times*, March 1, 1975, p. A30; and Johnson, "Executive Order 12,333," p. 408.

responsible for international conflict and therefore least innocent. Nevertheless, the ethical stigma against assassination is more likely to dissuade a state from bumping off a high state official than a functionary or a troublesome private citizen. While some members of the British government, for example, steadfastly opposed the idea of eliminating Hitler, considerable evidence exists that the Special Operations Executive made at least occasional use of assassination during World War II.[97] Among contemporary states, Israel has gained notoriety for its willingness to resort to assassination. Nevertheless, there are limits on when—and against whom—violence is used. In 1991 Yossi Melman, an expert on Israeli intelligence, pointed out that "Israel, in forty-three years of independence, has never been involved in political killings of foreign leaders." The article quoted a former Mossad agent's opinion that "it's wrong for Israel to be involved in assassinations against Arab leaders of sovereign countries," and noted that "a tacit understanding has been reached between Arab states and Israel—if you don't kill our leaders, we won't kill yours."[98] Remarkably, although the most common targets of Israeli assassination attempts have been figures affiliated with the Palestine Liberation Organization, this forbearance has usually extended to upper-echelon PLO leaders.[99]

The second major point of divergence between the norm against assassination and international law concerns the personal targeting of national leaders during armed conflicts. From a legal standpoint, this practice is within the rights of belligerent states as long as the targeted individual is in the chain of command and the means used are not "treacherous" as defined by the laws of war. Such an attempt, therefore,

---

[97] The SOE was probably involved in two of the best-known assassinations during that conflict: the killing of German military governor Reinhard Heydrich by Czech commandos in May of 1942; and of Admiral Jean-François Darlan, the head Vichy administrator in Northern Africa, in December of the same year. Anthony Verrier, *Assassination in Algiers: Churchill, Roosevelt, de Gaulle, and the Murder of Admiral Darlan* (New York: W.W. Norton, 1990); Stephen A. Garrett, *Conscience and Power: An Examination of Dirty Hands and Political Leadership* (New York: St. Martin's Press, 1996), chap. 3; Phillip Knightley, *The Second Oldest Profession: Spies and Spying in the Twentieth Century* (New York: W. W. Norton, 1987), pp. 123–24. Verrier quotes one "distinguished member" of the SOE's recollection of being told when he was recruited, "You shouldn't object to fraud—and you mustn't object to murder" (p. 92).

[98] Melman, "Why the Plot to Kill Hussein Failed," p. M2. Twice in the late 1950s, Israeli leaders considered assassinating Egyptian President Gamal Abdel Nasser, but both times decided against it. Ben-Yehuda, *Political Assassinations by Jews*, pp. 302–7.

[99] Dan Fisher and John M. Broder, "Killing of Wazir Ruthless and Efficient," *Los Angeles Times*, April 22, 1988, pp. 4, 12.

would not properly be termed an "assassination."[100] In practice, however, attacks of this nature have been surprisingly uncommon.[101] In effect, the norm against assassination appears to spill over to create a stigma against even the lawful targeting of enemy leaders. This stigma is a manifestation of the second-strand concerns that led Gentili and Grotius to express such apprehension for the safety of princes and generals. Moreover, it is not a recent development but goes back almost as far as the norm against assassination itself. Mid-eighteenth-century jurist Emmerich de Vattel, apart from the issue of assassination per se, also weighed the question of "consideration for the person of the enemy's King."[102] While acknowledging that "it is not a law of war that the person of the enemy's King must be spared," Vattel nevertheless observed that a clear standard had evolved that strongly encouraged it:

> In former times he who succeeded in killing the King or general of the enemy was commended and rewarded . . . Nothing could have been more natural than such an attitude; for the ancients almost always fought for the very existence of the State, and frequently the death of the leader put an end to the war. At the present day the soldier would not dare, ordinarily at least, to boast of having killed the enemy's King. It is thus tacitly agreed among sovereigns that their persons shall be held sacred.[103]

Vattel further noted that this standard applied particularly strongly to surprise attacks on leaders, which, unlike assassinations, were "doubtless, perfectly lawful in warfare."[104] While such attacks technically remain permissible under the law of war to the current day, the spillover of the assassination taboo has made them, along with more conventional means of targeting enemy leaders, extremely infrequent. At the battle of Waterloo, the Duke of Wellington reportedly refused to allow British artillery to fire on Napoleon, declaring that, in the words of one

---

[100] Schmitt, "State-Sponsored Assassination," pp. 639–41; Zengel, "Assassination and the Law of Armed Conflict," p. 627; Beres, "The Permissibility of State-Sponsored Assassination," p. 237.

[101] One commentator observes that "while a civilian head of state who serves as commander-in-chief of the armed forces may be a lawful target . . . as a matter of comity such attacks generally have been limited." Parks, "Memorandum of Law," p. 6. The word "comity" here can be defined as courtesy or civility, but it also implies a sense of reciprocity in the observance of such courtesies.

[102] Vattel, *Le droit des gens*, p. 290.

[103] Ibid.

[104] Ibid., p. 287.

account, "no one knew what would become of battles if people went about killing Commanders-in-Chief."[105] And in the Second World War, on several occasions the Allies refrained from targeting top German leadership in bombing raids.[106] The U.S. operation that killed Admiral Isoroku Yamamoto stands out as so exceptional in this regard that, although it is uniformly agreed that it was not an assassination under the law of war, most subsequent considerations of assassination in international law at least mention the case.[107]

Although willingness to target opposing leaders during hostilities seems to be increasing, it is clear that the association of this practice with assassination continues to render it ethically problematic, irrespective of its legality. This ambiguity was apparent in both the 1986 air strike on Tripoli and the 1990–91 Persian Gulf crisis. In each case, the United States clearly chose certain targets with the hope that the raids would result in the death of the opposing leader, yet in each case officials denied this intent, sometimes with considerable indignation. While the legal justification for going after Qaddafi has generated considerable disagreement,[108] the grounds for targeting Saddam Hussein seem clearer. As the uniformed head of the armed forces of a state engaged in hostilities, Saddam was not only a legitimate target of non-treacherous attack but a strategically valuable one.[109] Yet U.S. officials went to great lengths to insist that coalition forces were not targeting Saddam personally. In September 1990 Secretary of Defense Richard Cheney fired Air Force Chief of Staff Michael Dugan after Dugan told reporters that U.S. war plans called for the bombing of Saddam, his family, and his mistress. Among the reasons Cheney gave for dismissing Dugan was that he "said

---

[105] W. E. Armstrong, "Letters," *Times* (London), August 13, 1969, p. 9.

[106] Stowell, "Comment: Military Reprisals and the Sanctions of the Laws of War," *American Journal of International Law* 6 (1942): 646; Leslie J. Douglas-Mann, "Letters," *Times* (London), August 8, 1969, p. 9.

[107] See, e.g., Zengel, "Assassination and the Law of Armed Conflict"; Eric L. Chase, "Should We Kill Saddam?" *Newsweek*, February 18, 1991, pp. 16–17; Parks, "Memorandum of Law," p. 5; Joseph B. Kelly, "Comments: Assassination in War Time," *Military Law Review* 30 (1966): 102–03; Johnson, "Executive Order 12,333," p. 419; and Newman and Van Geel, "Executive Order 12,333: The Risks of a Clear Declaration of Intent," p. 433.

[108] Brandenburg, for example, argues that it constituted an unlawful assassination attempt, while Parks maintains that the raid was a lawful action in self-defense against a continuing threat pursuant to Article 51 of the UN Charter.

[109] On the legality of targeting Saddam, see Schmitt, "State-Sponsored Assassination"; Ross, "The Case for Targeting Leadership in War"; Eric Chase, "Should We Kill Saddam?"; and Turner, "Killing Saddam: Would It Be a Crime?"

we would violate the executive order banning participation in assassinations."[110] According to the law of war, he had done no such thing.[111] But the fact that Cheney did not recognize this distinction demonstrates that the spillover of the norm can cause the line between unlawful assassination and lawful personal targeting to become blurred, even in the eyes of foreign policy elites.[112] The irony in this case was that the legal distinction worked to the favor of the United States, which was within its rights as a belligerent to target Saddam. More fundamentally, however, legality was less important than *legitimacy*, for it was legitimacy that defined the scope of positions that could be publicly expressed as policy goals.[113]

Of course, given that the United States *did* target both Qaddafi and Saddam, one must conclude that the spillover stigma against targeting leaders by conventional means is not as strong as the assassination norm itself.[114] Nevertheless, the desire to publicly disassociate these attacks from the intent to kill any particular individual speaks to the sensitivity that the norm has engendered. Moreover, these examples show that the rhetoric of government officials regarding assassination is important. Attention should be paid to rhetoric that is deferential to a norm, even

[110] Woodward, *The Commanders*, p. 294. Dugan's comments were also irksome to Cheney because they mentioned the role that Israeli intelligence was playing in preparations for war and expressed the "arrogant assumption that the Army and Navy would be relegated to secondary roles as the Air Force won the war all by itself." Bruce van Hoorst, "Ready, Aim, Fired," *Time*, October 1, 1990, p. 55.

[111] Of course, the targeting of Saddam's family and mistress, who were noncombatants and therefore immune from attack, would in fact have constituted a violation of the law of war.

[112] Similar confusion was apparent among the press, who routinely spoke of the targeting of Saddam in terms of "assassination," and on Capitol Hill, where Representative Bob McEwen (R-Ohio) introduced a resolution that would suspend the executive order forbidding assassination for the duration of the Gulf War on the grounds that it "prevents us from targeting the sources of attack upon the American forces." Quoted in Schmitt, "State-Sponsored Assassination," pp. 673–74. McEwen added, "I don't want some American pilot pulling two G's over Baghdad to be hauled up before some congressional inquisition a few years from now because he got Saddam Hussein." Tom Kenworthy, "From Capitol Hill, a Potshot at Saddam," *Washington Post*, February 27, 1991, p. A23

[113] The importance of legitimacy was reinforced by the need to preserve the tenuous coalition and the status of acting under the imprimatur of United Nations resolutions.

[114] On the targeting of Saddam during the Gulf War, see Michael R. Gordon and General Bernard E. Trainor, *The Generals' War: The Inside Story of the Conflict in the Gulf* (New York: Little, Brown, 1995), pp. 313–15; Bruce Atkinson, *Crusade: The Untold Story of the Persian Gulf War* (New York: Houghton Mifflin, 1993), p. 273. On the targeting of Qaddafi in 1986, see Seymour M. Hersh, "Target Qaddafi," *New York Times Magazine*, February 22, 1987, p. 17.

in the face of actions that suggest ambivalence. When U.S. officials decried assassination even as they targeted Qaddafi and Saddam, it was clear not only that they were mindful of the norm but also that it exerted influence in complex and subtle ways. Such rhetoric is not simply hypocrisy. Rather it is evidence that national decision makers must often navigate a careful path through a maze whose contours are defined not only by material factors but also by the norms of international politics.

A NORM IN DECLINE?

Despite its continuing influence, evidence has mounted in recent decades that the norm against assassinating foreign leaders may be waning. One sign is the increasing frequency of calls by lawmakers and commentators to consider assassination as a foreign policy option. Although the term still has a strongly negative connotation, there appears to be a greater willingness to accept it as a necessary evil. The ethical disconnect between recoiling at the thought of assassinating a despot while barely batting an eyelash at bombing casualties in the thousands has led some to question what should truly count as "honorable."[115] In the United States in the late 1990s, for example, the dual conundrums presented by an intransigent Saddam Hussein and increasingly dangerous terrorists such as Osama bin Laden raised calls in Congress and the editorial pages for a reassessment of the ban on assassination.[116]

Another indication that the norm may be in decline is the rising number of assassinations and assassination attempts in international politics in the second half of the twentieth century. The 1960 assassination of Jordanian prime minister Hazzah Majali, for example, was traced to Egyptian president Gamal Abdel Nasser, who was also reportedly involved in several other assassination intrigues either as the instigator

---

[115] See, for example, Peters, "A Revolution in Military Ethics?"; Ross, "The Case for Targeting Leadership in War"; Turner, "Killing Saddam"; and Stephanopoulos, "Why We Should Kill Saddam."

[116] Congressional Republicans who argued for a reconsideration of the ban on assassination included Senators Orrin Hatch and Richard Shelby; Democrats included Senator Dianne Feinstein and Representative Lee Hamilton. "Congress Ponders Whether the U.S. Should Ease Ban on Assassinations," *Los Angeles Times*, September 18, 1998, p. A6; "Rethinking the Ban on Political Assassinations," *New York Times*, August 30, 1998, p. D3. For columns and editorials advocating assassination, see "Fight Plan for a Dirty War," *Washington Post*, August 24, 1998, p. A19; "A Case for Assassination?" *Boston Globe*, August 30, 1998, p. E1; "Kill the Bad Guys," *Pittsburgh Post-Gazette*, September 6, 1998, p. E1; and Stephanopoulos, "Why We Should Kill Saddam."

or the intended victim.[117] In radio broadcasts, Nasser repeatedly urged the assassination of Jordan's King Hussein; and he himself was the subject of plots funded by King Saud of Saudi Arabia and of abortive plans by France, Israel, and Britain.[118] In the Middle East, Israel's bungled 1997 attempt to assassinate an official of the Palestinian opposition group Hamas, and its alleged role in other killings, caused embarrassment to the Netanyahu government and impeded the peace process.[119] In 1998, allegations surfaced in Britain that Her Majesty's Secret Service plotted to kill Moammar Qaddafi in 1996,[120] while former British intelligence officers have told of plots to assassinate the Libyan leader as early as 1971.[121] Press reports also raised the possibility of French government complicity in the plane crash that killed the presidents of Rwanda and Burundi in 1994, triggering horrific ethnic violence.[122] Perhaps the most compelling evidence that the norm is declining, however, is the fact that the United States was willing to attempt assassination several times during the Cold War. The revelations of the Church committee concerning CIA involvement in these plots raise a crucial question: if the norm against assassination protects the interests of great powers, why would the strongest state in the system be prepared to violate it?

Some have claimed that the answer lies in the exceptionally grave nature of the threats facing the United States (and other states) since

[117] Willard A. Heaps, *Assassination: A Special Kind of Murder* (New York: Meredith, 1969), p. 106; and Richard P. Hunt, "Hussein Weighing Break with Cairo," *New York Times*, September 1, 1960, p. 1.

[118] William Crotty, ed., *Assassinations and the Political Order* (New York: Harper and Row, 1971), pp. 18–19; Ben-Yehuda, *Political Assassinations by Jews*, pp. 305–7; and Peter Wright, *Spycatcher: The Candid Autobiography of a Senior Intelligence Officer* (New York: Viking, 1987), pp. 160–61.

[119] "Botched Assassination by Israel Gives New Life to Hamas," *Washington Post*, October 6, 1997, p. A1; "The Daring Attack That Blew up in Israel's Face," *New York Times*, October 15, 1997, p. A1.

[120] "Former Spy Says British Tried to Have Khadafy Assassinated," *Boston Globe*, August 9, 1998, p. A13; "Paper Trail Leads to British Secret Service Connection," *Sunday Times Internet Edition* (London), August 9, 1998, http://Sunday-times.co.uk/news . . . /08/09 stifocnws03001.html? 2522508; "Shayler in TV Interview on Gadafy Plot," *The Guardian* (London), August 8, 1998, p. 2. British government officials denied the allegations. "Gaddafi Death Plot Claims 'Pure Fantasy'—Cook," *BBC News Online Network*, August 9, 1998, http://news.bbc.co.uk/hi/english/uk/newsid_147000/147940.stm.

[121] "Paper Trail Leads to British Secret Service Connection."

[122] "Missiles from French Armoury Hit African Leaders' Jet, Paper Says," *Toronto Star*, April 1, 1998, p. A10; "Ex-French Officials Defend Rwanda Role; Charges of Complicity in Massacres Denied," *Washington Post*, April 22, 1998, p. A18.

World War II.[123] In the wake of the revelations of the Church committee, for example, there were many efforts to explain, if not excuse, American involvement in assassination plots as a manifestation of the intense and unprecedented pressure posed by the threat of international communism. To convey a sense of the very high stakes perceived to be involved, the Church Committee Report quoted from the Korean War—era Report of the Second Hoover Commission:

> It is now clear that we are facing an implacable enemy whose avowed objective is world domination by whatever means at whatever cost. There are no rules in such a game. Hitherto acceptable norms of human conduct do not apply. If the U.S. is to survive, long-standing American concepts of "fair play" must be reconsidered. We must develop effective espionage and counterespionage services and must learn to subvert, sabotage, and destroy our enemies by more clever, more sophisticated, and more effective methods than those used against us. It may be necessary that the American people be made acquainted with, understand and support this fundamentally repugnant philosophy.[124]

While this statement hardly reflected the sentiments of all Americans at the time, there is little doubt that it had its share of proponents. Desperate times can indeed call for desperate measures. Still, this explanation is less than satisfying. In order to ascribe the roots of the decline of the assassination norm to the extenuating circumstances of the Cold War alone, one must assume that those circumstances were more extenuating than others in the past that did not significantly alter the norm. This is a difficult assumption to make. In the three and a half centuries since the norm arose, the international system has faced three major crises that posed risks to global order at least as great as the Cold War— the Napoleonic Wars and the First and Second World Wars. Moreover, in two of these there were significant ideological dimensions to the crisis that rivaled those of the Cold War. Yet, as I have shown, the assassination norm survived these crises intact. Surely times were no

---

[123] This explanation is consistent with the neorealist view, which sees norms as inconsequential in the face of perceived threats to national security.

[124] Quoted in Scott D. Breckenridge, *The CIA and the U.S. Intelligence System* (Boulder: Westview Press, 1986), pp. 294–95.

more desperate in the 1950s than they had been in 1938, and no enemy could have been more ruthless and implacable than Hitler.

If the norm against assassination is losing currency, this suggests instead that changes in the international political environment may be pushing toward a different normative equilibrium. Simply put, if the norm is declining it is probably because it does not fit into the structure of the international system as well as it once did. Indeed, at least two structural changes in the post–World War II international system may be undermining the norm.

Terrorism and Unconventional Violence

The first structural change is the increasing prevalence of nontraditional modes of violence such as guerrilla warfare and terrorism, particularly by nonstate actors. The rise of terrorism in a sense represents the explicit rejection of norms that seek to prohibit certain means of violence as illegitimate. Terrorist groups refuse to play by the rules of international politics partly because they are unable to; the means at their disposal are not amenable to resolving disputes by the large-scale clash of troops. This refusal to play by the rules, along with the nonterritorial nature of many groups employing such tactics, places state actors in a difficult position in terms of responding. Seldom are easily identifiable armed forces involved that can be defeated in conventional combat. Nor are there often discrete geographical strongholds that can be attacked to neutralize the threat. When there are, they are likely to be predominantly civilian areas within the territory of a state that is a third party to the dispute, raising difficulties associated with violating another state's sovereignty.[125] As a result, threatened states may feel pressured to respond with similar tactics. The first known assassination plot sponsored by U.S. officials, for example, was against Mexican bandit Pancho Villa during the 1916 Punitive Expedition.[126] The expedition, which sought to bring Villa to justice for deadly border raids, was stymied by Villa's elusiveness and the desire to avoid armed contact with regular Mexican forces. It was a conventional response to an unconventional threat, and its failure frustrated U.S. authorities. General John Pershing, the expedition commander, finally resorted to hiring several Mexicans

---

[125] This issue arose, for example, with the United States' August 1998 cruise-missile strikes in Afghanistan and Sudan, and with Israel's early 2000 attacks on villages in southern Lebanon.

[126] Knott, *Secret and Sanctioned*, p. 155.

to poison Villa's coffee. The plot, which was unknown to Pershing's superiors, failed.[127]

The Villa episode presaged both the difficulty that powerful states would have in dealing with unconventional threats in the post–World War II era and the frequent temptation to respond to such threats in kind. The plots reported by the Church committee were one manifestation of the difficulty the United States experienced in countering national liberation movements during the 1950s and 1960s. In Vietnam the United States responded to the use of terror by the Vietcong with the "Phoenix program," a counterinsurgency effort that included the assassination of VC figures.[128] Perhaps following Israel's example, in the 1980s and 1990s the United States at least flirted with the use of assassination as a response to terrorism. In the mid-1980s, the Reagan administration launched efforts to ensure that the executive order banning assassination was not interpreted as forbidding antiterrorist operations.[129] Furthermore, reports in 1984 and 1985 suggested that Reagan signed secret intelligence findings with deliberately ambiguous language that might have circumvented the assassination ban in raids against terrorists.[130] Although the administration vehemently denied the reports, its own publicly proposed 1985 interpretation of the executive order would have permitted almost exactly the sort of actions reportedly authorized by the secret intelligence findings.[131] Finally, a 1991 article by the former operations officer of a "classified Pentagon counter-terrorist unit" strongly implied that assassination was part of the "sensitive retaliation operations" against those responsible for the 1983 bombing of the U.S. Marine barracks in Beirut.[132] All these examples suggest that

---

[127] Ibid.

[128] Lewy, *America in Vietnam*, pp. 279–85.

[129] Doyle McManus, "Assassination Ban May Not Apply in Anti-Terror Raids," *Los Angeles Times*, July 13, 1985, p. A1; Linda Greenhouse, "Bill Would Give Reagan a Free Hand on Terror," *New York Times*, April 18, 1986, p. A9; and Stephen Engelberg, "U.S. Order on Anti-Terror Strikes Is Disclosed," *New York Times*, October 6, 1988, p. A13.

[130] "Report on Covert Operations Denied," *Los Angeles Times*, October 5, 1988, p. 1; Engelberg, "U.S. Order on Anti-Terror Strikes Is Disclosed," p. A13; and Lee May, "Reagan Denies He Gave CIA a 'License to Kill,' " *Los Angeles Times*, October 6, 1988, p. 7.

[131] See McManus, "Assassination Ban May Not Apply in Anti-Terror Raids." Former Deputy Director of Central Intelligence John McMahon notes that the CIA received a directive from the National Security Council staff in 1985 "telling us to go knock off terrorists in pre-emptive strikes." McMahon declined to act on the directive. Weiner, "Rethinking the Ban on Political Assassinations."

[132] William Cowan, "How to Kill Saddam: Stalking the Dictator: Scenarios from a Former Counter-Terrorist," *Washington Post*, February 10, 1991, p. C2.

the assassination taboo may not apply as strongly in responses to terror-ism.[133] Still, the norm itself may not be so easily "divisible." Even actions taken against nonstate terrorist targets are, in the long run, likely to undermine the norm as a whole, thus eroding the barriers to the use of assassination in other circumstances.

Modern War and the Personal Responsibility of Leaders

The second structural change that threatens the norm against assassi-nation has its basis in the immensely destructive nature of modern war. World Wars I and II brought death and hardship of a magnitude previ-ously unimaginable, and the advent of nuclear weapons threatened even greater horrors. These material changes were accompanied by a closely related ideational change: the post–World War II transformation in international law that outlawed aggressive war as a means of pursuing state goals.[134] This development strikes at the heart of the Westphalian idea that war is a legitimate activity for sovereign states, and that national leaders should not be held personally accountable for it. The post–World War II judgment at Nuremberg stripped leaders of the shield of *raison d'etat* as a justification for war, making aggression a crime and exposing them to personal responsibility as war criminals.[135] The idea that leaders can and should be held accountable for transgressions committed in the name of the state is a significant blow to the ideational foundation on which the assassination ban is based.

The effects of modern war also diminish the unquestioning accept-ance that assassination is morally wrong. Specifically, they bring into relief the anomaly of forbidding the murder of one person while allow-ing the deaths of many thousands far more innocent. What is at stake is, in Michael Walzer's terms, the "moral plausibility" of the norm. Walzer argues that while any rule limiting the use of force will be useful as long

[133] Even when the intended targets are terrorists, however, states sometimes resist the idea of selective killing in cold blood. For this reason, counterterrorist operations by strong states often make use of conventional military means rather than cloak-and-dagger intrigues.

[134] See Walzer, *Just and Unjust Wars,* chaps. 4–6, 18; Telford Taylor, "Just and Unjust Wars," in *War, Morality, and the Military Profession,* ed. Malham Wakin, (Boulder: Westview Press, 1979).

[135] For an example of the application of this principle to targeting foreign leaders, see Robert F. Turner, "Deterring Humanitarian Law Violations: Strengthening Enforcement" (paper presented at the Center for National Security Law, Charlottesville, Virginia, November 4–5, 1994).

as it is commonly accepted, "no limit is accepted simply because it is thought that it will be useful. . . . [The] convention must first be morally plausible to large numbers of men and women; it must correspond to our sense of what is right. Only then will we recognize it as a serious obstacle to this or that military decision, and only then will we debate its utility in this or that particular case."[136] Recent debates suggest that a hard-and-fast rule against assassinating foreign leaders may not "correspond to our sense of what is right" as strongly as in the past. As a result, the temptation to strike directly at those most responsible for international mischief appears to be growing.

These structural changes help to explain why assassination has resurfaced on the international relations landscape after an absence of over three centuries. At the very least, it is likely that the norm is less internalized by policy makers than it was in previous eras. It is possible to believe that the British never seriously entertained the benefits of killing Hitler in 1938. On the other hand, one would expect a contemporary leader faced with a modern-day Hitler—or even George Bush confronted by Saddam Hussein—to weigh assassination as a possible, if extreme and desperate, course of action. In this sense it is accurate to say that whereas Bush decided against assassination, in 1938 there was no real decision to be made. This is an important distinction, and it is the measure of the extent to which commitment to the norm has begun to waver among national decision makers.

Still, Bush *did* decide against assassination, and this, too, is important. So is the fact that few national leaders would ever publicly admit to considering it in the first place. Changes in attitudes notwithstanding, for most states assassination would become a serious option only in exceptional circumstances, if at all. Clearly, the assassination taboo remains a powerful constraint in international politics. There are at least two reasons for this. First, the strength of the norm over several centuries has invested assassination with connotations that remain heavily negative, even if slightly less so than before. Second, occasional frustrations notwithstanding, the norm continues to serve the interests of powerful actors by providing a barrier to actions that would introduce considerable unpredictability into the international system. Great powers, understandably, tend to value predictability highly and therefore still derive a comparative advantage from the presumptive illegitimacy of

---

[136] Walzer, *Just and Unjust Wars*, p. 133.

assassination. In large part, therefore, the strength of the norm can be ascribed to the fact that it has, since its inception, served a *power-maintenance* function in international society. Those most attracted to assassination are typically actors who lack the resources that strong states possess, especially military power. U.S. State Department attorney Abraham Sofaer made this point during the Persian Gulf War, when calls for the assassination of Saddam Hussein were heard with increasing frequency. Sofaer argued that although targeting Saddam was legally and morally defensible, "the United States has a substantial interest in discouraging acceptance of the killing of political leaders as a routine measure, even in self-defense. Tyrants and terrorists are likely to be better than Americans at this sort of thing."[137] Because of its power-maintenance effects, moreover, the norm against assassination is strong enough that it is generally viewed as intrinsically obligatory, rather than contingent upon the reciprocal compliance of others. In the terminology of Chapter 2, in other words, the norm is not "convention-dependent": it is considered binding even if a foreign antagonist violates it first.[138]

For these reasons the norm remains strong despite flagging commitment among the general public in some countries. While public opinion may reflect general moral judgments, it is less attuned to issues of international legitimacy, which necessarily weigh heavily on the minds of national leaders, as well as to longer-term systemic consequences of short-term solutions. As convenient as assassination may occasionally seem for solving difficult problems, no state wishing to use it could reserve this right to itself. If a government were to embrace assassination as an instrument of policy, it would not only subject itself to acts of reprisal by aggrieved nations in the short term but might also hasten the

[137] Abraham Sofaer, "Thinking Past the Moment," *U.S. News and World Report,* February 18, 1991, p. 28. Other commentators have argued that the CIA's failure to actually kill any of the foreign leaders it plotted against in the 1950s and 1960s proves Sofaer's point. A 1986 *Newsweek* article noted that "even in its glory days, the CIA was markedly inept when it came to murder." The article quoted a former CIA official's assessment of the problem: "Harvard and Yale graduates are poor hit men." "Assassination: Is It a Real Option?" *Newsweek,* April 28, 1986, p. 21.

[138] Saddam Hussein's involvement in the plot to assassinate former President Bush, for example, was not seen by the U.S. government as warranting a reciprocal attempt, notwithstanding public support for one, and in 1995 CIA officials refused to support a plot by Iraqi dissidents to assassinate Saddam. "Hussein Directed Plot to Kill Bush, U.S. Says," *Los Angeles Times,* June 29, 1993, p. A1; "FBI Probed Alleged CIA Plot to Kill Hussein," *Los Angeles Times,* February 15, 1998, p. A1.

de-stigmatization of the practice in the international system as a whole. For great powers such as the United States, such a policy would likely prove self-defeating, because it would exchange the advantages of normative legitimacy and superior conventional military capability for a playing field slanted decidedly in the other direction. Consequently, despite temptations to the contrary, we should expect great powers to continue to resist the return of assassination to the repertoire of international power politics.[139]

[139] As one international legal scholar has pointed out, in this regard the words of Shakespeare's Macbeth are well considered:

> If it were done, when 'tis done, then 'twer well,
> It were done quickly: If th'Assassination
> Could trammell up the Consequence, and catch
> With his surcease, Successe: that but this blow
> Might be the all, and the end all, here,
> But here, upon this Banke and Schoole of time,
> Wee'ld jumpe the life to come. But in these Cases,
> We still have judgment here, that we but teach
> Bloody instructions, which being taught, returne
> To plague th'Inventer. This even-handed Justice
> Commends th'Ingredience of our poyson'd Challice
> To our owne lips.

Quoted in Johnson, "Executive Order 12,333," p. 401.

CHAPTER 4

Aerial Bombing to 1945
"A Frightful Cataclysm"

The military balloon, by the very nature of it, will always have a
weakness which will be a sort of compensation for the almost
limitless freedom of movement which it enjoys. It will never be
as formidable as a war-ship; the projectiles which it can discharge will never be as effective as those discharged with terrifying swiftness from guns of large and small caliber; always subject to the control of its pilot, it will not present for neutrals any
of the dangers threatened by anchored or floating contact
mines; there is therefore no reason to be greatly frightened if
they cannot be forbidden. I understand very well how terrifying
to the popular mind is the idea that some fine day there may
fall out of the sky without any warning some sort of bomb which
will blow up its houses and desolate its crops; but considering
the matter coolly one will be easily convinced that this new
engine of war is no more terrible than those already in use.
> Marius de Robilant, *The Proceedings of the*
> *Hague Peace Conferences,* 1907

Strange how quickly shocking things become casual things. There
was horror aplenty over the early bombings of the war. Today we
announce similar bombings . . . and we casually shrug it off.
> *America,* August 1943

In the early morning hours of February 13, 1991, less than a month into
the Persian Gulf War, two U.S. F-117 stealth fighters each dropped one
two-thousand-pound, laser-guided bomb on the Al Firdos bunker, which
intelligence sources had identified as a newly operational Iraqi com-
mand-and-control center. Unbeknownst to U.S. officials, the bunker was
also serving as a shelter for Iraqi civilians. The F-117s scored a direct hit,
destroying the bunker and in the process killing over two hundred Iraqi
civilians, including scores of women and children.[1]

[1] Atkinson, *Crusade*, pp. 285–86.

Even before CNN began airing grisly scenes of corpses being carried from the bunker, U.S. theater commander General Norman Schwarz-kopf "recognized that the coalition had major press and political prob-lems."[2] Chairman of the Joint Chiefs of Staff Colin Powell shared this concern and reminded Schwarzkopf of the "policy and political over-tones" of targeting decisions, emphasizing that the allies could not afford "to take a chance on something like this happening again."[3] Henceforth, both Schwarzkopf and Powell would exercise target-by-tar-get approval of all sorties against sites in Baghdad, and strikes against strategic targets would be greatly curtailed. Bridges and bunkers that could potentially be serving as bomb shelters were placed off-limits for the remainder of the war. There were no strikes on targets of any kind in Baghdad for five days after Al Firdos, and none against leadership tar-gets for ten days. In all, only five more targets in Baghdad were hit before the war ended some two weeks later.[4] The Gulf War Air Power Survey later concluded that "the strategic consequences of this attack were considerable. To all intents and purposes the civilian losses ended the strategic air war campaign against targets in Baghdad," and with it went the effort to "decapitate" the Iraqi military, a major goal of air force officials since the first provisional plans were drawn up the previous August.[5]

Despite the dramatic reaction by U.S. officials to the Al Firdos bomb-ing, it is doubtful that the action constituted a violation of international law. Clearly, a serious intelligence error was made, but there was no indi-cation that it had been the result of gross or criminal negligence. Fur-thermore, evidence existed that the bunker was in fact being used for military activity, a fact that might have permitted it to be attacked under the laws of war, the presence of civilians notwithstanding.[6] The crucial issues at stake, however, were not legal but ethical and political. One commentator described Powell's concern that "another massacre like

[2] Gulf War Air Power Survey (GWAPS), *Volume II: Operations* (Washington, D.C.: Gov-ernment Printing Office, 1993), p. 220.

[3] Quoted in Atkinson, *Crusade*, p. 289.

[4] GWAPS, *Operations*, p. 222; Atkinson, *Crusade*, pp. 294–95.

[5] GWAPS, *Operations*, p. 206; Robert A. Pape, *Bombing to Win: Air Power and Coercion in War* (Ithaca: Cornell University Press, 1996), chap. 7.

[6] Atkinson, *Crusade*, pp. 275–77. For the argument that the raid may have violated the laws of war, see Middle East Watch, *Needless Deaths in the Gulf War: Civilian Casualties during the Air Campaign and Violations of the Laws of War* (Washington: Human Rights Watch, 1991), pp. 128–48.

Al-Firdos would destroy the allies' moral standing"[7]—and this concern was enough to significantly change the way the war was fought.

Some of the same questions posed at the beginning of the last chapter about George Bush's unwillingness to assassinate Saddam Hussein may be applied to the Al Firdos episode. Are we to view the concerns of U.S. officials as expressions of moral judgment, political judgment, or both? If they reflect both moral and political sensibilities, how do we account for the nexus between the two? For students of international politics, what should be striking about this episode is that although we can understand the U.S. reaction to the bombing, we have a hard time explaining it with the theories at our disposal. How, for example, does the U.S. reaction fit with the assumption that states, especially states at war, pursue their short-term strategic interests? Moreover, if the raid did not violate international law, why did the civilian casualties represent such a public relations nightmare for the United States—and such a propaganda windfall for Saddam Hussein?

It is impossible to answer these questions without recognizing the role of norms in international politics, and in particular the norm against the aerial bombing of civilians during wartime. The bombing of civilians has been the subject of an immense amount of attention not only among historians and political scientists but also philosophers, artists, and writers of fiction. For proponents of norms, an abundance of drama and pathos is ordinarily not a healthy sign, and thus has it been with bombing. Indeed, the conventional assessment of what I will call "the bombing norm" is a story of norm failure, focusing on the dramatic disintegration of the norm during the Second World War, when millions of noncombatants died in bombing raids carried out by both sides. The conventional view holds that the original prohibition against bombing civilians, which reflected long-standing humanitarian rules designed to protect innocents from the horrors of war, fell away quickly—and inevitably—when confronted by strategic necessity, as the interests of states fighting for their survival overpowered moral concerns. The death of the norm was sealed by technological limitations that left belligerents with little choice but to hit the largest and most accessible targets available: enemy cities. The fact that civilians bore the brunt these attacks is seen as a tragic but unavoidable consequence of this particular manifestation of modern war. The following passage illustrates this view:

[7] Atkinson, *Crusade*, p. 288.

The fall of France in 1940 left Britain alone against Germany. The ensuing Battle of Britain, culminating in the Blitz, left England reeling. Surrender was unthinkable, but it could not retaliate with its outnumbered and overstretched army and navy. The only hope of hitting back at Germany and winning the war lay with Bomber Command. But operational factors quickly demonstrated that prewar doctrine [emphasizing precision bombing of military objectives] had been hopelessly unrealistic. . . . Aircrew survival dictated night area attacks, and, in truth, there was little alternative other than to not attack at all. Moral constraints bowed to what was deemed military necessity, which led air leaders down a particularly slippery path.[8]

With the notable exception of the portrayal of British prewar bombing doctrine, there is nothing terribly wrong with this account, as far as it goes. But such accounts are often taken no further, and the breakdown of bombing restraint is held out as perhaps the apotheosis of the impotence of ethical norms in general in the face of the exigencies of war.

There are two main problems with the conventional view of the bombing norm. First, it ascribes the failure of the norm in World War II to the shortcomings of ethical norms in general, portraying the episode as the simple triumph of necessity over morality. This both buys into and reinforces a view of norms that relies on the facile dichotomy pitting power and interest against moral principle (described in Chapter 1). The pull of strategic interests was an important aspect of the story of the bombing norm in World War II, but it was not all there was to it. Although the bombing norm was an early casualty of the war, other ethical norms, such as those against assassination and the use of chemical weapons, held up far better.[9] This suggests that something in the nature of the bombing norm itself made it particularly brittle. It is important, therefore, to examine more closely the construction of the norm itself, rather than treating it as a generic moral injunction untouched by geopolitical or technological considerations. The second problem is that the conventional approach does not follow the story long enough. It closes the book on the bombing norm after the cataclysms of Hiroshima and Nagasaki, sometimes adding as an epilogue the nuclear "balance of terror" as conclusive evidence that the targeting of civilians is here to stay.

[8] Phillip S. Meilinger, "Winged Defense: Airwar, the Law, and Morality," *Armed Forces and Society* 20, no. 1 (Fall 1993): 106–7.

[9] On assassination, see Chapter 3, supra. On chemical warfare, see Legro, *Cooperation under Fire*, chap. 4; and Price, *The Chemical Weapons Taboo*, chap. 5.

In fact, the norm against bombing civilians has enjoyed a gradual revitalization in the decades since World War II. The reasons for this, again, relate less to the power of norms in general than to conditions favorable to this norm in particular. Bringing the story of the bombing norm up to date provides valuable insights into the construction and operation of ethical norms, and further exposes the shortcomings of the view that sees norms as mere moral fetters on state power.

Chapters 4 and 5 address each of these problems in turn. In this chapter I argue that the failure of the bombing norm in the Second World War was caused not only by the strategic interests of the belligerents but also by the inherent weakness of the norm itself—a weakness attributable to the fact that it did not mesh well with the geopolitical, technological, or normative conditions prevailing in the first decades of the twentieth century. As a result, although there was a clear *legal* prohibition against the bombing of noncombatants, this prohibition was not internalized by the military and political institutions of major states, and it gave rise to only a very tenuous understanding that such actions were inappropriate. By the eve of World War II, the bombing norm was what I have referred to in Chapter 2 as a "convention-dependent" norm; that is, contingent upon mutual compliance and not strong enough to deter any state from reciprocating if another state breaks the norm first. This, better than reference to strategic necessity alone, explains both the initial period of relative restraint in bombing observed by the warring powers and the eventual spiral into unrestrained bombing that culminated in the firebombing raids on Dresden and Tokyo and the atomic bombings of Hiroshima and Nagasaki.

The remainder of this chapter contains three sections. First, I examine the roots of the bombing norm and the principle of noncombatant immunity. I argue that while noncombatant immunity directly embodies a priori moral judgments, it nevertheless contains ambiguities that make its application to aerial warfare problematic. In the second section I trace the development of the bombing norm from 1899 to the eve of World War II, focusing on the rise of air power theory and the frustrated attempts to arrive at a normative consensus among states about how aerial warfare was to be conducted. I then consider the breakdown of the norm during the war, showing how the pattern of bombing can be explained by the convention-dependent nature of the norm. I also consider alternative explanations for the dramatic failure of the norm, arguing that none can serve as a satisfactory account in its own right.

NONCOMBATANT IMMUNITY AND
THE ROOTS OF THE BOMBING NORM

While the bombing norm itself is, of course, a twentieth-century development, its roots go back much further to the doctrine of the just war and the principle of noncombatant immunity. The principle can be stated most simply as "prohibit[ing] directly intended attacks on noncombatants and nonmilitary targets."[10] Some version of this principle has existed since antiquity; both Plato and Roman authors argued that the violence of war should be visited only upon those who were "guilty" in the sense of having actively borne arms in battle.[11] The references to guilt and innocence in these early formulations makes clear that the restriction was seen as bearing a close relationship to an underlying moral principle. This relationship was made explicit by Saint Augustine in his influential fourth-century work on the doctrine of just war. Starting from the a priori position that the taking of human life was wrong, Augustine reasoned that although some license for killing must be given to Christian soldiers in just wars, this license was strictly limited to that which was necessary to redress injustice and restore peace. By this reasoning, noncombatants were protected from violence.[12] The protection of noncombatants as a class was later the object of the Roman Catholic Church's Peace of God movement. Originating in the eleventh century, this movement promulgated a series of doctrinal pronouncements aimed at humanizing the conduct of war, including the proposition that those who are not in a position to do harm should have no harm done to them.[13] This moral proposition—reinforced by the medieval code of chivalry, which saw war as a contest between equals based upon military virtue—eventually evolved into a common normative understanding in European society that the violence of war should be limited as much as possible to those who participate in it directly, and that others should be spared.[14]

In this form, it is tempting to see the rule of noncombatant immunity as a concrete embodiment of an abstract moral principle: that human life is intrinsically valuable, and killing without justification is morally

---

[10] Pierce, "Just War Principles and Economic Sanctions," p. 101.
[11] McElroy, *Morality and American Foreign Policy*, p. 149.
[12] Ibid., pp. 149–50.
[13] Parker, "Early Modern Europe," p. 41.
[14] McElroy, *Morality and American Foreign Policy*, p. 150.

wrong. Indeed, the rule undoubtedly derives much of its strength from, in Michael Walzer's words, people's "sense of what is right." It is worth considering, however, that both the Peace of God movement and chivalric norms actually reflected the interests of important social actors of the time. As James Turner Johnson writes:

> The idea of noncombatant immunity had only the most hesitant beginnings in ecclesiastical thinking, and the first canonical attempts to define such a doctrine are transparently the result of a churchly self-interest. Similarly, the protection accorded noncombatants by the chivalric code was rooted in self-interest, though this time it was in the interest of the knightly class to hold chivalry separate from the rest of medieval society and superior to it. The church's definition was, to be sure, of a somewhat more absolute nature than the chivalric: so long as the persons named in the canons took no part in war, protection from harm in war was a right not to be violated. Meanwhile, the chivalric code allowed for actions outside the bounds set by noncombatant immunity if necessary for the higher purpose of the code: knightly superiority. This was a doctrine of relative, not absolute, protection of noncombatants.[15]

When ecclesiastical and chivalric codes ceased to exert a strong influence on actors in European society, the norm of noncombatant immunity survived partly because it continued to conform to people's sense of justice, but also because it was compatible with new social structures emerging at the time. As we saw in Chapter 3, an important idea that grew up around the institution of sovereign statehood was the fiction of states as actors and the disassociation of war between states with personal antipathy between citizens of those states. Because warring armies were seen as agents of the state, licensed to use violence only for the purpose of pursuing state interests, the protection of noncombatants was easily incorporated into the treatises of such writers as Vitoria and Grotius and thereby into the legal and normative structure of the new Europe. Moreover, there were compelling military reasons for respecting noncombatant immunity. The larger armies of the time were required to forage to sustain themselves, a task that would be extremely difficult if wanton violence destroyed the local economy and alienated the local population. Another problem was that such actions severely undermined discipline within the ranks, a pressing issue in such large organizations, especially

---

[15] Johnson, *Just War Tradition and the Restraint of War*, pp. 199–200.

ones that drew from classes ignorant of the norms of chivalry. Noncombatant immunity therefore served the interests of military leaders faced with novel logistical and command problems.[16] Even such an apparently fundamental humanitarian principle as noncombatant immunity, therefore, was to a large degree the product of processes of social and political construction.

The nexus between the norm of noncombatant immunity and pragmatic concerns helps to explain some of the ethical ambiguities in its application. For example, the interests of military necessity that usually serve to protect civilians also sometimes place them in harm's way. Thus the rule has always admitted of exceptions for cases when harm to noncombatants cannot be avoided without seriously compromising the military effort. Likewise, the rule only protects noncombatants from being targeted in "directly intended" attacks, meaning that the rule is violated neither by their accidental death nor if their death is incidental to a legitimate act of war.[17] It is unnecessary here to go into the details of how these exceptions are worked out in practice. The point is simply that the norm of noncombatant immunity, as morally fundamental as it may seem, has never taken the form of an absolute prohibition but instead has always been filtered through the lens of pragmatic concerns in concrete historical circumstances. Consequently, a considerable amount of divergence exists between the abstract moral principle and the rule as it is sometimes applied. Michael Walzer states the point well:

> The historical specifications of the principle [of noncombatant immunity] are, however, conventional in character, and the war rights and obligations of soldiers follow from the conventions and not (directly) from the principle, whatever its force. Once again, war is a social creation. The rules actually observed or violated in this or that time and place are necessarily a complex product, mediated by cultural and religious norms, social structures, and formal and informal bargaining between belligerent powers, and so on. Hence, the details of noncombatant immunity are likely to seem as arbitrary as the rules that determine when battles should start and stop or what weapons may be used.[18]

[16] Terry Nardin, "The Moral Basis of the Law of War," *Journal of International Affairs* 37 (Winter 1984): 304.

[17] For an explanation and critique of this "principle of double effect," see Walzer, *Just and Unjust Wars*, pp. 151–59.

[18] Ibid., p. 43.

A good example is the treatment of civilians under the rules of siege warfare. Customary laws of war dating back to the medieval period held that inhabitants of cities taken by siege were entitled to no protection whatsoever, even from outright slaughter.[19] This rather dramatic exception to noncombatant immunity was often justified by its strategic utility in deterring other towns from resisting occupation in the future, but in any case the extent to which the practice departed from its underlying moral principle is striking. Of course, this in no way diminishes either the strength or the validity of the moral impulse to protect noncombatants; it does, however, show how difficult it has been to translate that impulse into specific rules.

Finally, even in its simplest form, noncombatant immunity can be ethically ambiguous. As George Mavrodes points out, the standard moral justification for the distinction between combatants and noncombatants, that of guilt and innocence, does not withstand moral scrutiny.[20] Some soldiers may be good and peaceful people forced to fight against their will, and some civilians may bear a large measure of responsibility for the war from which they find themselves protected.[21] Referring to all noncombatants as "innocents," Mavrodes argues, is simply another way of stating the rule that they should not be exposed to danger rather than an independent moral assessment.[22] Still, Mavrodes argues, there may be worthwhile ethical reasons for respecting the distinction between combatants and noncombatants if by doing so we can to some extent limit the destructiveness and suffering of war. Mavrodes sees noncombatant immunity, then, as a "convention-dependent obligation related

---

[19] Parker, "Early Modern Europe," pp. 48–49. As an illustration of the prevailing practice, Parker quotes from Henry's ultimatum to the besieged town of Harfleur in Shakespeare's *Henry V*:

> If I begin the batt'ry once again,
> I will not leave the half-achieved Harfleur
> Till in her ashes she lie buried.
> The gates of mercy shall be all shut up
> And the flesh'd soldier, rough and hard of heart,
> In liberty of bloody hand shall range
> With conscience wide as hell, mowing like grass
> Your fresh fair virgins and your flow'ring infants.

[20] Mavrodes, "Conventions and the Morality of War."

[21] Walzer refers to this as "an example of class legislation." *Just and Unjust Wars*, p. 138.

[22] Mavrodes, "Conventions and the Morality of War," pp. 122–23. As Walzer says, in this sense, "innocent" is a term of art. Ibid., p. 146.

to a convention which substitutes for [unlimited] warfare a certain form of limited combat."[23] Because of the ethical benefits derived from it, the rule does give rise to a moral obligation, but one that rests less on any deep-seated and immutable moral distinctions and more on the consequences of the rule.

In some circumstances, of course, the association of noncombatants with innocence may be clearer—as in the case of children, for example, whom we may safely assume to be innocent in any relevant sense of the word. There are strong independent moral reasons why we would wish to forbid soldiers to shoot at children. The choices confronted in war, however, are not always this clear, especially in the modern age. When the contemplated target is not an individual but a building, a military installation, a factory, or a city, it becomes highly likely that both innocent and guilty people—whether they are combatants or noncombatants—will die as a result. In such cases, Mavrodes's interpretation of noncombatant immunity as an essentially result-oriented rule becomes highly relevant, and helps to explain some of the conundrums of the application of the rule to aerial bombing.

Noncombatant Immunity and Aerial Bombing: Problems of Application

Early attempts at applying the rule of noncombatant immunity to aerial bombing raised even more vexing questions. Specifically, three issues made the application of the rule difficult. The first was the increasing murkiness of the line between combatants and noncombatants. Nationalist ideology, especially in Europe, not only brought a larger percentage of a nation's populace into the armed forces but also served to undermine the understanding that war was the business of armies alone, divorced from the concerns of everyday citizens. This trend was complemented by the effects of the industrial revolution and the ensuing industrialization of war, which meant that many civilians played an increasingly important role in the war effort. Moreover, the late 1800s saw the rise of the guerrilla and partisan warfare that was to become so prominent in the twentieth century. The Franco-Prussian War of 1870–71, for example, witnessed both guerrilla action and the occasionally brutal treatment of the civilian population. As Italian air power theorist Giulio Douhet wrote in 1921, "The prevailing forms of social organization have given war a character of national totality—that is, the entire population and all the resources of a nation are sucked into the maw of war. And,

---

[23] Mavrodes, "Conventions and the Morality of War," p. 127.

since society is now definitely evolving along this line, it is within the power of human foresight to see now that future wars will be total in character and scope."[24] The implications of this trend were profound, as the phenomenon of "total war" forced a reexamination of almost every element of noncombatant immunity, including the fundamental question of what should count as a legitimate military target.

A second difficulty encountered in applying noncombatant immunity to aerial bombing was that specific applications of the rule developed in other technological contexts provided questionable precedents. For example, the law of land warfare outlawed the bombardment of "undefended" towns but permitted attacks on "defended" towns—an obvious vestige of the prevalence of sieges in medieval and Renaissance warfare. When it came to bombing from the air, however, it was far from clear what constituted a defended town, or what ethical or legal significance should attach to whether it was defended or not. Some argued that the existence of antitank and antipersonnel fortifications at national borders meant that the entire nation was considered defended and open to attack from the air; others maintained that the existence of a national air force had the same effect; still others held that the presence of antiaircraft artillery was the relevant criterion.[25] By any measure, as Tami Davis Biddle points out, "a too-literal interpretation leads to an absurd situation. If a nation provides its town with an air defense, does it open them to attack? If it provides no defense, are military targets within the towns immune from attack?"[26] Nevertheless, much of the early debate over the permissibility of aerial bombing centered on the "defended town" criterion. Even by the time of World War II, this standard, long since outdated, remained technically in effect.

This example illustrates the problems encountered when customary standards that have evolved over time confront a fundamentally different mode of warfare. As M. W. Royse observed in 1928: "Fundamental in the regulation of warfare is the fact that the employment of each major

---

[24] Giulio Douhet, *The Command of the Air*, trans. Dino Ferrari (New York: Coward-McCann, 1942), pp. 5–6.

[25] Donald Cameron Watt, "Restraints on War in the Air before 1945," in *Restraints on War: Studies in the Limitation of Armed Conflict*, ed. Michael Howard (Oxford: Oxford University Press, 1979), p. 63; Paul W. Williams, "Legitimate Targets in Aerial Bombardment," *American Journal of International Law* 23, no. 3 (July 1929): 573; Major Richard H. Wyman, "The First Rules of Air Warfare," *Air Force Review* 35, no. 3 (March/April 1984):96.

[26] Tami Davis Biddle, "Air Power," in *The Laws of War*, p. 144.

weapon brings about the restrictions or limitations upon its use. . . . Thus, to attempt to regulate aerial bombardment by the customary practices which have grown out of land or naval warfare is to lay down a set of artificial regulations which will hardly stand the strain of war."[27] In other words, existing norms refer to practices that reflect a balance among capabilities, interests, and humanitarian concerns that in turn has become accepted and internalized. A new technology may lead to a quite different balance and therefore to different understandings and expectations—different norms—concerning how the weapon is to be used. While existing legal provisions may be expanded to incorporate new weapons, therefore, it is difficult to establish an effective norm in this manner, especially for a mode of warfare with unproven potential.

A final and closely related obstacle to applying the principle of noncombatant immunity to aerial bombing was the uncertainty attending the introduction of a completely novel technology. Manned flight represented such a profound departure from previous modes of warfare that accurately assessing its potential applications was nearly impossible. This had effects of two very different types. First, the inability to predict what the airplane (and, in the years before World War I, the airship) would and would not be capable of doing exacerbated political uncertainties and impeded efforts to limit the possession or use of the new technology. In the early years of the century there were huge differences of opinion as to whether the development of air power was an indispensable step or an utter waste of time and money. Because technology was developing so quickly, moreover, there was always the possibility that a technological breakthrough could vault some states ahead and leave others behind the curve. Under these circumstances, there was an incentive to approach arms control and regulation cautiously for fear of giving up a potentially useful, if unproven, technology.

The second effect was that technological uncertainty complicated calculations of military effectiveness. It was not known, for example, how many airplanes it would take to accomplish certain missions, what the proper composition of an air force was, or whether bigger planes would be more capable than smaller planes. Moreover, there was no clear way of distinguishing between aircraft designed for commercial purposes and those capable of being used for military missions, particularly bombing. All this meant that "air power did not lend itself to the sorts of limi-

---

[27] M.W. Royse, *Aerial Bombardment and the International Regulation of Warfare*, (New York: Vinal, 1928), p. 239.

tations that could be placed on battleships."[28] Just as important, uncertainty about the military capabilities of aircraft confused the calculations of necessity, effectiveness, and proportionality that are necessary to apply the rule of noncombatant immunity. This was especially true of bombing. How, for example, can a belligerent know whether a bombing mission promises sufficiently significant military gains to justify the risk of civilian casualties if both the risk of casualties and the prospective gains are matters of conjecture? And, given this type of uncertainty, is it realistic to expect belligerents to err on the side of restraint, resolving all questions in favor of protecting noncombatants even at the expense of strategic gain?

All these factors, then, made the regulation of air warfare more complicated than simply plugging a new weapon into an old equation. As a result, while the principle of noncombatant immunity provided a general context of ethical judgment, norms specific to aerial bombing were created more or less from scratch in the first years of the twentieth century. Unfortunately, the ensuing decades would not be conducive to the establishment of a strong regulatory regime, as technological uncertainty and geopolitical volatility combined to frustrate efforts to generate a normative consensus.

UNCERTAINTY AND FRUSTRATION: THE BOMBING NORM BEFORE WORLD WAR II

The first significant occasion on which states considered the regulation of air warfare was the Hague Peace Conference of 1899. Acting on a proposal by Russia, the conferees agreed to prohibit the discharge of explosives or projectiles from balloons for a period of five years.[29] While ostensibly humanitarian in nature, the prohibition was very much shaped by practical strategic considerations. Not long before proposing the measure, for example, Russia's program to develop a dirigible had failed miserably, while similar French and German programs were nearing success.[30] Not surprisingly, the Russian proposal generated considerable difference of opinion. Delegates from France, Germany, the

---

[28] Lee Kennett, *A History of Strategic Bombing* (New York: Charles Scribner's Sons, 1982), p. 63.
[29] Biddle, "Air Power," p. 141.
[30] Watt, "Restraints on War in the Air before 1945," p. 60.

United States, and Britain opposed restrictions, while smaller states sided with Russia in favoring an absolute prohibition. A five-year ban was eventually proposed by the American delegate as a compromise solution, but this was opposed by the British, who believed that the use of balloons as military platforms might offset the numerical inferiority of the British army relative to the continental powers. British resistance was finally overcome by an American pledge to support Britain in fighting a ban on dum-dum bullets.[31] The five-year limitation was, in the end, crucial to the conclusion of an agreement but also made it much less meaningful. Because of the primitive state of aircraft development at the time, an agreement to refrain from using them in combat meant very little.[32] Still, the five-year limit showed that states were aware that a technological breakthrough might change matters considerably, and they were unwilling to sacrifice a potentially useful weapon into the indefinite future. Consequently, there was less to even this modest provision than meets the eye.

When the provision came up for renewal at the Second Hague Conference in 1907, the situation had indeed changed dramatically. Some states had made great progress in the use of dirigibles, and the Wright Brothers' flight of 1903 had shown the feasibility of heavier-than-air flight. Still, not all states had pursued aviation with equal vigor, and consequently states came to the 1907 conference with a variety of negotiating positions reflecting their different strategic situations.[33] Leading the pack in terms of air power were the French, who possessed a full fleet of airships and had the only military airplanes in existence at the time. Close behind were the Germans, whose Zeppelin and Parseval airships gave them perhaps the most capable technology. Russia, the moving force behind the balloon ban eight years earlier, had modernized its military after the humiliation of the Russo-Japanese War and was moving aggressively on airplane and airship development. The Italians were also beginning an ambitious airship building program. Moreover, Italy was probably the European nation least vulnerable to raids by dirigibles, which could not fly over the Alps or the Dolomites while carrying full bombing loads and could be intercepted relatively easily if they

---

[31] Ibid.

[32] Royse, *Aerial Bombardment and the International Regulation of Warfare*, p. 121.

[33] The best single account of the situation of the major states with regard to air power in 1907 is found in Royse, *Aerial Bombardment and the International Regulation of Warfare*, chap. 3.

approached from over the sea. Not surprisingly, all of these states opposed renewing the prohibition of 1899.[34]

Leading the fight on the other side of the question were Great Britain and Austria-Hungary, which shared some important strategic similarities. Neither were militarily weak states, but both were "status quo" powers whose strength rested on traditional means of warfare. Neither had invested much in either military or civilian air capabilities, despite the fact that Austria-Hungary was a center for experimentation in aerodynamics. Finally, each felt that the advent of air power left it significantly more vulnerable than it had been before. Austria-Hungary, a traditional land power, suddenly found itself practically surrounded by states with burgeoning aerial capabilities. For Britain the situation was even more menacing, as air power threatened to end the long period of security assured by the English Channel and the Royal Navy. Consequently, Britain and Austria-Hungary pushed for the bombing ban of 1899 to be extended indefinitely. In this they were joined by weaker states such as Greece, Portugal, China, and Turkey, all of which either lacked the resources to build a capable air force or were vulnerable to attack from states that did not. In a third category were the United States and Japan. Despite being the home of the Wright Brothers, as well as a strong opponent of an unlimited bombing ban in 1899, the United States had shown little interest in developing air power and possessed no aeronautical equipment whatsoever in 1907, except for some balloon material. The situation was the same in Japan, where the military had strongly resisted developing an aerial capacity. Still, the relative geographical isolation of each nation afforded the luxury of watching the development of European air forces with a sense of detachment rather than alarm. As a result, the United States and Japan remained more or less indifferent to the debates of 1907.

Technically, the issue at stake in "legitimizing" aerial bombing was not whether it was to be permitted without any restrictions whatsoever. Rather, the choice was between regulation or prohibition: whether it was to be subject to the same restrictions as other modes of warfare or outlawed altogether by the indefinite extension of the 1899 ban.[35] The "air power" states—France, Germany, Russia, and Italy—argued that

---

[34] For debates on the renewal of the bombing ban, see *The Proceedings of the Hague Peace Conferences: The Conference of 1907*, vol. 3 (New York: Oxford University Press, 1920), 37, pp. 143–53.

[35] Ibid., p. 120.

since the advance of technology might soon make it possible for air power to be used effectively in a military context, there was no reason to treat it differently than any other type of weapon, such as artillery. In one sense, there is an undeniable logic to this position: Why should one means of delivering an explosive shell be subject to an entirely different set of restrictions than another? The problem, of course, was that in the case of air power the means of delivery was in fact so dramatically different that the humanitarian issues raised would be of an entirely different character. This problem was recognized in the context of naval bombardment, which as a result was governed by different rules than bombardment on land. While land forces were prohibited from attacking undefended towns, the relevant criterion for naval gunnery was not defense or fortification but whether the prospective target was a valid military objective.[36] While it would eventually become apparent that this was an appropriate standard for aerial bombing as well, this was less obvious in 1907, several years before the first use of aircraft in combat.

While advancing rapidly, aeronautical technology was still so primitive that meaningful military applications were few. Airplanes were still viewed more as a novelty than a useful tool; by the summer of 1907, the longest heavier-than-air flight to take place in Europe had been less than a quarter-mile.[37] Consequently, airplanes were hardly mentioned at all at the conference, and it was not deemed necessary to update the 1899 Hague Declaration's reference to "balloons or other new methods of a similar nature."[38] Understandably, air doctrine was even less developed than technology. In 1907, it was as reasonable to assume that aircraft would be used solely as an adjunct to ground forces than to anticipate a dramatically different, independent bombing role. In fact, the United States' first military aviation arm was established in 1907 as a section of the Army's Signal Corps—a designation it retained throughout World War I.[39] Even as late as 1914, a leading expert argued that military aircraft would be used "first, and chiefly, as scouts: the service of information will be their special and most important role."[40]

[36] Biddle, "Air Power," p. 143; James B. Scott, *The Hague Peace Conferences: American Instructions and Reports* (New York: Oxford University Press, 1916), p. 112.

[37] Royse, *Aerial Bombardment and the International Regulation of Warfare*, p. 75.

[38] William I. Hull, *The Two Hague Conferences* (Boston: Atheneum Press, 1908), pp. 79–82; *Proceedings*, vol. 1, pp. 109, 678.

[39] Thomas H. Greer, *The Development of Air Doctrine in the Army Air Arm, 1917–1941* (Washington, D.C.: Office of Air Force History, 1985), p. 1.

[40] J. M. Spaight, *Aircraft in War* (London: MacMillan, 1914), p. 8.

If the military implications of advances in aircraft technology were uncertain, the same was at least as true of the humanitarian implications. Predictions at the conference ranged from the benign to the apocalyptic, but given the modest capabilities of the aircraft of the day, the most pessimistic scenarios required a leap of imagination. The sober assessment of the future of air power that opened this chapter, offered by the Italian delegate Robilant, was closer to the prevailing view. Indeed, the remarks of many conference delegates are striking for the belief that aerial warfare would have little effect on the humanitarian aspects of war. They are striking to the modern observer, however, because we view them with the benefit of hindsight: we know what air power was to mean to the twentieth century, but the delegates at the Hague in 1907 could not. This fact alone illustrates a major obstacle to establishing a normative consensus on a mode of warfare that is new and changing rapidly. The fact that it remained for the most part an unknown quantity made it nearly impossible to know what was at stake in any regulatory regime. And, as Robilant candidly explained, "The Powers which have realized the greatest progress in the art of managing balloons will not easily give up the right to use them at a time when their progress in this difficult work gives them an undoubted advantage over the others."[41] Under these circumstances, the chances for negotiating meaningful restrictions on air warfare in 1907 were remote. In the end, aerial bombing was brought under the rules of land warfare, thus codifying the preference of the air power states.[42] The result was a set of rules for aerial warfare that was, in the words of one commentator, "consciously ineffectual."[43]

World War I

The first significant test of air power came with World War I. At the beginning of the war the use of aircraft was limited primarily to reconnaissance and pursuit missions, but soon the desire to strike at the enemy's homeland led to the first bombing raids.[44] In 1915, Germany

---

[41] *Proceedings*, vol. 3, p. 150.

[42] This was accomplished by amending the language of the 1899 Land Warfare Convention to read: "The attack or bombardment, *by whatever means*, of towns, villages, dwellings or buildings which are undefended is prohibited." Biddle, "Air Power," p. 142 (emphasis added).

[43] William V. O'Brien, "The Meaning of 'Military Necessity' in International Law," *World Polity* 1 (1957): 134.

[44] David MacIsaac, "Voices from the Central Blue: Theorists of Air Power," in *Makers of Modern Strategy*, p. 628.

launched zeppelin raids against towns in England and France that caused numerous civilian casualties and prompted the British Home Office to protest that "almost all the unfortunate people who have been killed were not only non-combatants, but non-combatants of a class who hitherto, in the honorable practice of civilized warfare, have been exempt from attack (women, children, small shopkeepers, working men), the sacrifice of whose lives serves no military purpose, either morally or materially."[45] Nevertheless, the British soon launched raids of their own against German towns. None of these, however, had the impact of the offensive launched against London and England's southeast coast by German Gotha bombers in the spring of 1917. Although the raids were relatively few (twenty-seven from May 1917 through the end of the war), and the total number of casualties was low compared to the military losses on the continent (1,413 killed and 3,407 injured), the psychological impact of the raids was devastating.[46] One Briton had written of the zeppelin raids two years earlier: "It is particularly humiliating to allow an enemy to come over your capital city and hurl bombs upon it. His aim may be very bad, the casualties may be few, but the moral effect is wholly undesirable. When the Zeppelins came to London they could have scored a galling technical triumph over us if they had showered us with confetti."[47] The effects of the Gotha raids were even more disconcerting, leading to a widespread panic in London, the temporary displacement of hundreds of thousands of Britons seeking shelter, and rampant absenteeism and declining production in war industries.[48] The Gotha raids spurred the pace of both technological development and bombing operations conducted by the Allies, who when the Armistice came were in the process of planning a major bombing offensive for 1919.

Through all of this, the concrete effects of the 1907 restrictions were negligible. The criterion of defended towns was, for the reasons discussed earlier, almost impossible to apply in any meaningful way. When the 1917 raids prompted neutral states to propose a renewed agreement to limit future bombing, for example, the British General Staff issued a memorandum expressing the opinion that "with trench lines stretching from Switzerland to the sea, in some sense every German town was

---

[45] Quoted in Royse, *Aerial Bombardment and the International Regulation of Warfare*, p. 179.
[46] Legro, *Cooperation under Fire*, p. 96.
[47] Quoted in Kennett, *A History of Strategic Bombing*, p. 24.
[48] Ibid., pp. 25–26.

defended."[49] For their part, the Germans proposed limiting future bombing to "military areas" only—which not only would have exposed the populations of Belgium and Northern France to bombing but was defined in such a way as to also include British cities such as London and Brighton while excluding German cities like Stuttgart and Karlsruhe.[50] Officially, Britain maintained throughout the war that it was bombing only legitimate military objectives, thus ostensibly applying the standard of naval warfare. France appealed to the same standard while also acknowledging some indiscriminate raids as reprisals for German raids on French towns.[51] Germany insisted that it, too, was bombing discriminately, but it admitted that the ultimate aim of the raids was to damage the morale of the civilian population—a goal that both Britain and France denied seeking.[52] The actual conduct of bombing by all sides, however, made such pronouncements meaningless. To a large extent this was a function of technology. Bombing in World War I suffered from severe limitations in navigation, bomb sighting, and bomb design. While the bombers in service late in the war represented significant improvements over earlier craft, they still suffered from major shortcomings that limited their effectiveness. The result was that no air force had the ability to hit specific military targets on the ground by anything other than sheer luck.[53] Targets were therefore chosen to maximize the chances of hitting something of value, and this meant dropping bombs on cities.

Limited technology, however, was only part of the picture. The panic and disruption caused by the Gotha raids on London made a profound impression on the Allies, and they doubtless wished to generate some of the same effects with their raids on Germany. Moreover, the raids gave rise to a new and powerful way of thinking about air power, leading to a series of organizational and doctrinal innovations that would extend far beyond World War I itself. Donald Watt explains that "the raids of 1917 led directly ... to the establishment of the Royal Air Force upon the amalgamation of the Royal Flying Corps and the Royal Naval Air Service, and to the establishment in October 1917 in France of the Independent Bombing Force to carry the strategic bombing offensive to the German

---

[49] Watt, "Restraints on War in the Air before 1945," p. 63.
[50] Ibid.; Williams, "Legitimate Targets in Aerial Bombardment," p. 573.
[51] Royse, *Aerial Bombardment and the International Regulation of Warfare*, p. 189.
[52] Ibid., p. 214.
[53] Kennett, *A History of Strategic Bombing*, p. 33.

people."[54] The goals and ambitions of the devotees of air power at the time are evident in the Smuts Memorandum of 1917, which was crucial to the founding of the RAF: "As far as can at present be foreseen there is absolutely no limit to its future independent war use. And the day may not be far off when aerial operations with their *devastation of enemy lands and destruction of industrial and populous centres on a vast scale* may become the principal operations of war, to which the older forms of military and naval operations may become secondary and subordinate."[55] It is clear that, protestations to the contrary notwithstanding, the belligerents in World War I sought from their bombing operations precisely the results that followed from dropping large numbers of bombs on large numbers of people—and would probably have tried to do so even if technological capabilities had allowed for far greater precision than was the case. While none of the belligerents officially asserted the right to bomb indiscriminately (without distinguishing between military and civilian targets) in order to damage enemy morale, there was little doubt that both sides sought this very effect.

In terms of both casualties inflicted and strategic impact, bombing played a negligible role in the First World War. With respect to the formation of bombing norms, however, the war had two important effects. First, while the city-bombing of World War I was limited and crude, it provided a glimpse of the potential for air power that was simultaneously intoxicating and terrifying. Second, the massive scale of the carnage of conventional ground combat in Europe increased receptiveness to alternative means of warfare that might prevent a similar nightmare the next time around. These two elements provided the impetus for the generation of interwar air power theorists that would shape the conduct of bombing in the next world war. And when combined with continuing rapid technological change and exceptionally volatile geopolitical conditions, they would make the conclusion of a binding agreement or the creation of a strong normative consensus on the bombing of noncombatants almost impossible.

The 1922–23 Hague Commission of Jurists
The clear failure of the 1907 Hague rules to constrain bombing in World War I led to calls for new guidelines that would specifically address the problems of aerial warfare. To this end, an international

---

[54] Watt, "Restraints on War in the Air before 1945," p. 62.
[55] Quoted in MacIsaac, "Voices from the Central Blue," pp. 628–29 (emphasis added).

commission of jurists was convened at the Hague from late 1922 to early 1923. It was charged with formulating updated rules that were consistent with the humanitarian goals of existing laws of warfare but also "conformed to actual practices" by recognizing the powerful influence of military necessity. The commission therefore explicitly set out to formulate realistic rules that states would actually agree to and abide by.

The commission immediately recognized that there were serious problems with the "defended city" test as a standard for aerial bombing. As one commentator explained, "It is clear that in the future, defense as a test for the legitimacy of an air attack is entirely inadequate. . . . Defense was an adequate criterion when the enemy attempted to capture, to force surrender, but it quite misses the point now that the enemy wishes simply to destroy."[56] The commission therefore rejected this test in favor of the standard used for naval bombardment—i.e., air attack would be permissible only against a "military objective," defined as "an object of which the destruction or injury would constitute a distinct military advantage to the belligerent."[57] In order to ensure that this rule adequately protected civilians, the commission added two other provisions: one prohibiting bombing for the purpose of terrorizing the civilian population, and the other forbidding even the bombing of legitimate military objectives if it would result in the incidental "indiscriminate bombardment of the civilian population."[58]

As commentators at the time noted, the Commission of Jurists' rules, unlike the confusing 1907 provisions, articulated standards that if followed would indeed provide a significant measure of protection for noncombatants.[59] Nevertheless, the rules met with almost immediate criticism. One complaint was that the definition of "military objective" was too vague to prevent attacks on a broad range of targets.[60] More fundamentally, it was objected that although the rules tried to take into account military necessity and the actual practices of belligerents, they placed unrealistic restrictions on a mode of warfare that might prove decisive in future wars. Some argued, for example, that the rule against striking military targets if it would result in the "indiscriminate bombardment" of civilians would, because of the destructiveness of bombs,

---

[56] Williams, "Legitimate Targets in Aerial Bombardment," p. 573.
[57] Quoted in Biddle, "Air Power," p. 148.
[58] Quoted in Williams, "Legitimate Targets in Aerial Bombardment," p. 575.
[59] See, e.g., Royse, *Aerial Bombardment and the International Regulation of Warfare,* chap. 6.
[60] Williams, "Legitimate Targets in Aerial Bombardment," pp. 576–77.

the inaccuracy of bombers, and the proximity of most military targets to populated areas, effectively forbid almost all bombing.[61] This was a sacrifice, it was argued, that states were not ready to make:

> It is inconceivable that nations which have come to regard the air service as a major means of attack will forgo the advantages derived from their predominance in that respect, and ultimately any such prohibition must be disregarded. . . . The better rule would be frankly to allow the bombing of military objectives wherever found and under whatever conditions. This would encourage their isolation and would recognize in law what is already true in fact, that a state possessed of a strong air force will not spare a military objective in however densely populated a district if the need is sufficiently urgent. . . . If states generally are not willing to forgo the use of advantages which they may be able to obtain from superiority in the air, then it is quixotic to draft a code which drastically curtails the operations of the aeroplane.[62]

The point was that the success of the commission's efforts ultimately depended upon the states that would be governed by them. The commission was, in Royse's words, "confronted with the task of restricting the most effective means of warfare of modern times."[63] But it was not the effectiveness per se of air power that hindered regulation, since aerial operations (particularly bombing) had not had that great of an impact on World War I, and matters had not changed that much by 1923. What made regulation so difficult was instead the *potential* effectiveness of air power and the fact that it remained for the most part an unknown quantity. This bred uncertainty not only as to future applications but also with regard to which states would benefit the most from air power and which would be the most vulnerable. An apt analogy might be poker players wagering on a hand without knowing which cards are wild; players might have a general idea of the strength of their hands, but would certainly hedge their bets if the stakes were high. Moreover, as in 1907, some players were holding more chips than others. France was again the strongest air power, with an air force organized around strategic bombing. Germany, while forbidden by the Versailles Treaty from possessing an air force, had begun laying a foundation for a strong future air presence immediately after the restrictions on building civilian aircraft were lifted in 1922. Italy, like France, had a strong bombing

---

[61] Royse, *Aerial Bombardment and the International Regulation of Warfare*, p. 230.
[62] Williams, "Legitimate Targets in Aerial Bombardment," pp. 577, 579.
[63] Royse, *Aerial Bombardment and the International Regulation of Warfare*, p. 174.

force. All of these states were opposed to strong restrictions such as those embodied in the Commission of Jurists' rules.[64]

In Britain, a pattern of intragovernmental squabbling over bombing was developing that would define that nation's air policy between the wars. The bombing panics of 1917 had left a mixed legacy. For most of the general public and much of the government, they had provided a glimpse of an apocalyptic form of warfare to which Britain, given the accessibility of its capital to bombing raids, was especially vulnerable. According to this view, bombing needed to be controlled—by arms limitations if possible, otherwise by regulation. For others, including the Air Ministry and the RAF, the raids had previewed a potentially decisive type of warfare that Britain could master if it took the lesson to heart and built up a strong bombing-intensive air force. To this constituency, limitations on air power were as unwise as they were futile. Furthermore, in the years after the war the RAF's aging bombers proved valuable in squelching indigenous resistance in British colonies such as Iraq and Somalia, making a total ban on bombing under any circumstances a costly policy move.[65] This combination of factors led Britain, wary both of restricting its own options and of being victimized by other states, to tentatively support the commission's rules. The United States and Japan also supported the rules, while the Netherlands objected that they did not go far enough in protecting neutrals against bombardment.[66]

The upshot of this jumble was that, despite widespread public approval of the provisions, no state ever ratified the Commission of Jurists' rules lest they put themselves at a relative disadvantage.[67] There was little confluence of interests among great powers, the lure of the new technology was strong, and there was no clear way to achieve the humanitarian goal of protecting civilians while also uniformly protecting the interests of states. In 1924 the adviser to the British delegation to the commission expressed the prevailing pessimism:

> It is doubtful whether such rules for air bombardment as those drawn up by the jurists at the Hague in January-February, 1923, will save the world's great cities. The doctrine of the "military objective," useful within its own limits, will be no adequate protection. Any belligerent who chooses will be able to keep within the rules which embody that

[64] Ibid., pp. 195–202.
[65] Watt, "Restraints on War in the Air before 1945," pp. 64–65.
[66] Wyman, "The First Rules of Air Warfare," p. 100.
[67] Ibid.

doctrine and yet use his air arms for a purpose quite distinct from the destruction of objects of military importance, namely, for the creation of a moral, political, or psychological effect within the enemy country. . . . The bombing of civilian objectives will be a primary operation of war carried out in an organized manner and with forces which will make the raids of 1914–1918 appear by comparison spasmodic and feeble. . . . The attacks on towns will be the war.[68]

The Interwar Air Power Theorists

This belief in the dominance of the bomber in future wars was the moving force behind a new type of strategic thought. The vision set forth in the 1917 Smuts Memorandum—of bomber fleets rendering armies and navies obsolete by striking directly at the enemy's homeland—captured the imagination of many proponents of aviation in the interwar years. The classic statement of strategic bombing doctrine from this period was provided by an Italian airman, Giulio Douhet, whose 1921 book *Command of the Air* drew heavily on the experiences of World War I. The central premises of his theory were that decisive offensive operations by ground forces were no longer possible, that there was no effective defense against aerial assaults, and that the scale of modern warfare no longer allowed for distinctions to be made between combatants and noncombatants. "The decision in this kind of war," he explained, "must depend upon smashing the material and moral resources of a people caught up in a frightful cataclysm which haunts them everywhere without cease until the final collapse of all social organization."[69] The logic behind the attack on material resources, especially industry and raw materials, was that it was easier and more efficient to prevent weapons from reaching the battlefield than destroying them once they got there. As Sir Hugh Trenchard, British Chief of Air Staff and the leading figure in the rise of the bombing-oriented RAF between the wars, reasoned:

> By attacking the sources from which armed forces are maintained infinitely more effect is obtained. In the course of a day's attack upon the aerodromes of the enemy perhaps 50 aeroplanes could be destroyed; whereas a modern industrial state will produce 100 in a day—and production will far more than replace any destruction we can hope to do

[68] Quoted in Kennett, *A History of Strategic Bombing*, p. 65; and Williams, "Legitimate Targets in Aerial Bombardment," p. 571.
[69] Douhet, *Command of the Air*, p. 61.

in the forward zone. On the other hand, by attacking the enemy's factories, then output is reduced by a much greater proportion.[70]

The belief in the effect of bombing on civilian morale was grounded on less rigorous analysis. The raids of World War I had seemed to confirm the observation of a late-nineteenth-century study on balloon bombing that "it undoubtedly produces a depressing effect to have things dropped on one from above."[71] This belief was increasingly complemented by the social and political upheavals of the 1920s and 1930s. In Britain, the General Strike of 1926 and the growing class tensions in industrial regions lent plausibility to the argument that modern industrial societies were inherently fragile and were liable to descend into chaos if targeted during wartime.[72]

While both the material and moral effects of bombing were important in all versions of strategic bombing doctrine in the interwar period, different air forces varied considerably in emphasizing one or the other. In Britain, Trenchard built the RAF and its early bombing doctrine around the "20 to 1 rule"—the belief that "the moral effect of bombing stands undoubtedly to the material effect in a proportion of 20 to 1."[73] Bombers would be most effective if they could generate a "state of panic" among civilians, because civilians "are not disciplined and it cannot be expected of them that they will stick stolidly to their lathes and benches under the recurring threat of air bombardment."[74] In the United States, on the other hand, doctrine focused on maximizing the material effects of bombing by identifying and targeting the "vital centers" of an enemy's industrial complex in order to bring its production to a grinding halt. While destroying the equilibrium of the enemy's delicately balanced economy might in turn lead to a breakdown in civilian morale, the emphasis on fewer crucial industrial "bottleneck" targets meant that morale was a secondary objective—not, as in the British case, a primary one.[75]

---

[70] Quoted in W. Hays Parks, "Rolling Thunder and the Law of War," *Air University Review* 33, no. 2 (Jan./Feb. 1982): 8.

[71] Quoted in Sheldon M. Cohen, *Arms and Judgment: Law, Morality, and the Conduct of War in the Twentieth Century* (Boulder: Westview Press, 1989), p. 91.

[72] Malcolm Smith, *British Air Strategy between the Wars* (Oxford: Clarendon Press, 1984), pp. 5, 46–47.

[73] Quoted in Biddle, "Air Power," p. 145.

[74] Quoted in Kennett, *A History of Strategic Bombing*, p. 76.

[75] See Mark Clodfelter, "Pinpointing Devastation: American Air Campaign Planning before Pearl Harbor," *The Journal of Military History* 58 (Jan. 1994): 75–101.

This difference in doctrinal emphasis had implications for ethical issues such as noncombatant immunity. Douhet made no bones about the fact that his theory of strategic bombardment called for the direct targeting of civilians as well as industrial and governmental resources; he even envisioned poison gas attacks on major cities.[76] British doctrine, however, was more ambiguous on the matter. Trenchard insisted that although the destruction of enemy civilian morale was the most significant contribution that strategic bombing could make to victory, this was to be accomplished by the bombing of legitimate military and industrial targets within cities rather than the indiscriminate bombing of urban populations per se.[77] Still, it was not clear how much protection this standard provided for noncombatants. First, Trenchard broadly defined valid military targets as "any objectives which will contribute effectively towards the destruction of the enemy's means of resistance and the lowering of his determination to fight," a formulation that seemed to have morale attacks on civilians specifically in mind.[78] Moreover, in order to maximize the effects on morale, bombing was to be spread among as many targets as possible, in contrast to the American desire to concentrate efforts on fewer crucial targets. The "incidental destruction of civilian life and property" that would inevitably result from such a targeting scheme, Trenchard believed, would only enhance the impact on morale.[79] Of course, this type of reasoning toed a fine and somewhat dubious ethical line, as it amounted to an acknowledgment that the primary goal of RAF bombing operations would be illegal and unethical if it were anything other than an incidental side effect of achieving its secondary goal.

As for U.S. doctrine, while it was based primarily on perceived efficiency, there was an undercurrent of moral concern that occasionally came to the surface. During World War I both Woodrow Wilson and Secretary of War Newton Baker had expressed disapproval of what they saw as the "promiscuous" bombing being carried out by the British, and interwar statements sometimes distinguished U.S. doctrine from the less ethical "morale bombing" orientation of other nations.[80] The military adviser to the American delegation at the 1922–23 Hague Commission

[76] MacIsaac, "Voices from the Central Blue," p. 630.
[77] Kennett, *A History of Strategic Bombing*, p. 76.
[78] Quoted in Parks, "Conventional Aerial Bombing and the Law of War," p. 112.
[79] Kennett, *A History of Strategic Bombing*, p. 76.
[80] McElroy, *Morality and American Foreign Policy*, p. 152; Biddle, "Air Power," pp. 149–50.

of Jurists declared that "among peoples in whom the spirit of sport has been strongly inculcated, it is peculiarly abhorrent to contemplate the waging of war on unarmed civilians of all ages and sexes."[81] On a similar note, a lecture at the U.S. Air Corps Tactical School in the 1930s explained that "direct attack of civilian populations is most repugnant to our humanitarian principles, and certainly it is a method of warfare that we would adopt only with great reluctance and regret."[82]

Proponents of morale bombing were not without their own ethical arguments, however. A predominant theme in the writings of early air theorists was that the advent of air power would make war so intensely destructive that it would either end quickly and with fewer casualties or would be deterred altogether.[83] Douhet argued, therefore, that bombing might paradoxically represent a humanitarian breakthrough: "Mercifully, the decision will be quick in this kind of war, since the decisive blows will be directed at civilians, that element of the countries at war least able to sustain them. These future wars may yet prove to be more humane than wars in the past in spite of all, because they may in the long run shed less blood."[84] While in other contexts it would be tempting to dismiss this line of argument as simple rationalization, in post–World War I Europe it took on a different tenor. So staggering was the death toll from the bloody stalemate in the trenches that possible alternatives, however horrifying, could not be dismissed out of hand. British military writer Basil Liddell-Hart, an early supporter of strategic bombing, wrote in 1925 that another experience like the First World War "must mean the breakdown of Western civilization." He continued:

> Of what use is a decisive victory in battle if we bleed to death as a result of it? . . . [The ethical objection to bombing cities] is based on the seeming brutality of an attack on the civilian population, and the harmful results to the aggressor of any outrage of the human feelings of the neutral peoples. The events of the last war have, however, acclimatized the world to the idea that in a war between nations the damage cannot be restricted merely to paid gladiators. When, moreover, the truth is realized that a swift and sudden blow of this nature inflicts a total of injury far less than when spread over a number of years, the

---

[81] Quoted in Kennett, *A History of Strategic Bombing*, p. 66.

[82] Quoted in Clodfelter, "Pinpointing Devastation," pp. 84–85.

[83] As early as 1864, for example, Victor Hugo predicted that the invention of aircraft would lead to the abolition of national borders, making war obsolete. MacIsaac, "Voices from the Central Blue," p. 626 n. 3.

[84] Douhet, *Commend of the Air*, p. 61.

common sense of mankind will show that the ethical objection to this form of war is at least not greater than to the cannon-fodder wars of the past.[85]

Arthur Harris, who as chief of the RAF's Bomber Command in the Second World War would become a strident defender of morale bombing, put the point more bluntly, saying that bombing cities was preferable to having "morons volunteering to get hung in the wire and shot in the stomach in the mud of Flanders."[86]

This line of moral argument, of course, constituted a rejection of noncombatant immunity and reflected the growing incoherence of the rule in the context of modern war. This owed not only to the increased risk to which civilians had been exposed in the bombing raids of World War I but also to the fact that, even when conducted by the rules, war in its modern form had become too costly a proposition to contemplate. The humanitarian objections to the targeting of civilians, therefore, could be met with a plausible countervailing moral argument in defense of strategic bombing. While far from universally accepted, this argument found a receptive audience among many in Europe who had lived through the last war, and was widely used by the RAF in justifying its fixation on morale bombing. By holding out the possibility of a humane alternative to trench warfare, it provided another impediment to the achievement of a normative consensus on bombing in the international community.

Some of the differences between British and American interwar bombing doctrine, therefore, can be explained by each nation's different wartime experiences and interwar strategic situations. Britain was strongly influenced by the knowledge that air power had destroyed its isolation and left it vulnerable to attack in the next war. Moreover, its own traumatic experience with bombing in World War I lent plausibility to the dramatic claims of morale bombing advocates, convincing many Britons that the outcome of the next war would hinge on their ability to give as good as they got. RAF bombing doctrine, in other words, reflected the perspective of those who viewed Britain as the once and future target of bombing raids and saw little chance that bombing was more likely to be constrained by humanitarian concerns in the next war

[85] Quoted in Barrie Paskins and Michael Dockrill, *The Ethics of War* (Minneapolis: University of Minnesota Press, 1979), pp. 5–7. Liddell-Hart later deemphasized bombing because he believed the tank would allow war to again become fluid and decisive.

[86] Quoted in Smith, *British Air Strategy between the Wars*, p. 64.

than it was in the last. The United States, on the other hand, was geographically far removed from any likely antagonists, and the American public had remained relatively insulated from the direct effects of World War I. These factors allowed a degree of detachment in thinking about strategic bombing, a luxury that doubtless contributed to a greater willingness to consider some of its ethical implications in the abstract.[87] Furthermore, because American losses in the war were far fewer than those suffered by European societies, the countervailing moral argument for the humanity of morale bombing was less compelling. The events of World War II were to demonstrate that there was less than meets the eye to the apparent normative distinctions between British and American bombing doctrines. What differences there were, however, were rooted less in discrepant views of abstract moral principle—or of the importance of moral principle generally—than in different historical and strategic perspectives.

Fits and Starts in the 1930s

While norms and international agreements are not always the same in content, the obstacles to the development of a strong bombing norm in the 1930s can be gleaned from the difficulties encountered in trying to conclude a convention on rules governing strategic bombing. Conditions for reaching a genuine consensus on rules were perhaps never more propitious than at the International Disarmament Conference convened at Geneva in 1932. While important conflicts of interest remained among the states of Europe, there was a growing sense that bombing constituted a threat to all nations, and that some of the earlier barriers to agreement had eased (temporarily, it would prove). France's dominance in air power was in decline, and Germany did not yet pose a substantial threat. In this atmosphere, all states but one expressed willingness to agree to a total ban on aerial bombing. Ironically, the lone holdout was Britain. Still fearful of air attack by continental powers,

---

[87] The geographical isolation of the United States also influenced bombing doctrine in a more indirect way. Because the strongest case to be made for bombers in the early interwar years was as a coastal defense force, American bombing advocates were forced to concentrate on developing the ability to bomb small naval targets accurately. This institutional emphasis on precision bombing created a bomber force that was seen as capable of knocking out specific military and industrial targets, instead of the more indiscriminate bombing to which less accurate bombers would be limited. World War II proved this belief to be overly optimistic. For an overview, see MacIsaac, "Voices from the Central Blue."

Britain pressed for disarmament but would not agree to a ban on bombing unless there was an exception carved out "for police purposes in certain outlying regions."[88] This provision was uniformly condemned by other states, and no agreement was reached. In light of the events of the later 1930s and World War II, British insistence on retaining bombers for controlling its colonies now seems like a case of misplaced priorities. Nevertheless, in the early interwar period Trenchard had sold the government on bombers largely on the strength of their policing role, and throughout the 1920s this role was seen as more important than preparing for a major war.[89] British fear of bombing, strong as it may have been, was in 1932–33 still an abstract fear, unrelated to any particular geopolitical threat.[90] In this context, bombers provided an imperial power like Britain a considerable advantage indeed over the forces of indigenous resistance in its colonial territories.[91] The relative significance of this application of air power changed dramatically in 1933, however, when Hitler came to power, withdrew Germany from the disarmament conference, and began an aggressive program of rearmament. Britain's fear of bombing suddenly took on an air of reality.

The frustrating pattern continued by the failure at Geneva only intensified during the remainder of the 1930s. Again, the fundamental problem was not disagreement on the moral implications of bombing civilians but discord resulting from the conflicting interests and vulnerabilities of strong states in the international system, especially in Europe. Air policy in Britain during this period provides an illustration of some of the difficult issues involved. For the British, the fear of air attack was a major foreign policy concern. Throughout the 1920s and 1930s, the ambitious predictions of the air power theorists in the RAF and the Air Ministry were supplemented by even more apocalyptic visions in sensationalistic newspaper accounts and popular literature of civilization ending in a fiery hail of bombs. Typical of this genre was "An

---

[88] Uri Bialer, *The Shadow of the Bomber: The Fear of Air Attack and British Politics, 1932–1939* (London: Royal Historical Society, 1980), p. 38.

[89] MacIsaac, "Voices from the Central Blue," p. 633; Smith, *British Air Strategy between the Wars*, p. 45.

[90] Uri Bialer writes: "Until the end of 1933, only the French air force could possibly endanger Britain—for the Luftwaffe had yet to come into being—and war with France had long been considered a very remote contingency. The discussions concerning the air peril throughout this period are notable for the absence of any mention of a potential enemy." Bialer, *The Shadow of the Bomber*, p. 40.

[91] Imperial policing was, therefore, one example of the way in which bombers served as tools of power-maintenance in the first half of the twentieth century.

Expert's Prophetic Vision of the Super-Armageddon That May Destroy Civilization," written by a retired air officer:

> A hideous shower of death and destruction falls screeching and screaming through space and atmosphere to the helpless, thickly populated earth below. The shock of the hit is appalling. Great buildings totter and tumble in the dust like a mean and frail set of ninepins. . . . The survivors, now merely demoralized masses of demented humanity, scatter caution to the winds. They are seized by a demoniacal frenzy of terror. They tear off their gas masks, soon absorb the poisonous fumes, and expire in horrible agony, cursing the fate that did not destroy them hurriedly and without warning in the first awful explosions.[92]

As melodramatic as this account seemed to be, there was at the time no way of saying that it would not prove accurate. As Uri Bialer argues, the rapid development of technology and the lack of much relevant inter-war experience meant that the actual effects of bombing in the future could only be speculated upon.[93] In this regard, the sensational prognostications of the air power theorists had an air of authority about them. It was therefore taken more or less on faith that bombing would play a decisive role in future war. In an influential speech in Parliament in 1932, Prime Minister Stanley Baldwin stated the prevailing opinion: "No power on earth can protect the man in the street from getting bombed. Whatever people may tell him, the bomber will always get through."[94] Again, given the vulnerability of London as a target, this was thought to place Britain particularly at risk.[95] This sense of vulnerability made bombing a dominant issue in British politics in the years before World War II and forced the reevaluation of traditional ways of thinking about foreign policy. A member of the Foreign Office wrote in 1933, "In the air the matter is urgent for here alone we cannot be isolated however isolationist we feel."[96] Sir Robert Vansittart, permanent under-secretary of state for foreign affairs, echoed this thought two years later:

[92] Quoted in Richard Overy, *Why the Allies Won* (London: Jonathan Cape, 1995), p. 105.

[93] Uri Bialer, "Elite Opinion and Defence Policy: Air Power Advocacy and British Rearmament during the 1930s," *British Journal of International Studies* 6 (April 1980): 37–38.

[94] Quoted in Bialer, *The Shadow of the Bomber*, p. 14.

[95] Churchill remarked that London resembled "a valuable fat cow tied up to attract the beasts of prey." Quoted in Legro, *Cooperation under Fire*, p. 118.

[96] Quoted in Bialer, *The Shadow of the Bomber*, p. 75.

"Air policy in its broadest aspects cannot now be divorced from foreign policy."[97]

This obsession with bombing gave rise to two powerful yet contradictory impulses in British politics. The first was a strong push for banning strategic bombers entirely, or, failing that, restricting bombing in such a way as to save the cities from destruction. This was throughout the 1930s the position overwhelmingly favored by British public opinion, which largely blamed uncontrolled arms buildups for the First World War and therefore saw disarmament, Bialer notes, as a "panacea."[98] For all the attention given to the interwar naval disarmament conferences, moreover, it was bombers, not battleships, that most concerned the public. As a cabinet secretary noted in 1932: "Compared with bombing aeroplanes the public interest in such matters as heavy guns or whether a battleship should be 35,000 or 25,000 tons is almost negligible."[99] As in the 1920s, many civilians in government, especially in the Foreign Office, generally shared the public's belief that, as Baldwin warned, the future of European civilization depended upon concluding a pact abolishing the bomber.[100] In other circles, however, the fear of bombing gave rise to exactly the opposite conclusion. If Baldwin was right that "the bomber will always get through," some reasoned, then Britain's prospective enemies were just as defenseless against British bombers as Britain would be against theirs. The answer, therefore, was not disarmament or negotiated restrictions, either of which would likely prove impotent in any case, but an aggressive program of rearmament focused on creating a powerful strategic bombing force. Only by deterring would-be foes by the threat of destruction, the reasoning went, could Britain itself be spared. Among the critics of aerial disarmament was J. M. Spaight, who wrote that if efforts were instead focused on building bombers, "the nations may fear to unleash the monsters they have bred. That would be the greatest, the most welcome contribution that air power could make to the next war—that the next war never in fact comes."[101] Not surpris-

---

[97] Ibid., p. 53.

[98] Ibid., p. 9.

[99] Ibid., p. 20. The strength of public opinion on the matter was illustrated by the results of a "Peace Ballot" in 1935, in which a proposition for the banning of military aircraft was favored by a ratio of nearly six to one. Smith, *British Air Strategy between the Wars*, p. 49.

[100] Kennett, *A History of Strategic Bombing*, pp. 68–69.

[101] Quoted in Smith, *British Air Strategy between the Wars*, p. 49.

ingly, the primary advocates of this view were the RAF and the Air Ministry.

These two apparently contradictory responses to the bombing threat were not mutually exclusive in practice. Especially after Hitler's rise to power in Germany, Britain pursued what could be called a two-track plan, setting out to build the most powerful bombing force in Europe even as it relentlessly pursued an agreement restricting the use of bombers. While the RAF and the Air Ministry, both of which adamantly opposed any sort of limitations upon air power until the late 1930s, were usually overruled when it came to international negotiations, they succeeded in getting a lion's share of the resources allocated to defense.[102] Moreover, both elements were part and parcel of the general policy of appeasement taking shape in the 1930s. If the overarching foreign policy goal was avoiding major war in Europe, a strong bomber force could help by serving as a deterrent. So along with calling for the banning of the bomber, Baldwin also vowed not to allow Britain to lag behind other European powers in air strength. "Let us not forget this," Baldwin said, "since the days of the air the old frontiers are gone. When you think of the defence of England, you no longer think of the white cliffs of Dover; you think of the Rhine."[103] Later, Neville Chamberlain himself noted that "if we possessed an overwhelming Air Force then the air menace would be less serious."[104]

There were two significant effects of this two-track policy. First, the emphasis on the bombers as a deterrent force led to relatively little attention being paid to how they would actually be used in a war if deterrence failed.[105] The result was what was sometimes pejoratively called a "shop-window force"—insufficiently trained in navigation and unable to bomb accurately even when unopposed and under the most favorable conditions.[106] Second, while pursuing both rearmament and negotiated restrictions simultaneously was possible in practice, the two tracks were based on fundamentally incompatible assumptions. Implicit in the push to build bombers was the belief that if war came, in the words of one newspaper editorial, "the nation that is the first to equip itself with an overwhelming force of this most flexible and decisive of all weapons will

[102] Ibid., chaps. 3–5.
[103] Quoted in ibid., p. 138.
[104] Quoted in Bialer, *The Shadow of the Bomber*, p. 63.
[105] Smith, *British Air Policy between the Wars*, chap. 4.
[106] Kennett, *A History of Strategic Bombing*, p. 92.

hold world power in the hollow of his hands."[107] To the extent that this belief had a hold on the great powers, any effort to establish a normative consensus that strategic bombing was an inappropriate means of warfare was doomed from the start. And to the extent that it was still a matter open to question, the gusto with which the British built bombers made any such effort that much less credible and more difficult.

France faced a somewhat similar situation as the 1930s progressed. As the dominant air power of the 1920s, it had opposed any efforts to place constraints on aerial warfare. By the 1930s, however, two things were changing. First, France was in the process of frittering away its air superiority through a series of policy and organizational blunders, including the disastrous nationalization of its aircraft industry in 1936.[108] Second, it was faced with a Germany that, shackled by the Versailles Treaty since the end of World War I, was now asserting its right to parity with the other European powers. This was an outcome the French wished to avoid at any cost, especially after Hitler assumed power in 1933. As in Britain, the fear of bombing raids on major cities, especially Paris, provided the backdrop for concerns about German rearmament.[109] The French faced a dilemma, however: Germany would only consider an agreement restricting strategic bombing if it was also agreed that Germany had the right to military parity with other European powers. This the French steadfastly refused to consider until it was a fait accompli, and even then they insisted that a ban on bombing be linked to arms reductions—a demand they were in no position to make.[110]

Germany, for its part, was amenable to significant restrictions on bombing. But even in the Weimar years it would not sacrifice its claims to parity in order to conclude an agreement on the matter. Once in power, Hitler refused to consider arms limitations, although he did express opposition to the bombing of noncombatants, even proposing a ban on strategic bombing in 1935.[111] This apparently humanitarian gesture was, of course, nothing of the sort. Unlike British and French leaders, Hitler and most other members of the Nazi hierarchy were skeptical

---

[107] Quoted in Bialer, "Elite Opinion and Defence Policy," p. 37.

[108] George H. Quester, "Strategic Bombing in the 1930s and 1940s," in *The Use of Force: International Politics and Foreign Policy*, 2d ed., ed. Robert Art and Kenneth Waltz (Lanham, Maryland: University Press of America, 1983), pp. 240–41.

[109] During the 1938 Munich crisis, for example, fear of bombing raids led to the evacuation of about one-third of the population of Paris. Ibid., p. 242.

[110] Bialer, *The Shadow of the Bomber*, chaps. 2–3.

[111] Quester, "Strategic Bombing in the 1930s and 1940s," pp. 242–44.

of the efficacy of strategic bombing and were instead building the Luftwaffe around a ground support role. Hitler's proposal, which would have limited aerial bombing to the zone of operations of ground forces, greatly favored a nation on the strategic offensive, since all the areas that could be legitimately bombed would be located in the defenders' territory.[112] Furthermore, Hitler saw the possibility of using the lure of a bombing pact as a means of driving a wedge between the British and the French.[113] Remarkably, Britain was so eager to conclude a bombing ban that it not only seriously entertained the German proposal in 1935, but at other times it considered using as inducements accession to German remilitarization of the Rhineland and a pledge to forgo the use of naval blockades in the event of war.[114] Ultimately, Britain was constrained not to conclude an agreement with Germany without the participation of the French because it would threaten the united front of the "Little Entente" with France and its allies.[115]

In any event, however, British interest in restricting bombing grew even more urgent in the late 1930s, as it became evident not only that war was likely but also that the RAF's bombing capabilities, despite the vaunted rearmament program, were woefully inadequate.[116] In 1937 the Air Staff was forced to concede that "any attempt to demoralise the German people before German air attacks could demoralise our own people would operate under severe handicap. . . . It is certain that mutual air attack, even at equal intensity, upon each other's vulnerable points would only lead to a far quicker reduction of the war effort in England than in Germany."[117] At this point even the Air Ministry desperately hoped for an agreement on bombing to buy time to catch up to what were thought (erroneously, as it turned out) to be vastly superior German bombing forces. Given the turbulent state of affairs in Europe, however, the best that could be done was a unilateral pronouncement by Chamberlain in June 1938 that if war came, the RAF would adhere to three principles: that the bombing of civilians per se was unlawful; that

[112] Ibid., p. 244.

[113] Bialer, *The Shadow of the Bomber*, p. 97.

[114] Watt, "Restraints on War in the Air before 1945," pp. 71, 73.

[115] Bialer, *The Shadow of the Bomber*, p. 87.

[116] The problems related not only to the number of bombers available but also to their likely ineffectiveness in carrying out their missions. In August 1939 the head of Bomber Command, Edgar Ludlow-Hewitt, revealed that in exercises more than 40 percent of RAF bombers could not locate a target in a friendly city in broad daylight, much less place their bombs on target. Biddle, "Air Power," p. 149.

[117] Quoted in Quester, "Strategic Bombing in the 1930s and 1940s," p. 239.

only targets capable of positive identification as military objectives could be bombed; and that reasonable care must be taken to avoid hitting the surrounding civilian population.[118] Although the moribund League of Nations adopted Chamberlain's principles by resolution in September 1938, the European powers descended into war without having concluded any binding agreement in the interwar period governing the conduct of aerial bombing.[119]

The Status of the Bombing Norm at the Beginning of World War II

From the standpoint of the norm against the bombing of civilians, the absence of an agreement on bombing principles was less important than the reasons why states failed to conclude one. It was not simply a matter of some states wanting to restrict bombing and other states resisting. All the major powers were interested in restrictions of some sort, but each wished the restrictions to be crafted in a way favorable to its particular interests. There was, notably, a core of consensus that the bombing of civilians was wrong, but geopolitical and technological circumstances made it impossible to operationalize this principle in a way that was neutral to the interests of a substantial majority of the great powers. To be sure, the mere fact that efforts had been made to ban bombing probably reinforced the understanding that the targeting of noncombatants was morally problematic, and may have contributed to the restraint shown in the early stages of World War II. But because norms are not simply reflections of moral principles but also rules based on expectations of actual behavior, conflicting state interests served to undermine the moral imperative to keep noncombatants safe. Consensus on a moral principle is a necessary but not a sufficient condition for the creation of a strong ethical norm. For this reason, even had an agreement been reached, it would probably have only marginally strengthened the bombing norm, which was weak not because its moral basis was uncertain but because the path from moral principle to concrete rule was strewn with insuperable obstacles.

Moreover, it is incorrect to state, as some have, that on the eve of the Second World War there was no international law whatsoever governing aerial bombing.[120] The problem, wrote J. M. Spaight in 1938, was not the

---

[118] Legro, *Cooperation under Fire*, p. 122.

[119] Parks, "Conventional Aerial Bombing and the Law of War," p. 108.

[120] See, e.g., Hamilton De Saussure, "The Laws of Air Warfare: Are There Any?" *Naval War College Review* 23 (Feb. 1971): 35–47; and Parks, "Conventional Aerial Bombing and the Law of War."

absence of law but "a multiplicity of laws," as the laws of land warfare applied in some cases, the standards for naval bombardment in others, and the 1923 Hague rules perhaps in some but perhaps not in others. The result, according to Spaight, was "a state of baffling chaos and confusion which makes it almost impossible to say what in any given situation the rule really is."[121] Despite this legal muddle, however, there did appear to be a clear consensus on one point: it was unlawful to make noncombatants the direct targets of aerial bombing.[122] Terror bombing of the civilian population in order to shatter morale was therefore impermissible. Again, this rule reflected the strength of the fundamental moral principle that civilians should be spared. Spaight commented with regard to allegations that Japan was guilty of indiscriminate bombing in Manchuria: "If Japan did deliberately bomb the civilian quarters of crowded Chinese cities, then she was guilty of barbarity, law or no law, and no one wishes to condone that."[123]

Clearly, as such comments suggest, there was a norm in existence that conformed to this moral principle. When it came to the application of the norm, however, the situation was far more ambiguous. First, what constituted the "deliberate" bombing of noncombatants was anything but clear, and specific application of the rule was unsettled and highly speculative. Moreover, few national air forces placed much emphasis, in either training or doctrine, on adherence to the laws of war. Arthur Harris, head of Bomber Command for much of World War II, himself believed that "in the matter of the use of aircraft in war, there is, it so happens, no international law at all."[124] Jeffrey Legro argues that, in any event, the principle of noncombatant immunity "had a relatively modest impact on expectations, preparations, and decisions in war."[125] Early in World War II, for example, when its instructions called for restraint in bombing, the RAF was forced to set aside twelve of its thirteen prewar plans because only the plan for attacks on the German navy did not

[121] J. M. Spaight, "The Chaotic State of the International Law Governing Aerial Bombardment," *Royal Air Force Quarterly* 9 (January 1938): 25.

[122] Manfred Messerschmidt, "Strategic Air War and International Law," in *The Conduct of the Air War in the Second World War*, ed. Horst Boog (New York: St. Martin's Press, 1992), p. 301; Legro, *Cooperation under Fire*, p. 99.

[123] Spaight, "The Chaotic State of International Law," p. 25.

[124] Quoted in DeSaussure, "The Laws of Air Warfare," p. 36. The 1944 British *Manual of Air Force* provided no rules for war in the air, noting in a footnote that it was impossible to include a chapter on international law on the subject in the absence of an international agreement. De Saussure, "The Laws of Air Warfare," p. 37.

[125] Legro, *Cooperation under Fire*, p. 122.

entail a significant risk of substantial civilian casualties.[126] For the RAF, the avoidance of bombing civilians was not only a low priority but in fact ran counter to doctrine, which, as we have seen, emphasized the effects on bombing on morale. This orientation predisposed the British toward area bombing: "For the British, area bombing fitted naturally with a doctrine that emphasised the impact of air power on civilian morale and the home front. . . . Throughout the 1920s and 1930s the RAF considered the enemy working class the weakest link within an opposing state, one that would remain vulnerable to the impact of a campaign that aimed not just to 'dehouse' but to kill."[127]

While the significance of noncombatant immunity in bombing was particularly low in the prewar RAF, the situation was not much different in other states. While the Luftwaffe was oriented more toward close infantry support than strategic bombing, the merits of terror bombing had been debated within the organization throughout the 1930s, with very few references to moral considerations.[128] Moreover, the German Condor Legion had carried out notoriously brutal bombing raids in the Spanish Civil War. As one historian comments, while terror bombing was not a prominent aspect of Luftwaffe doctrine, "there is no reason to believe that the decision stems from a willingness to uphold international law."[129] Even in the U.S. Army Air Corps, whose bombing doctrine emphasized precision strikes against limited numbers of crucial military and industrial targets, the avoidance of civilians was most often explained in terms of efficiency, not morality: other targets simply presented a better use of resources. It was also believed that indiscriminate bombing was liable to backfire, stiffening the resolve of the civilian population and prolonging war. In the war plans devised before U.S. entry into the war, however, a role was seen for morale bombing after the civilian population had already been weakened by the destruction of its industrial network.[130] Moreover, as Tami Davis Biddle relates, in teaching materials at the Air Corps Tactical School (ACTS), "the possibility of attacking capitals and centers of population was left open; students were informed that such targeting would be governed by political considera-

---

[126] Ibid., p. 123.

[127] Williamson Murray, "The Influence of Pre-War Anglo-American Doctrine on the Air Campaigns of the Second World War," in *The Conduct of the Air War in the Second World War*, p. 244.

[128] Messerschmidt, "Strategic Air War and International Law," pp. 301–3.

[129] Ibid., p. 303.

[130] Clodfelter, "Pinpointing Devastation," p. 91.

tions during the course of a future war."[131] Indeed, the ACTS curriculum in the 1930s reflected a general lack of concern with legal issues: students were given only one lecture on the international law of aerial warfare, but they were required to take one hundred hours of horsemanship.[132]

In sum, the norm against bombing civilians, while present, was weak and not internalized by the organizations responsible for the planning and prosecution of the air war. Notwithstanding the technical requirements of international law, there was no strong understanding or expectation about what constituted proper or improper conduct of aerial warfare. There was clearly some moral aversion to the idea of raining bombs down on civilians, but many states were prepared, both materially and doctrinally, to do so. By 1939, a norm existed, but it was fragile. In terms of the discussion in Chapter 2, the pre–World War II bombing norm was a convention-dependent ethical norm: based on moral principle, but having an ambiguous relationship, at best, to the interests of strong states in international society.[133] The expectation for such a norm, it will be recalled, is that patterns of adherence and violation are heavily dependent upon reciprocity. So while the norm may cause actors to behave with restraint as long as others do the same, violations of the norm are also likely to be reciprocated. For this reason, convention-dependent normative regimes can be as tenuous as a house of cards, collapsing quickly after the first violations occur.

THE BOMBING NORM IN WORLD WAR II

The conduct of aerial bombing in World War II, in fact, closely fits the pattern one would expect in dealing with a convention-dependent norm. Bombing early in the war was remarkably restrained, but belligerents on both sides clearly assumed that any departure from this pattern would bring about reciprocal attacks and that thereafter restraint would be irretrievably lost. A study conducted by the German General Staff in the first months of the war therefore "warned that a bombing offensive against the British Isles would open up Western Germany to air attacks

---

[131] Biddle, "Air Power," pp. 250–51.

[132] Ibid., pp. 150, 257 n. 34.

[133] Jeffrey Legro also argues that bombing norms were weak at the beginning of the war. Legro classifies the strength of norms according to three criteria: "concordance," "specificity," and "duration." On each measure, he contends, bombing norms either scored "very low" or could not be measured. Legro, *Cooperation under Fire*, pp. 99–100.

that would seriously hinder army preparations for the Western offensive."[134] This warning rested on several noteworthy assumptions: that a bombing offensive represented a qualitatively distinct mode of warfare that would be recognized as such by the enemy; that if Germany didn't launch such an offensive, the enemy probably wouldn't, or at least was less likely to; and that if it *did* launch such an offensive, the enemy almost certainly would as well. Similar assumptions were implicit in British communications on bombing in the same period. Churchill worried in May of 1940, for example, that "it would be very dangerous and undesirable to take the initiative in opening unrestricted air warfare at a time when we possessed only a quarter of the striking power of the German Air Force . . . [as it] might result in the wholesale indiscriminate bombing of this country."[135] The logic of reciprocity, therefore, is central to understanding the pattern of bombing in the first year or two of the war, as both sides were careful not to undertake any bombing raids that might be seen as indiscriminate.

This restraint was due partly to the fact that none of the three major belligerents in the first months of the war saw itself as likely to benefit from a no-holds-barred bombing exchange. Britain and France remained terrified of the effects of bombing on their capital cities, and perceived their own bombing forces as terribly inferior to those of the Luftwaffe.[136] Moreover, the frequency with which Hitler and Luftwaffe chief Hermann Goering used the threat of bombing as a diplomatic bullying tactic in the years prior to the war led the Allies to believe that, once the Germans started bombing, they would go all out in targeting Allied cities.[137] Germany, however, had its own reasons for not throwing down the bombing gauntlet. First, in the early months of the war, Hitler clung to the hope of reaching an accommodation with Britain, and feared that the passions aroused by city bombing would make this impossible.[138] Second, Hitler had pledged "perfect safety" for the Ger-

[134] Williamson Murray, "British and German Air Doctrine between the Wars," *Air University Review* 31 (March/April 1980): 51.

[135] Quoted in Legro, *Cooperation under Fire*, p. 128.

[136] Britain, especially, had grossly overestimated both the size of the Luftwaffe and the extent to which it was oriented toward strategic bombing. This error in net assessment, combined with the long-standing fear of bombing, was an important factor in the decision to appease Hitler over the Sudetenland in 1938. Smith, *British Air Strategy between the Wars*, p. 224.

[137] Quester, "Strategic Bombing in the 1930s and 1940s," p. 253.

[138] Ibid., p. 105.

man civilian population and may have wished to avoid any action that would cause the war to be carried directly to the people, who might then become disenchanted with his regime.[139] Third, as the General Staff study quoted above shows, it was feared that an Allied bombing offensive, even if not decisive, might interfere with offensive operations of the Wehrmacht, which were the focus of German efforts. Finally, as noted earlier, the German leadership simply did not place much stock in strategic bombing as a decisive weapon, and as a result, Allied perceptions notwithstanding, the Luftwaffe was not a strong strategic bombing force.[140]

There was, however, another significant incentive for restraint, one that applied with almost equal force to both sides. As Jeffrey Legro explains, "Despite the absence of a well-developed air-warfare regime, there was a stigma attached to bombing noncombatants."[141] While the bombing norm was weak, it still garnered a fair amount of respect and support by virtue of its connection to a valued moral principle. As a result, the norm served as a constraining influence in its own right, since any party breaking it might suffer not only reciprocation at the hands of the enemy but also sanctions by third parties. In a conflict of the magnitude of the Second World War, one might think that this consideration would mean very little. On the contrary, it is clear that on the bombing issue both sides felt constrained by the desire to stake out the moral high ground. The most significant audience for this restraint was public opinion in neutral countries, especially the United States. Britain desperately hoped for U.S. entry into the war on the Allied side as well as continuing material aid, but these depended to a large extent on American public opinion remaining favorably disposed toward Britain. If Britain was seen as taking the war to civilian populations, this goodwill might be jeopardized. This point was recognized by an interservice committee convened late in the summer of 1939 to draw up instructions for the conduct of air operations in the coming war. Citing the need to avoid offending public opinion in neutral states, the committee issued restrictive instructions for bombing, including the omission of targets in populated areas.[142]

---

[139] Quester, "Strategic Bombing in the 1930s and 1940s," pp. 243–44, 250.

[140] David MacIsaac argues that "German capability to conduct long-range air operations of the sort that had any hope of producing decisions independently of surface forces was nil throughout the war." "Voices from the Central Blue," p. 637.

[141] Legro, *Cooperation under Fire*, p. 141.

[142] Ibid., pp. 123–24.

Even after the restraint of the first year of the war started to give way to more indiscriminate city bombing, some vestiges of the concern for public opinion remained. Sir Alexander Cadogan, permanent under-secretary of the British Foreign Office, wrote in his journal in December 1940, "We're not bombing tonight or tomorrow. Wonder whether the Germans will fall into the trap! . . . If they bomb and we don't, we can score on it."[143] Moreover, the possibility of America staying out of the war gave Germany a corresponding interest in not further antagonizing public opinion by indiscriminate bombing.

Nevertheless, as W. Hays Parks writes, "Neither Germany nor Great Britain harbored any illusions that restrictions would survive anything more than the early stages of the . . . war."[144] There were advantages to be gained by strategic bombing, and it was hardly doubted that it would play an important role in the war. The bombing norm, however, created a disincentive to be seen as the side that bombed first. It was understood and more or less accepted that a belligerent whose cities were bombed would be entitled to respond in kind, but the costs of violating the norm would weigh heavily on the nation that let the genie out of the bottle. Both sides, therefore, took precautions to protect against this perception. The shelving of twelve out of the thirteen original RAF war plans has already been mentioned. And although the RAF was authorized to operate against the German navy, attacks on ships in drydock were prohibited because of the likely proximity of civilians.[145] From the beginning of the war until the German offensive against France in May of 1940, the use of bombers on both sides was more or less limited to reconnaissance missions, although during the winter the British and French also used them to shower German cities with propaganda leaflets.[146] Allied bombers flying over German airspace were forbidden to carry bombs.[147] These precautions, as Malcolm Smith relates,

---

[143] Quoted in ibid., p. 124. Legro notes that this shows how norms can be used strategically to advance state interests: "In this instance, the norms of restraint shaped the calculations of states on how power might be accrued. By adhering to restrictions on air warfare, Britain hoped to attract, or at least not lose, the support of other countries. Had the norms been different or absent, Britain's actions might have been different."

[144] Parks, "Conventional Aerial Bombing and the Law of War," p. 106.

[145] Cohen, *Arms and Judgment*, p. 94.

[146] Ibid.; Quester, "Strategic Bombing in the 1930s and 1940s," p. 245. Arthur Harris, the RAF's champion of morale bombing, later complained that the leaflet campaign served only "to supply the Continent's requirements for toilet paper for the five long years of the war." Quoted in Cohen, p. 94.

[147] Cohen, *Arms and Judgment*, p. 94.

did not mean that Britain would not be prepared to retaliate in kind if
any such attack should be unleashed by the enemy, but for the sake of
the propaganda initiative in the case of major neutrals like the USA, as
well as in a real attempt to give a city like London some measure of
paper protection, it was essential that Britain should not strike
first. . . . It was expected that at the beginning of a war there would be
an initial "gloves-on" stage, which would end when the Germans committed some "mad dog" act that would justify full-scale retaliation.[148]

The Germans, in their own right, exercised similar restraint, and
Hitler himself insisted on retaining personal control over when and for
what purpose bombing restrictions would be lifted.[149] While the Luftwaffe inflicted considerable damage in raids on Warsaw in September
1939 and Rotterdam the following spring, these were in support of German ground offensives and were not generally seen as violations of the
bombing norm.[150] The Nazi offensive against France in May 1940 placed
greater pressure on both sides to abandon restrictions, but although
bombing operations were expanded, they remained limited to military
targets. The Germans struck only a few RAF bases in southeast England,
and refrained from bombing Paris altogether. The British, facing an
increasingly dire strategic situation, escalated somewhat, launching
night raids on some military targets in the heavily industrial Ruhr region
of northwest Germany. Still, they were careful to avoid larger cities,
especially Berlin, and RAF pilots were ordered not to drop their bombs
unless they could find the specific target they were looking for.[151] Even
during the first several months of the Battle of Britain in the summer of
1940, the Germans maintained a "no-cities" policy, while the British,
close to being pressed to the wall, still kept Berlin off the target list.[152]

---

[148] Smith, *British Air Strategy between the Wars*, p. 283.

[149] Legro, *Cooperation under Fire*, p. 102.

[150] Although the moral logic can be questioned, such use of "tactical" air power has generally been viewed as more legitimate and less ethically problematic than independent
"strategic" raids. Possible rationales are that civilians in a battle zone are already exposed
to the dangers of combat, and that bombing in such circumstances is more clearly seen as
aimed at military objectives, even if civilians are harmed as a result. In any case, it is important to note that the British considered air operations in neither Warsaw nor Rotterdam
sufficient justification to claim that the Germans had opened the door to unrestrained
bombing. Messerschmidt, "Strategic Air War and International Law," p. 303.

[151] Quester, "Strategic Bombing in the 1930s and 1940s," p. 247; Biddle, "Air Power,"
p. 151.

[152] Quester, "Strategic Bombing in the 1930s and 1940s," p. 247; Legro, *Cooperation
under Fire*, p. 137.

The pivotal events in the breakdown of the norm were the Luftwaffe raid on London on the night of August 24, 1940, and the British response. Up to that point, although Germany had bombed shipping resources and aircraft factories throughout England, care had been taken to avoid hitting London. Growing losses during daytime raids, however, prompted the Luftwaffe to begin flying missions at night, when increased difficulty in navigation greatly reduced bombing accuracy. On one of the first nighttime raids, about a dozen bombers strayed from their intended course and dropped their bombs within the London city limits.[153] The British responded immediately, attacking Berlin with ninety-five bombers the next night, and with similar numbers five times in the following fortnight. Hitler followed with retaliatory raids of his own, shifting the focus of Luftwaffe bombing raids from RAF fighter bases to a large-scale offensive against London that began on September 7.[154] While missions on both sides were still publicly characterized as precision raids against industrial targets, the period of restraint produced by the bombing norm was over. As Sheldon Cohen puts it, "The gloves were off. These attacks ushered in a momentous change in the strategic air war, which from then on would be directed to a large extent at cities."[155]

The events of August 1940 fit the pattern that would be expected in the breakdown of a convention-dependent norm. That restraints on bombing lasted as long as they did is evidence of the considerable influence that even a relatively weak norm can exercise on state behavior. Because periods of restraint based on convention-dependent norms are fragile, however, they are likely to endure only as long as certain conditions prevail. First, restraint in such cases rests on an equilibrium of interests and capabilities that is easily disrupted. In the case of bombing in 1939–40, restraint obtained because given the totality of the circumstances— including bombing capabilities, vulnerability to bombing, and the particular exigencies of their strategic situations—none of the belligerents felt that initiating unrestricted bombing would clearly be preferable to waiting for the other side to do so. If any of these conditions changed, one country might be willing to act first, especially if a pretext could be found that allowed it to blame the lapse on its oppo-

---

[153] Hitler was reportedly so infuriated by this error that he ordered the responsible bomber crews reassigned to the infantry. Legro, *Cooperation under Fire*, p. 102.

[154] Quester, "Strategic Bombing in the 1930s and 1940s," p. 247.

[155] Cohen, *Arms and Judgment*, p. 99.

nent. This raises a second condition for continued restraint: a belligerent's desire to adhere to the norm must be clearly perceived. If, on the other hand, actions intended to be non-threatening are seen as norm violations, the effects may be the same as if the norm had been violated deliberately. Given the difficulty of discerning states' motivations, combined with the confusion and ill will present in wartime, the danger of such misperception is great. This is especially true in cases involving relatively untested means of warfare, such as bombing in World War II. In 1929, an American commentator provided this account of the likely difficulties inherent in maintaining limits on bombing exchanges:

> A pilot may not always be aware of the immediate proximity of a large civilian population; he may overestimate the accuracy of his aim or he may not intend to be accurate, and who shall judge of his intent? In view of the fact that intention is generally better than the results, as evidenced by mutual recriminations in the recent war, you cannot in any given case judge with certainty of the intent by the results. The tendency will be for each belligerent to become as convinced of the baseness of his enemies' intentions as of the purity of his own, and the bombed, being in the best position to judge of the damage done to innocent lives and property, may conceivably be goaded to indiscriminate bombardment by way of retaliation.[156]

This, of course, is an apt description of the sort of misperception that may have prompted the British retaliation for the August 24 raid.

Finally, as would be expected when dealing with a convention-dependent norm, the first seemingly indiscriminate attacks on capital cities began a spiral that quickly led to the loss of almost all restraint in the conduct of bombing. German raids on London and other major cities continued throughout the fall and winter, eventually ending in the spring as Hitler concentrated his forces for the offensive against the Soviet Union. During this period, which came to be known as "the Blitz," about forty thousand Britons were killed in bombing raids.[157] While the first British attacks on German cities were described as reprisals for raids on London, within weeks the RAF's doctrinal inclination toward morale bombing came to the fore. Charles Portal, then-chief of Bomber Command, urged Churchill in September 1940 that the primary focus of British bombing should be breaking the will of the German people.[158]

[156] Williams, "Legitimate Targets in Aerial Bombardment," p. 578.
[157] Kennett, *A History of Strategic Bombing*, pp. 119–22.
[158] Messerschmidt, "Strategic Air War and International Law," p. 304.

The following month, motivated by both the desire to crush German morale and increasingly apparent limitations on bomber accuracy, the RAF determined that targets should be chosen by virtue of the possible "supplementary effects" of bombs that missed their target.[159] While it avoided saying so, this policy was for all intents and purposes tantamount to targeting heavily populated areas that happened to contain legitimate military or industrial objectives. On December 16, 1940, RAF bombers struck Mannheim in a raid designed as a test of techniques intended to inflict maximum destruction on a German city.[160] In February 1942 an RAF directive formally endorsed "the morale of the enemy civilian population" as the primary objective of the bombing campaign, specifying that bombers should aim for the "built-up areas" of German cities in an attempt to "render the German industrial population homeless, spiritless, and, in so far as possible, dead."[161] In fact, this only formalized a practice that was already commonplace; George Quester writes that "meaningful limits on the air war were at an end" as early as the winter of 1940–41.[162] Still, the directive was remarkable for all but abandoning the fiction that bombing raids were directed at military or industrial targets. What followed in the European theater was a steady progression of bombing restrained only by the availability of aircraft and the limits of existing technology, culminating in some of the most destructive attacks in military history in Hamburg, Dresden, and Berlin.

The Paradox of American Bombing in World War II

To a great extent, the ferocious city-busting campaigns waged by British Bomber Command reflected the interwar emphasis on morale bombing in RAF doctrine. The pattern of bombing carried out by the United States Army Air Forces (USAAF), however, presents a different problem. The USAAF entered World War II with a doctrine emphasizing precision attacks on industrial targets, yet American bombing is most commonly remembered for the cataclysmic atomic bomb attacks on Hiroshima and Nagasaki in August 1945. How, one might ask, is this

[159] Quester, "Strategic Bombing in the 1930s and 1940s," p. 248.

[160] Ibid.

[161] Quoted in Tami Davis Biddle, "British and American Approaches to Strategic Bombing: Their Origins and Implementation in the World War II Combined Bomber Offensive," in *Airpower: Theory and Practice*, ed. John Gooch (London: Frank Cass, 1995), p. 117. This goal was also described more antiseptically as trying to "de-house" German workers. Biddle, "Air Power," p. 152.

[162] Quester, "Strategic Bombing in the 1930s and 1940s," p. 248.

paradox explained? From the time of the U.S. entry into the war there were often significant differences of opinion between USAAF officials and their British counterparts about the relative merits of precision and morale bombing, and these differences were sometimes expressed in moral terms.[163] In the summer of 1944, for example, USAAF leaders vetoed Operation Thunderclap, the RAF plan for the bombing of Berlin, on the grounds that it was "contrary to our national ideals to wage war against civilians."[164] Moreover, it was relatively common for USAAF leaders to speak publicly about the moral dimensions of strategic bombing, something that was not true of their RAF allies. It is possible, however, to make too much of these pronouncements. The fact remains that by the last year of the war there were very few differences between the RAF and USAAF in terms of respect for the bombing norm. As Ronald Schaffer argues, "Virtually every major figure concerned with American bombing expressed some views about the moral issue . . . [but] moral constraints almost invariably bowed to what people described as military necessity."[165]

In both the European and Pacific theaters the USAAF initially sought to implement precision bombing doctrine, with varying success. Although its long-standing emphasis on precision, and technology such as the Norden bombsight, made it possible for the USAAF to bomb more accurately than the RAF, accuracy still required flying daylight missions in good weather, which made American bombers vulnerable to fighter interceptors and antiaircraft artillery. While the British responded to these threats by switching primarily to night bombing, the Americans stayed for some time with daylight missions by heavily armed "self-escorting bombers" flying in close formations—an unsuccessful tactic that led to heavy losses.[166] Moreover, even under optimal conditions, U.S. bombing was too inaccurate to be described as "precise."[167] Over

---

[163] See, e.g., McElroy, *Morality and American Foreign Policy*, chap. 6; and Conrad Crane, "Evolution of U.S. Strategic Bombing of Urban Areas," *The Historian* 50 (November 1987): 14–39.

[164] Quoted in McElroy, *Morality and American Foreign Policy*, p. 159.

[165] Quoted in Crane, "Evolution of U.S. Strategic Bombing of Urban Areas," p. 15.

[166] Paskins and Dockrill, *The Ethics of War*, pp. 30–31.

[167] According to the United States Strategic Bombing Survey (USSBS), from January to September of 1943 only 20 percent of U.S. bombers on daylight missions dropped their bombs within a fifth of a mile of the intended target. Cohen, *Arms and Judgment*, p. 103.

time, American officials became less insistent on precision and more receptive to the idea of damaging enemy morale, so that by late 1944 and 1945 there was little practical difference between British and U.S. bombing. To be sure, the USAAF never officially embraced morale as a primary bombing objective, and many American officials remained publicly disdainful of such a suggestion.[168] Nevertheless, late in the war the USAAF was willing to bomb just as destructively as the RAF, as long as it could be claimed that missions were directed at legitimate targets. It was therefore possible for the USAAF to sign off on the plan that would lead to the bombing of Dresden (in which the United States participated) by, as Robert McElroy writes, "producing plans that combined terror bombing with elements of 'legitimate' military targeting so that it was difficult to identify where selective targeting left off and terror bombing began. . . . Thus the benefits of morale bombing could be obtained without the reputational risks or moral dilemmas that Thunderclap had entailed."[169] The insistent reliance on such fictions as a means of differentiating U.S. from British bombing led one British historian of the air war to condemn the American approach as "moral hair-splitting."[170]

In the Pacific, compunctions about the bombing of civilians were even less relevant to the U.S. air campaign. Once bases became available from which to launch raids against Japan, precision bombing was attempted at first. But it was hindered by several operational difficulties, including high jet-stream winds, bad weather, and the prevalence in Japan of home-based "cottage industries," which presented fewer large industrial targets.[171] The decision was therefore made to switch to incendiary "fire-bombing" raids on Japanese cities, starting with Tokyo in early March 1945. The results, as one account puts it, were "spectacular."[172] The Tokyo raid created a fireball that left eighty thousand dead and leveled 63 percent of the commercial center of the city.[173] It was followed by raids on other Japanese cities, sixty-six of which were incinerated by the time of the atomic bombings five months later.[174] To an extent, the severity of these firebombing raids was made possible by virulent Ameri-

---

[168] McElroy, *Morality and American Foreign Policy*, chap. 6.

[169] Ibid., pp. 160–61.

[170] Hastings, *Bomber Command*, p. 124.

[171] Crane, "Evolution of U.S. Strategic Bombing of Urban Areas," pp. 34–36.

[172] Ibid., p. 35.

[173] Cohen, *Arms and Judgment*, pp. 109–10.

[174] Biddle, "Air Power," p. 154.

can public opinion toward Japan, which reflected anger over the attack on Pearl Harbor and Japanese atrocities as well as, many historians argue, a strong element of racism.[175] On the other hand, the normative difference between the European and Pacific bombing campaigns was relatively small. Conrad Crane argues that the Japanese fire raids simply "marked another stage in the evolution of total war and represented the culmination of trends started in the air war against Germany. Although target selection late in the European campaign showed less effort taken to avoid civilian casualties, [General Curtis] Lemay's planning [in the Pacific] ignored such considerations altogether."[176] In light of this "evolution," by August 1945 the decision to drop atomic bombs on Hiroshima and Nagasaki was less epochal than it now seems in retrospect. Most officials did not see the atomic bombs as presenting any ethical dilemma that had not been resolved long before.[177]

Although the bombing of civilians undeniably raised troubling moral questions, after the collapse of the bombing norm early in the war these questions seldom intruded meaningfully into policy debates. While public opinion in the 1930s was strongly opposed to bombing, this changed dramatically with the coming of war. Polls taken during the war showed that an overwhelming majority of Americans favored the strategic bombing campaigns against Germany and Japan.[178] Many U.S. officials did express unease with the extent of civilian casualties caused by the air war. While in isolated cases this may have made a difference, it was not enough to serve as a brake on unrestrained bombing in the absence of a system-wide norm reinforcing these individual beliefs. Moreover, if American public opinion is any indication, it is likely that many people's moral stance more or less mirrored the status of the norm itself: a clear but ultimately shallow distaste for bombing in the abstract, eventually giving way to acceptance or even enthusiasm when faced with the pressures of war. This seems to describe, for example, the attitude of President Franklin Roosevelt. Richard Overy writes:

[175] Crane, "Evolution of U.S. Strategic Bombing of Urban Areas," p. 34; George E. Hopkins, "Bombing and the American Conscience During World War II," *The Historian* 28, no. 3 (1966): 463–71; and Michael S. Sherry, *The Rise of American Air Power: The Creation of Armageddon* (New Haven: Yale University Press, 1987), passim.

[176] Crane, "Evolution of U.S. Strategic Bombing of Urban Areas," p. 36.

[177] See, e.g., Barton J. Bernstein, "The Atomic Bombings Reconsidered," *Foreign Affairs* 74, no. 1 (Jan./Feb. 1995): 135–52.

[178] Hopkins, "Bombing and the American Conscience during World War II."

It is still not entirely clear why Roosevelt, a man of peace and good-neighborliness, who had long campaigned to get aerial bombing outlawed by international agreement, should have become so enthusiastically committed not just to air power but to its unlimited use against civilians. But there seems little doubt that this is what happened. His confidant Harry Hopkins reported in August 1941 that the President was "a believer in bombing as the only means of gaining a victory." Roosevelt told his Treasury Secretary, Henry Morgenthau, that "the only way to break the German morale" was to bomb every small town, to bring war home to the ordinary German.[179]

While Roosevelt's change of heart may have been especially striking, the scale and relentlessness of the bombing campaigns undoubtedly had a numbing effect on moral sensibilities.

The pattern of bombing by U.S. forces in World War II, like the bombing by other states, is consistent with what would be expected from a norms analysis, and illustrates the critical role played by international norms in restraining state behavior. By the time the United States entered the war, the bombing norm had already been abandoned by the other belligerents, removing any *external normative incentive* for scrupulously avoiding civilian casualties. Had the norm remained intact longer, U.S. precision doctrine or the moral qualms of USAAF officials might have had a greater influence on U.S. bombing operations. Neither, however, was strong enough to induce restraint by itself, especially if it meant placing the United States at a strategic disadvantage relative to states not similarly constrained. By the time the Americans were forced to deal with the ethical dilemmas of bombing, these dilemmas had already effectively been settled, for better or worse.

ALTERNATIVE EXPLANATIONS FOR THE COLLAPSE OF THE
BOMBING NORM IN WORLD WAR II

To recapitulate, I have argued that at the beginning of the Second World War, although international law prohibited the aerial bombing of civilians, the corresponding *norm* was weak and hung by a slender thread of reciprocity. While this was sufficient to restrain bombing for the first year of the war, after the first violations it broke down quickly in a flurry of retaliatory attacks. Once the norm crumbled, systemic incentives for restraint in bombing disappeared, leaving operational and strategic con-

[179] Overy, *Why the Allies Won*, pp. 109–10.

siderations unchecked by any ethical counterweight. The result was a bombing spiral that ended in the virtual absence of any normative restraint, even on the part of the USAAF, which began the war as champions of precision bombing. Before moving on in Chapter 5 to examine the revival of the bombing norm in recent decades, I will consider three alternative explanations for the breakdown of restraint in aerial bombing in World War II. While none of these explanations is necessarily *incorrect*, all are at least somewhat *incomplete*. Indeed, they must be complemented by a norms-based explanation in order to provide a coherent account of the pattern of bombing in the war.

The Argument from Strategic Interests

Perhaps the most common view reflects the influence of the realist position, which holds that ethical notions of right and wrong have little relevance in foreign policy, especially during wartime. While people may therefore agree that bombing civilians is wrong in the abstract, the exigencies facing belligerents dictate that wartime decisions are driven solely by considerations of strategic interests, without regard for normative preferences. Therefore, it is argued, the early period of restraint in World War II simply reflected the fact that no country believed that it was in its interests to begin bombing vigorously, while the massive scale and destructiveness of air raids later in the war likewise was driven by the strategic needs of those conducting them. If bombing in World War II seemed exceptionally cruel, this was because the stakes of the war were exceptionally high. A January 1943 article in *Harper's* magazine captured this rationale: "It seems brutal to be talking about burning homes. But we are engaged in a life and death struggle for national survival, and we are therefore justified in taking any action which will save the lives of American soldiers and sailors. We must strike hard with everything we have."[180]

It is foolish to deny that states at war are extraordinarily constrained by their strategic interests. However, there are several problems with the appeal to non-normative strategic interests as the sole criterion for state decision making, even in circumstances as desperate as in World War II. First, as mentioned earlier, if the norm against bombing noncombatants was an inevitable casualty of strategic necessity, there is no reason to expect other normative constraints to have fared any better under the

---

[180] Quoted in Hopkins, "Bombing and the American Conscience during World War II," p. 463.

same circumstances. Yet other norms did hold up, including the norm against assassinating foreign leaders and the norm against the use of chemical weapons.[181] Second, the argument from strategic interests itself often implicitly assumes the influence of norms. The restraints of 1939–40, for example, are typically attributed to the desire of belligerents on both sides to avoid provoking an all-out bombing exchange, which none saw as in its interests. This assumes reciprocity: that one side's restraint is contingent upon the other's, and that bombing by one belligerent would likely bring about reciprocation. The assumption of reciprocity is difficult to explain, however, unless one also assumes the presence of a norm designating a certain type and level of activity—in this case, the strategic bombing of populated areas—as prima facie illegitimate. Otherwise, the notion of a "retaliatory response" or reprisal would be nonsensical.[182] Without the assumption of norms and convention-dependency, therefore, it is difficult to see how both sides saw city bombing as contrary to their interests in August 1940 but perfectly consistent with their interests just one month later. This, along with the way in which the norm served as a focal point of the struggle to court neutral (especially American) public opinion, shows that norms often do not compete with strategic considerations but rather *alter the strategic calculus itself,* becoming a part of the entire strategic situation that a state must consider in making policy decisions.

Finally, *purely* strategic interests alone (as opposed to strategic interests shaped by norms) cannot explain the pattern of bombing over the course of the war. If the bombing of urban areas was simply a regrettable step made necessary by the requirements of the strategic situation, then we should expect a state's willingness to bomb civilians to be strongest at times when its strategic situation is most pressing. Michael Walzer refers to this as the "back-to-the-wall argument," after the words of Stanley Baldwin in 1932: "If a man has a potential weapon and has his back to the wall and is going to be killed, he will use that weapon, whatever it is and whatever undertaking he has given about it."[183] This, however, does not describe what happened in World War II. Britain's situation was clearly most dire in the spring and summer of 1940 after the defeat of France and the evacuation of Dunkirk, yet its bombing remained restrained throughout the summer. By the same token, Allied bombing

---

[181] Note 14, supra.

[182] See, e.g., Price and Tannenwald, "Norms and Deterrence."

[183] Quoted in Walzer, *Just and Unjust Wars*, p. 252.

of populated areas in both the European and Pacific theaters increased steadily over the course of the war, even after the gravest strategic crises had passed and other means of warfare had become more important. Churchill acknowledged as much in July 1942 but remained adamant about the continuation of city bombing:

> In the days when we were fighting alone, we answered the question: "How are you going to win the war?" by saying: "We will shatter Germany by bombing." Since then the enormous injuries inflicted on the German army and manpower by the Russians, and the accession of the manpower and munitions of the United States, have rendered other possibilities open. All the same, it would be a mistake to cast aside our original thought . . . that *the severe, ruthless bombing of Germany on an ever-increasing scale will not only cripple her war effort . . . but will create conditions intolerable to the mass of the German population.*[184]

Consequently, about 60 percent of the total tonnage of bombs dropped on Germany in the war was dropped between September 1944 and April 1945.[185] The pattern of early restraint giving way to the eventual disappearance of any meaningful restraint at all is consistent with the breakdown of a convention-dependent norm, but cannot be fully accounted for by purely strategic interests alone.

The Argument from Technological and Operational Limitations

The essence of this argument is that the belligerents in World War II did not wish to bomb civilians but were forced to do so by a combination of strategic necessity (which is often simply implied) and conditions that made it impossible to bomb with the precision they would have liked. The conditions usually cited are technological limitations on accuracy and the presence of enemy defenses, which made daylight bombing prohibitively costly and further diminished precision. Sheldon Cohen, for example, argues that "RAF Bomber Command resorted to night raids only because of the high losses sustained in daylight raids. Area bombing was not Bomber Command's preferred option but a consequence of the furious German defense."[186] He adds:

---

[184] Quoted in ibid., p. 261 (emphasis added).

[185] Clodfelter, "Pinpointing Devastation," p. 98. Of course, some of the dramatic increase in the pace of Allied bombing late in the war must be attributed to the increased availability of aircraft and the achievement of air superiority over the Luftwaffe, but neither of these accounts for the nature of decisions concerning how the bombers would be used.

[186] Cohen, *Arms and Judgment*, p. 114.

The fact is, as was proven over and over again during the war, that the night bombing of the period was so inaccurate that when it was conducted in the vicinity of a city, the difference between bombing the city itself and bombing military installations or docks in or near the city was a theoretical difference rather than a practical one. . . . Once losses forced bombers into night missions, discriminatory attacks were virtually impossible. They could only have occurred if the target were miles from the nearest town, and even then the target would almost certainly be missed. Night bombers could not, unless they were extremely lucky, hit a target much smaller than a medium-sized city.[187]

W. Hays Parks goes a step further, asserting that civilians were never intentionally targeted in the war but were truly incidental victims of attacks on legitimate military targets. Moreover, Parks argues, the military principle of economy of force would prevent any rational belligerent from ever intentionally targeting civilians, "for the attack of the civilian population as such would constitute a highly inefficient use and unnecessary risk of the limited military assets available, assets which are better used against high-value targets most likely to affect the enemy's ability to wage war. . . . Not even the sternest bombing advocate in past conflicts has suggested such a militarily inefficient use of bombing."[188] According to this interpretation, then, the norm against the bombing of civilians did not actually break down, because civilians were never the direct object of attack. Nevertheless, the explanation goes, when faced with a choice between bombing that would cause incidental civilian deaths and no bombing at all, the World War II powers were forced by necessity to choose the former.

It is undoubtedly true that the technological and operational limitations on precision bombing in the early years of the war were as daunting as Cohen describes, and that they influenced the manner in which the bombing campaigns were conducted. There was, however, more at work in the bombing of cities than the simple inability to bomb anything smaller. First, this explanation overlooks the extent to which interwar air power theory emphasized the morale of the enemy civilian population as a direct target of strategic bombing, as well as the extent to which this theory was reflected in prewar doctrine, especially of the RAF. If it is believed, as it clearly was by Trenchard and other leading British offi-

---

[187] Ibid., pp. 100, 102.
[188] Parks, "Conventional Aerial Bombing and the Law of War," p. 114.

cials (as well as by many air power theorists of other nations), that urban populations were the weakest and most vulnerable cogs in the war-making machinery of modern states, then Parks's argument gets it absolutely backward: the population is then the most valuable and economical strategic target, whereas targeting traditional military objectives is an inefficient diversion of resources. This, after all, is what makes bombing such a vexing moral issue: civilian populations suffer not simply because irrational or evil men wish it but because rational men who are not necessarily evil believe that it is strategically effective to make them suffer.

In any case, there is little doubt that the RAF's orientation toward morale bombing, and the ambivalence toward noncombatant immunity that it produced, was carried into the conduct of bombing in World War II. It is true that in the immediate prewar years the RAF was compelled, by the requirements of public relations and the realization that a disarming first strike was beyond its capabilities, to formally disavow morale as a target. Still, as Malcolm Smith argues, "The speed with which it reappeared once the war broke out implies that the importance of the supposed vulnerability of civilian morale remained a powerful underlying assumption in Air Staff minds."[189] It was so powerful, in fact, that within a few weeks after the declaration of war in 1939, a general in the British army was heard to complain that "the Air Ministry are now hypnotized by action against morale and will hear of nothing else."[190] Moreover, while limited accuracy was indeed a major obstacle to a successful precision bombing campaign, it was to a certain extent an obstacle of the RAF's own creation. As Jeffrey Legro points out, "The emphasis on morale bombing gave few incentives for developing the necessary equipment and skills for accuracy."[191] And when confronted with the problem of heavy losses on daylight missions, the RAF rapidly switched to nighttime attacks without seriously considering other possible solutions to the problem, such as building new long-range escort fighters or equipping existing fighters with drop-tanks to extend their range.[192] While certain things were beyond the RAF's control, Williamson Murray argues, "the doctrine had already established the proclivities before the war, and it would push RAF leaders, particularly those within [Arthur] Harris'

---

[189] Smith, *British Air Strategy between the Wars*, p. 63.

[190] Quoted in Legro, *Cooperation under Fire*, p. 136.

[191] Ibid., p. 131.

[192] Murray, "The Influence of Pre-War Anglo-American Doctrine on the Air Campaigns of the Second World War," p. 240.

realm, into a single-minded effort to bludgeon Germany into surrender."[193]

The argument from technological and operational limitations also seriously understates the degree to which bombing operations made the devastation of cities, rather than the destruction of specific military and industrial targets *within* cities, their primary goal. A report by the British Air Staff in the first week of 1941 clearly emphasized the importance of enemy civilian morale to the war effort, ranking it second in targeting priority only to German oil facilities—and ahead of the Luftwaffe, German industry, transportation, and the German navy.[194] Arthur Harris, head of Bomber Command from February 1942 through the end of the war, went even further, adamantly resisting any efforts to divert bombers from city raids to missions aimed at what he derisively referred to as "panacea targets" such as oil, transportation, or crucial industrial plants.[195] Although Bomber Command raids were usually ostensibly aimed at specific military or industrial targets, it was clear that city-busting was the actual goal, not just an incidental effect. In a 1943 progress report to Churchill, instead of a list of military targets, factories, railyards, refineries, or other such objectives, Harris provided a list of almost fifty German cities classified under the headings "virtually destroyed," "seriously damaged," and "damaged."[196] Moreover, while most factories were located on the outskirts of towns or in the suburbs, bombs were typically targeted on town centers to maximize the destruction. Harris said that the actual destruction of factories "could be regarded as a bonus."[197] While this may have made sense strategically, it strains credulity to insist under such circumstances that the aim-point is still an industrial target. Such a contention calls to mind the joke about the fellow who loses his keys in a dark alley but looks for them under a streetlamp, where the light is better. Anyone who doubts the nature of Bomber Command objectives would do well to consider the 1944 proposal for Operation Thunderclap:

[193] Ibid., p. 245.

[194] "Report by the Chiefs of Staff on Air Bombardment Policy, 7th January 1941," in Charles Webster and Noble Frankland, *The Strategic Air Offensive against Germany, 1939–1944*, vol. 4 (London: Her Majesty's Stationery Office, 1961), pp. 188–93.

[195] Murray, "The Influence of Pre-War Anglo-American Doctrine on the Air Campaigns of the Second World War," p. 247.

[196] Messerschmidt, "Strategic Air War and International Law," pp. 306–7.

[197] Ibid.

The attack must be delivered in such density that it imposes as nearly as possible a one hundred percent risk of death to the individual in the area to which it is applied. The target chosen should be one involving the maximum association, both traditional and personal, for the population as a whole. Considerations of economic destruction must not be permitted to influence the selection of the target. Subject to [the above], the area selected should embrace the highest density of population.[198]

Bomber Command staff determined that Berlin would be the ideal target for the operation because of its population density: "If we assume that the daytime population of the area attacked is 300,000, we may expect 220,000 casualties. Fifty per cent of these or 110,000 may expect to be killed. It is suggested that such an attack resulting in so many deaths, the great proportion of which will be key personnel, cannot help but have a shattering effect on political and civilian morale all over Germany."[199]

Nor was the focus on the indiscriminate destruction of cities limited to the British. Early German attacks on British cities, although small by contrast to later Allied raids, were by and large terror raids. Moreover, the German V-1 and V-2 rockets, both of which lacked the accuracy to hit specific targets, were purely terror weapons.[200] As for the Americans, despite their claims of precision in the European theater, the goals and assessment of the U.S. firebombing raids on Japanese cities were very similar to the RAF focus on city-busting in Europe. An article in a magazine published by an arm of the USAAF conceded that U.S. goals in the bombing of Japan "basically . . . were the same as those of British area bombing."[201] And in the postwar report by the United States Strategic Bombing Survey, the March 1945 raid on Tokyo was assessed by the same criterion as Harris applied to the bombing of German cities, being called "the most effective mission ever accomplished in terms of area totally damaged per bomb tonnage dropped."[202]

Finally, the argument from technological and operational limitations ignores the fact that the limitations in question had been more or less overcome by the time bombing operations really began to hit their

---

[198] Quoted in McElroy, *Morality and American Foreign Policy*, p. 158.

[199] Quoted in Hastings, *Bomber Command*, p. 301.

[200] Richard Overy, *The Air War, 1939–1945* (New York: Stein and Day, 1980), p. 81.

[201] Quoted in Crane, "Evolution of U.S. Strategic Bombing of Urban Areas," p. 17.

[202] Quoted in Messerschmidt, "Strategic Air War and International Law," p. 306.

stride. By the late winter of 1944, Allied air forces, aided by a new generation of long-range escort fighters such as the U.S. Mustang, had won command of the air from the Luftwaffe, and new navigational aids and bombsights greatly increased accuracy. This made it possible to bomb with precision, as was demonstrated by the spring 1944 campaign against French marshaling yards in preparation for the invasion of Normandy.[203] While this capability was put to use in raids on heavy industry and oil, advocates of city bombing, most notably Harris, continued to view such efforts as a waste of time and resources, even in the face of evidence that morale bombing was not having as great an impact as envisioned.[204] Consequently, the most intense and deadly attacks on cities occurred after it was possible to use bombers as something more than the blunt instrument they had been earlier in the war.

The Argument from Organizational Culture

Finally, Jeffrey Legro has argued that the degree of adherence to norms in World War II, including the norm against the bombing of civilians, is best explained by reference to the dominant outlooks or "cultures" of the military organizations charged with conducting the war. Legro therefore emphasizes the culture of morale bombing within the RAF as the basis for Britain's willingness to violate the norm in 1940 despite its relative vulnerability and numerical inferiority, as well as its later "promiscuous" conduct of bombing. On the other hand, the focus on tactical close air support within the Luftwaffe is seen to be at the core of Germany's relatively more restrained bombing, even though it stood to enjoy a strategic advantage in a large-scale bombing exchange.

Legro's argument is a valuable contribution to the debate on bombing in the war, adding an important perspective that is often neglected in explaining the actions of the major belligerents. Still, there are limitations to the organizational culture approach. First, Legro uses organizational culture as an alternative to realist (interest-based) and institutionalist (norm-based) perspectives. However, none of these perspectives operates independently of one another; each evolves in constant and recursive interaction with the others. So treating organizational culture as an independent variable may understate the extent to which interests and norms influence policy *through* organizational culture. In other words, just as it is important to know where interests and

---

[203] Paskins and Dockrill, *The Ethics of War*, p. 34.
[204] Biddle, "Air Power," p. 154.

norms come from, it is also important to know where organizational culture comes from. Williamson Murray points out, for example, that British and German air doctrines in World War II were shaped by the states' respective strategic situations. Britain's emphasis on strategic air power reflected its status as an island nation whose primary vulnerability was through the air, whereas Germany, surrounded by hostile powers and bent on territorial expansion, developed an air culture that thought first in terms of tactical support rather than independent air operations such as bombing.[205] By the same token, some of the normative obstacles to the culture of morale bombing were minimized by the countervailing moral argument that the decisiveness of strategic air warfare would make wars shorter and more humane, thereby avoiding a repeat of the nightmare of the World War I trenches.

A second limitation of the organizational culture argument is that it fails to account for similar behavior by organizations with quite different cultures. Although the RAF and the USAAF both emphasized strategic bombing, for example, the differences between the morale-bombing orientation of the former and the precision, "bottleneck" targeting of the latter were significant. Nevertheless, by the end of the war the bombing practices of the two forces had more or less converged. Moreover, focusing on organizational culture relegates other important actors, such as national leaders outside of a particular organization, to subservient roles. This is less of an issue in the cases of the RAF and Luftwaffe, whose orientations toward bombing were shared by Churchill and Hitler, respectively.[206] In the American case, however, it may be worth considering the effect Roosevelt's support for morale bombing may have had in the evolution of USAAF bombing practices over the course of the war.

Finally, Legro's account emphasizes the tension between organizational culture and strategic, or realist, factors in the period leading up to the beginning of unrestrained bombing in August 1940. For him, as for my norms-based approach, the errant bombing of London on August 24

---

[205] Murray, "British and German Air Doctrine between the Wars," pp. 40–41.

[206] To be fair, Legro does argue that Churchill's views on morale bombing were "swayed" by the RAF upon taking over as prime minister in May 1940. *Cooperation under Fire*, p. 139. Legro may, however, understate the extent of Churchill's enthusiastic support for the air arm and independent air warfare throughout the 1930s. See, e.g, Bialer, *The Shadow of the Bomber*, and Bialer, "Elite Opinion and Defence Policy." In any event, the relationship of Churchill's opinions to the culture of an organization of which he was not a member remains unclear.

and the British retaliatory raid on Berlin the next day were pivotal.[207] According to Legro, after this the organizational culture of the RAF came to the fore, overwhelming the realist reasons why Britain should have avoided a bombing exchange. At the same time the Germans also abandoned restrictions, in spite of their continued ambivalence to bombing. What remains unclear from an organizational culture approach is why the August 24–25 exchange was such a crucial turning point. For example, why, before this time, was the British proclivity toward bombing suppressed? Even if the British used the August 24 raid as a pretext to let loose, why was a pretext seen as necessary? Why after the British response was the German disinclination to bomb less relevant? To answer these questions it is necessary to supplement the organizational culture approach with the norms approach I have set forth. This allows us to appreciate that the bombing norm itself, however weak and convention-dependent, did in fact exercise considerable influence on the warring powers, but that this influence declined precipitously with the first clear violations of the norm.

The norms-based perspective of this chapter is not, any more than the alternative explanations considered above, a comprehensive explanation of the conduct of strategic bombing in World War II. It would be wrong to argue that factors such as strategic interests, technological limitations, and organizational culture are not important influences on state behavior. Norms, too, however, play a significant part in the structural environment within which states act. The example of World War II shows two ways in which this is so. First, norms are shaped by other factors and shape them in return: considerations of strategic interest influenced the way in which the interwar norm took shape, but the existence of the norm early in the war created incentives for restraint that became part of the strategic environment in which interests were defined. Second, norms can act as more or less independent constraints, much the same as other constraints on state action. In World War II the bombing norm exerted considerable influence for a while, but because it was a weak and poorly developed norm it soon cleared the stage for military and organizational pressures.

[207] Legro, *Cooperation under Fire*, p. 140.

CHAPTER 5

Aerial Bombing since 1945
A Norm Revived

Every bomb is a political bomb.
              US. Air Force Colonel John Warden, August 1990

The future of the bombing norm could not have looked bright when viewed from the rubble of European and Japanese cities. At the least, international law on aerial warfare was in a state of disarray. Bombing in World War II seemed to make a mockery of the idea of customary law, as the actual practices of states had shown little evidence of legal constraint. The chief counsel at the Nuremberg Tribunal reported:

> Many of the provisions of the 1907 Hague Convention regarding unlawful means of combat . . . were antiquarian. Others had been observed only partially during the First World War and almost completely disregarded during the Second World War. . . . If the first badly bombed cities—Warsaw, Rotterdam, Belgrade, and London—suffered at the hands of the Germans and not the Allies, nonetheless the ruins of German and Japanese cities were the results not of reprisal but of deliberate policy, and bore witness that aerial bombardment of cities and factories has become a recognized part of modern warfare as carried on by all nations.[1]

[1] Quoted in Biddle, "Air Power," p. 155.

Three years later, one speaker at the meeting of the American Society of International Law was able to state without contradiction: "As you are all probably aware, there are no rules governing aerial warfare."[2] Clearly, the bombing norm itself was in equally bad shape. If the bombing of cities was indeed "a recognized part of modern warfare," there was little basis for any reasonable expectation of restraints in the future.

While the norm lay in shambles, what did remain was the underlying moral principle that innocent people should if possible be spared the horrors of war—a belief that may indeed have been strengthened by the ordeal of the war and the prospect of future destruction. From this foundation, the bombing norm has slowly recovered from the catastrophe of World War II. While far from absolute, the reborn norm has in recent decades engendered a sensitivity to noncombatant casualties that not only constrains states from targeting civilian populations per se but also creates pressures to minimize incidental casualties in general. In this chapter, I briefly survey the conduct of aerial bombing in the post–World War II world, arguing that it shows the increasingly strong influence of the bombing norm, with the Persian Gulf War of 1991 a particularly important watershed. I conclude with an analysis of why the norm has bounced back so vigorously, focusing on the interaction between changes in technology and the effects of the bombing norm on the distribution of power in the international system.

KOREA

The Korean War is often differentiated from World War II by its status as a "limited war." The term is, however, somewhat misleading. Even in total wars such as World War II, as we have seen, not all possible means are employed (chemical weapons and assassination, for example), whereas limited wars can involve the use of immensely destructive means. Limited war is not necessarily limited in every way. While bombing in the Korean War is often associated with restrictive rules of engagement, these restrictions more often reflected political imperatives (such as avoiding antagonizing China and the Soviet Union) than humanitarian concerns. Thus while U.S. bombers were forbidden to cross the Yalu River, the North Korean capital of Pyongyang and other towns were subjected to annihilating incendiary raids that resulted in the deaths of

---

[2] Quoted in Parks, "Conventional Aerial Bombing and the Law of War," p. 99.

hundreds of thousands of Korean civilians.[3] At the same time, however, there were stirrings of sensitivity over noncombatant casualties, particularly among the civilian leadership and the international community, that portended a future trend.

The first major U.S. strategic bombing campaign against North Korea, begun in late July 1950, was conceived much along the lines of the major offensives of World War II. Although the specific targets were industrial sites, and accuracy had improved enough to provide a realistic chance of actually hitting them, a primary objective of the raids was once again civilian morale. The Far East Air Forces (FEAF) plan for the attacks employed reasoning evocative of the interwar air theorists: "The psychological impact of bringing the war to the people is a catalyst that destroys the morale and will to resist. . . . [D]estruction of urban areas adjoining industrial plants would erode the morale of the North Korean people and undermine their obedience to the communist government."[4] Major General Emmett O'Donnell, one architect of the plan, described the goal as "putting a very severe blow on the North Koreans, with an advance warning, perhaps, telling them that they had gone too far . . . and we now have at our command a weapon that can really dish out some severe destruction, and let us go to work burning five major cities in North Korea to the ground, and to destroy completely every one of about 18 major strategic targets."[5] Civilian leaders in Washington, however, rejected the use of incendiary bombs out of fear that heavy civilian casualties would provide the North Korean government with a valuable propaganda tool.[6] Although incendiary munitions were later used many times after China's intervention in the war, the 1950 decision was interesting. The concern with propaganda clearly implies the influence of a normative judgment: being seen as bombing civilians might, U.S. officials believed, lead to ethical condemnation that would prove politically costly. So while still quite destructive, the 1950 raids remained confined to industrial areas, with fewer effects on the civilian population than FEAF planners had envisioned.[7] Nevertheless, the raids were sharply criticized by segments of the international media, even in

---

[3] Max Hastings, *The Korean War* (New York: Touchstone, 1987), p. 268.

[4] Quoted in Pape, *Bombing to Win*, p. 145.

[5] Quoted in Conrad C. Crane, *American Airpower Strategy in Korea, 1950–1953* (Lawrence: University Press of Kansas, 2000), p. 23.

[6] Robert F. Futrell, *The United States Air Force in Korea, 1950–1953*, rev. ed. (Washington, D.C.: Government Printing Office, 1983), p. 187.

[7] Pape, *Bombing to Win*, p. 151.

friendly countries. The London *News Chronicle*, for example, remarked that "the B-29s might be doing more damage to the democratic cause than to the Communists," and a RAND study of press reaction in Germany complained that "editors have apparently been reluctant to present a positive image of air power. Many of them must feel that such an undertaking is futile in a country which has suffered so heavily from bombing."[8]

Two years later, with the war mired in a stalemate and peace talks stalled, the United States launched a three-pronged strategic bombing offensive aimed at dashing any hope North Korea might have for a favorable resolution on the battlefield. The three parts of the plan were: attacks on five hydroelectric plants beginning on June 23, 1952; Operation "Pressure Pump," a series of incendiary raids on Pyongyang in July; and Operation "Strike," consisting of attacks on seventy-eight towns and villages used by communist forces as supply sites.[9] As in World War II, the nominal objectives of the raids were military targets, but these were selected with an eye toward their impact on morale. The FEAF plan specified that "whenever possible attacks will be scheduled against targets of military significance so situated that their destruction will have a deleterious effect upon the morale of the civilian population."[10] The first two elements went off as planned, resulting in extensive damage to an already battered Pyongyang and a two-week-long electrical blackout throughout North Korea.[11] The United States failed to anticipate, however, the intense criticism that these operations would generate in the international community. Former British Prime Minister Clement Attlee stood in the House of Commons to demand an explanation for bringing "misery and distress to hundreds of thousands of civilians,"[12] while French Foreign Minister Robert Schuman warned Secretary of State Dean Acheson of "unfavorable public and legislative opinion" in his country as a result of the attacks.[13] In India, where press reports condemned the conduct of the war as evincing American racism, Prime

---

[8] Futrell, *The United States Air Force in Korea*, p. 198; Eric Willenz, *German Press Reaction to the Air War in Korea* (Santa Monica: RAND Corp., 1951), p. 2.

[9] Pape, *Bombing to Win*, pp. 160–61.

[10] Quoted in ibid., p. 160.

[11] Clay Blair, *The Forgotten War: America in Korea, 1950–1953* (New York: Times Books, 1987), p. 969.

[12] "Why the British Were Not Told of Plans to Bomb Power Plants," *Newsweek*, July 7, 1952, p. 35.

[13] James F. Schnabel and Robert J. Watson, *The History of the Joint Chiefs of Staff, Vol. III: The Korean War* (Wilmington, Del.: Michael Glazer, 1979), p. 846.

Minister Jawaharlal Nehru said that his Parliament "was aghast" at the attacks.[14] Moreover, the publication of the list of seventy-eight targets for impending attacks in Operation Strike, while intended to facilitate the evacuation of civilians, allowed the Chinese to claim that the U.S. effort was "becoming a war against Korean women and children and the old people in the rear."[15] Consequently, the raids were discontinued at the urging of the State Department after only two villages had been hit because of concerns that public fallout from the campaign and communist manipulation of it were harming the U.S. position.[16]

These episodes show that, by the time of the Korean War, an international sensibility was emerging that bombing attacks resulting in many civilian deaths, even if they were not aimed at the civilian population per se, were not a legitimate means of warfare. Although the bombing norm was still not powerful enough to prevent states from thinking in terms of using air power to wither enemy morale, it was beginning to force them to limit the means by which they could accomplish this and make them consider the political costs they might incur by offending international opinion on the issue. By the same token, however, as illustrated by the FEAF plans and the differences of opinion between civilian and military authorities on the conduct of bombing, the norm was far from being internalized by military organizations, which still often assumed the relative absence of normative restrictions on bombing.[17] The shifting normative ground was apparent in a 1952 exchange between William Parsons, who as a member of the crew of the *Enola Gay* had participated in dropping the atomic bomb on Hiroshima seven years earlier, and representatives of MGM studios, who were filming a biography of Paul Tibbets, the airplane's pilot. Parsons objected to the film's characterization of the crew as "all mixed up emotionally," noting that crew members had been focused on winning the war and had no misgivings about their mission. The studio replied that "we dare not portray in an American

---

[14] C. H. Heimsath, "Indo-American Relations: Effects of the Korean Conflict," *Journal of International Affairs* 6 (Spring 1952): 154; "Nehru Says India 'Dislikes' Korean Power-Plant Raid," *New York Times,* June 27, 1952, p. 3.

[15] "Korea Foe Charges New Air Violation," *New York Times,* August 18, 1952, p. 2. Ironically, the practice of dropping leaflets warning civilians of impending raids was a source of considerable controversy, since it could be interpreted as threatening mass bombings of non-military targets. Crane, *American Airpower Strategy in Korea,* pp. 42, 77–78, 125.

[16] Pape, *Bombing to Win,* p. 161.

[17] As early as the summer of 1950, O'Donnell complained that political and humanitarian restraints left the FEAF "fighting distinctly 'under wraps.'" Quoted in Futrell, *The United States Air Force in Korea,* p. 475.

film today, an American airman killing eighty thousand Asiatics in a flash, and expressing no feelings of conscience about this, without seriously playing into the propaganda hands of the Kremlin." The story, therefore, would have to accommodate the feelings of "moral conflict" that the bombing would raise in audiences in 1952.[18]

VIETNAM

United States bombing in Vietnam remains controversial to this day, often being criticized as indiscriminate and disproportionately harmful to Vietnamese civilians. Nevertheless, far more than in Korea, sensitivity to civilian casualties served as an important constraint on bombing operations from the start. The Rolling Thunder bombing campaign, which ran from March 1965 to October 1968, was a combination of interdiction and industrial bombing designed not only to degrade North Vietnam's ability to prosecute the war but also to signal the seriousness of the U.S. commitment and to induce the North to seek peace. While it was hoped that bombing might also erode civilian morale, the rules developed to govern bombing operations made clear that direct harm to civilians and the civilian economy was to be avoided to as great an extent as possible. Here the commitment to noncombatant immunity went beyond the nominal restriction of raids to military targets that typified World War II and Korea. In Rolling Thunder, operations were subject to a number of significant limitations. Areas within thirty miles of Hanoi and ten miles of Haiphong were designated "restricted areas," the targeting of which required White House approval, with limited authority granted to "restrike" the target if it was not destroyed on the first run. Areas within ten miles of Hanoi and four miles of Haiphong were "prohibited areas," where the required White House approval for bombing was reserved for exceptional cases and came with no restrike authority. Targets in populated areas were to be generally avoided, and surface-to-air missile (SAM) sites located in populated areas could only be hit if they were in the act of firing at U.S. planes (a restriction opposed strongly, but unsuccessfully, by the Joint Chiefs of Staff).[19] Although the late stages of the Korean War had seen numerous raids on dams and reservoirs intended to create floods and destroy crops, the vulnerable Vietnamese dam and dike system was placed off-limits to bombing

---

[18] Crane, *American Airpower Strategy in Korea*, p. 184.
[19] Parks, "Rolling Thunder and the Law of War," pp. 9–11.

throughout the war, despite occasional North Vietnamese claims to the contrary.[20] In fact, the North Vietnamese became so confident that these targets would not be struck that they placed antiaircraft batteries on top of dikes to protect the batteries from attack.[21] The target selection process itself, moreover, was designed so that almost as much weight was given to avoiding civilian casualties as to military effectiveness, and sometimes more.[22]

An illustration of the priority placed on avoiding civilian casualties is the set of instructions, formulated by the White House, that was given to planners of a June 1966 raid on petroleum facilities in Hanoi and Haiphong:

- execute strikes only under optimum weather conditions, with good visibility and no cloud cover;
- make maximum use of experienced Rolling Thunder pilots;
- stress the need to avoid civilian casualties in detailed briefing of pilots;
- select a single axis of attack that would avoid populated areas;
- make maximum use of [electronic countermeasures] to hamper SAM and AA [antiaircraft] fire control, in order to limit pilot distraction and improve bombing accuracy;
- make maximum use of high-precision delivery munitions consistent with mission objectives;
- ensure minimum risk to third-country nationals and shipping; and
- limit SAM/AA suppression to sites outside populated areas.[23]

Moreover, when American bombing did result in considerable collateral damage, instructions were often amended to prevent a recurrence of

---

[20] Lewy, *America in Vietnam,* p. 399.

[21] Parks, "Rolling Thunder and the Law of War," p. 12.

[22] The target list review process had many steps. First, recommendations from local commanders went through the chain of command within Vietnam before going to the Joint Chiefs of Staff, who would review the proposed targets with political as well as military factors in mind. The list would then be reviewed by civilians in the office of the Assistant Secretary of Defense for International Security Affairs, who would revise estimates of probable civilian casualties upward from the JCS estimate by adding likely casualties among civilian factory workers. (Because workers in their factories are generally not considered immune under the laws of war, they were not included in the JCS estimates of "collateral damage.") Finally, at White House "Tuesday Lunches," everyone present would rank targets according to four criteria, two of which were estimated civilian casualties and danger to third country nationals. Ibid., pp. 13, 23.

[23] Quoted in ibid., p. 14.

the problem.[24] The focus on avoiding civilian casualties helped make Rolling Thunder, in the words of one legal expert, "one of the most constrained military campaigns in history."[25] Even some critics of U.S. involvement were forced to concede that the bombing was discriminately conducted. Telford Taylor, the former chief counsel at Nuremberg who opposed the U.S. presence in Vietnam, called the rules of engagement given to pilots "virtually impeccable."[26] James Cameron, an antiwar British journalist, toured the North and admitted: "It was my impression . . . that United States attacks on North Vietnam had been, as they claimed, aimed generally at what they could define as military objectives. . . . I do not believe that the Americans set out to bomb homes and hospitals; if they had wished to do so it would have been extremely easy to do so."[27] In all, the three-year campaign resulted in an estimated 52,000 civilian deaths, or 0.3 percent of North Vietnam's population. By contrast, bombing in World War II cost Japan an estimated 3 percent of its population; Germany, 1.6 percent.[28]

The Linebacker bombing campaigns of 1972 generated even more controversy than Rolling Thunder, being generally perceived as less restrained.[29] This perception, however, arguably has more to do with the pace of bombing than the targets chosen. While neither Linebacker I nor Linebacker II featured the "bombing stops" and measured progression that defined Rolling Thunder, the avoidance of civilian casualties remained a priority. Most of the restrictions from Rolling Thunder also applied to Linebacker, and some additional precautions were added, such as the use of precision-guided munitions (PGMs) in attacks on targets in heavily populated areas and stricter requirements for bomb damage assessment of all targets.[30] Again, the emphasis on safeguarding non-

[24] See, e.g., Lewy, *America in Vietnam*, pp. 233–34.
[25] Parks, "Rolling Thunder and the Law of War," p. 21.
[26] Quoted in Lewy, *America in Vietnam*, p. 233.
[27] Quoted in ibid., p. 406.
[28] Pape, *Bombing to Win*, p. 190.
[29] Linebacker I was a large-scale interdiction campaign that lasted from May to October 1972 and focused on military and some large industrial targets in both North and South Vietnam, including logistics, transportation, fuel dumps, warehouses, marshaling yards, power plants, petroleum products, SAM and antiaircraft sites. Linebacker II—the notorious "Christmas Bombings"—was an intense two-week campaign lasting from December 18 to December 29, 1972, aimed at many of the same targets as Linebacker I but concentrated on Hanoi and Haiphong. Ibid., pp. 198–200.
[30] W. Hays Parks, "Linebacker and the Law of War," *Air University Review* 34, no. 2 (Jan./Feb. 1983): 13.

combatants resulted in relatively few civilian casualties. Bombing attacks against the North in 1972 caused about thirteen thousand casualties, and the intense Linebacker II campaign killed 1,623 civilians in Hanoi and Haiphong—a remarkably low number considering the total tonnage of ordnance dropped and the density of urban targets.[31] A *Baltimore Sun* correspondent in Hanoi at the time of the bombings wrote: "Hanoi has certainly been damaged, but evidence on the ground disproves charges of indiscriminate bombing. Several bomb loads obviously went astray into civilian residential areas, but damage there is minor, compared to the total destruction of selected targets."[32]

In Vietnam, in sum, there was clearly greater emphasis placed on the avoidance of civilian casualties than in Korea some fifteen to twenty years earlier. Moreover, the restrictions on bombing in Vietnam were for the most part considerably more stringent than required by international law. Many targets that could have been lawfully struck were placed off-limits, and U.S. pilots were required to follow rules of engagement that subjected them to risks beyond those demanded by the law of war.[33] This was because, on a fundamental level, constraints on bombing in Vietnam were not based upon international law, or even, as some have argued, a misunderstanding of international law.[34] It is clear from the restrictions on U.S. air crews, as well as from accounts of the political processes from which those restrictions emerged, that priority was placed not simply on the avoidance of *unlawful* civilian casualties but the avoidance of civilian casualties, period. For the Johnson and Nixon administrations, international law on this point was not really the issue. What was at stake were the political costs that could be incurred by the perception that civilians were being targeted. In other words, by the

---

[31] Pape, *Bombing to Win*, p. 208. The actual number of noncombatant casualties caused by U.S. bombing, in fact, may have been even lower, since the North Vietnamese figures probably included some civilians who were taking part in hostilities, as well as some killed by errant North Vietnamese SAMs exploding in populated areas. Parks, "Linebacker and the Law of War," p. 25. On the other hand, civilian casualties surely would have been significantly greater had much of the population of Hanoi not been evacuated prior to the raids. Martin F. Herz and Leslie Rider, *Prestige Press and the Christmas Bombing, 1972: Images and Reality in Vietnam* (Washington, D.C.: Ethics and Public Policy Center, 1980), p. 55.

[32] Quoted in Lewy, *America in Vietnam*, p. 414. Both American and foreign journalists who toured Hanoi after the bombings reported that earlier accounts had "grossly overstated" the damage done to civilian areas. Stanley Karnow, *Vietnam: A History*, rev. ed. (New York: Viking Penguin, 1991), p. 668.

[33] Parks, "Rolling Thunder and the Law of War," pp. 16–21.

[34] See, e.g., ibid.

time of Vietnam, the norm against bombing civilians had become more important than international law governing the issue.[35]

Given the divisive impact of the Vietnam War upon American society, domestic political concerns constituted one avenue of normative pressure. Robert Pape comments that in 1972 Nixon was "keenly aware" of the domestic problems he would face if bombing caused large numbers of civilian deaths, and the desire to avoid domestic criticism likewise weighed on Johnson's mind during Rolling Thunder.[36] But U.S. officials were also concerned with the impact of bombing upon opinion in the international community. In an October 1966 memo Secretary of Defense Robert McNamara advised Johnson against unrestricted bombing, arguing that "to bomb the North sufficiently to make a radical impact upon Hanoi's political, economic, and social structure, would require an effort which we could make but which *would not be stomached either by our own people or by world opinion,* and it would involve a serious risk of drawing us into open war with China."[37] As in Korea, opponents of the United States launched concerted efforts to portray American bombing as indiscriminate and cruel. While such accusations generally had less merit in Vietnam than they had in Korea, they nevertheless made an impact. Charges that the United States had indiscriminately bombed North Vietnamese dikes, for example, were both false and, because dikes were lawful targets, legally incoherent. Nevertheless, such charges subjected the United States to increasing criticism and influenced the way in which the war was conducted.[38] The condemnation of bombing in the American and international press had begun early in the Rolling Thunder campaign,[39] and reached a crescendo during Linebacker II. The *New York Times* decried the bombing as "Stone Age bar-

[35] Even among the air crews actually dropping the bombs, international law itself was less significant than the general avoidance of civilian casualties, as embodied in the rules of engagement. This is illustrated by the plight of captured pilots charged with war crimes by the North Vietnamese. Despite having to fly their missions under restrictions designed to protect against civilian deaths, the pilots typically "lacked sufficient knowledge of the law to reject the charges out of hand." Parks, "Conventional Aerial Bombing and the Law of War," p. 101.

[36] Pape, *Bombing to Win,* pp. 208, 180.

[37] Quoted in Lewy, *America in Vietnam,* p. 382 (emphasis added).

[38] Parks, "Conventional Aerial Bombing and the Law of War," p. 107; Lewy, *America in Vietnam,* pp. 398–414.

[39] A December 1966 editorial in London's *Sun* newspaper urged, "In the name of humanity and of the British people—who know what bombing means—[British Prime Minister] Harold Wilson must warn President Johnson that Britain cannot support the bombing policy." Quoted in Lewy, *America in Vietnam,* p. 400.

barism," while the *Washington Post* hyperbolically termed it "the most savage and senseless act of war ever visited . . . by one sovereign people on another."[40] Pope Paul VI condemned the bombings from the Vatican, and one German newspaper branded them "a crime against humanity."[41]

The international and domestic outcry against the bombing of North Vietnam, along with the willingness of U.S. authorities to allow such concerns to significantly constrain the conduct of the war, evinced a sensitivity to civilian bombing casualties that had grown more profound in the years since Korea. This sensitivity, in turn, imposed higher political costs for the use of bombing than in the past. As Guenter Lewy explains:

> The bombing of North Vietnam strained U.S. relations with other noncommunist nations and greatly exacerbated domestic tensions. The accusations of indiscriminate bombing of civilian targets can now be shown to have been false, but during the years of the air war they were widely believed, and they *seriously impaired the moral authority of the U.S.. . . .* Despite discomfort and dislocations, the bombing brought North Vietnam valuable political dividends.[42]

The evidence suggests, furthermore, that even from the start of the war U.S. civilian officials were aware of the potential political significance of civilian casualties. This was less true of military officials. While the requirements of international law were for the most part internalized in U.S. military culture and doctrine, by the time of Vietnam the more exacting standards of international opinion seemed a more arbitrary constraint. As a result, the military often chafed under what it saw as unreasonably restrictive bombing rules.[43] Typical of the military position was a March 1968 request by Secretary of the Air Force Harold Brown that restrictions on bombing be eased "so as to permit bombing

---

[40] Karnow, *Vietnam*, p. 667; Mark Clodfelter, *The Limits of Air Power: The American Bombing of North Vietnam* (New York: Free Press, 1989), p. 191.

[41] Karnow, *Vietnam*, p. 667; Clodfelter, *The Limits of Air Power*, p. 191.

[42] Lewy, *America in Vietnam*, p. 396 (emphasis added).

[43] See, e.g., Parks's two articles, "Rolling Thunder and the Law of War" and "Linebacker and the Law of War," especially the former. These articles show that, the subsequent restraint of Operation Desert Storm notwithstanding, a strong current of opinion remained within the military (at least as of the early 1980s) that the restrictions on bombing in Vietnam were unreasonable. The cover illustration of the volume of *Air University Review* in which the "Linebacker" article appears, for example, features U.S. B-52 bombers straining against ropes tied to their tails.

of military targets without the present scrupulous concern for collateral civilian damage and casualties."[44] Such requests, Lewy notes, were invariably denied.[45]

THE PERSIAN GULF WAR

The coalition air campaign in the Gulf War of 1991 continued the trend toward increasingly restrained bombing in order to minimize direct casualties to noncombatants.[46] The planning and conduct of air operations included a wide array of safeguards. Many potential targets, including those that were culturally or religiously sensitive, were placed on a protected "joint no-fire target list" formulated by Central Command (CENTCOM) intelligence analysts in consultation with the State Department and national intelligence agencies. Moreover, all targets were reviewed for the presence of schools, hospitals, or mosques within a six-mile radius "to identify targets where extreme care was required in planning . . . [and when] targeting officers calculated the probability of collateral damage as too high, the target was not attacked."[47] Officials also

> timed strikes to maximize their effectiveness and minimize civilian casualties, employed weapons systems with the best delivery accuracy (F-117a and F-111Fs with laser-guided bombs) against targets in densely populated areas, reduced the likelihood of target misidentification through aircrew familiarization with flight routes and targets and used attack axes that lessened the chance of weapons landing outside targeted areas.[48]

By and large, these measures yielded impressive results. The number of civilian casualties incurred directly by the coalition air campaign was relatively low, reflecting the restraint and precision with which strikes on targets in populated areas had been planned and carried out. Although estimates of civilian deaths from bombing varied from fewer than 1,000 to the between 5,000 and 15,000 estimated by Greenpeace, most ana-

---

[44] Quoted in Lewy, *America in Vietnam*, p. 403.

[45] Ibid.

[46] The most serious and telling objections to the conduct of the air campaign have focused not on direct but "indirect" casualties—deaths caused by the medium-to-long-term effects of destroying Iraq's electrical system. For a consideration of this issue, see pp. 165–66 and p. 178, infra.

[47] U.S. Department of Defense, *Conduct of the Persian Gulf War: Final Report to Congress* (Washington, D.C.; Office of the Secretary of Defense, 1992), p. 100.

[48] Gulf War Air Power Survey, *Volume I: Planning* (Washington, D.C.: Government Printing Office, 1993), p. 93.

lysts now put the number somewhere around 3,000.[49] By any of these counts, one commentator points out, civilian casualties were "remarkably low compared to [both] the amount of ordnance dropped and the casualties in other wars."[50] In all, coalition air forces dropped 88,500 tons of bombs, more than four times the tonnage used in Linebacker II in 1972, and over twice the amount that fell on Great Britain during the Blitz. (See table 5–1.) Paradoxically, therefore, Operation Desert Storm was one of the most intense air campaigns in history and at the same time perhaps the most restrained.

The limitation of noncombatant casualties was clearly a major concern for the United States from the earliest planning stages of the air campaign. This time around, however, it was a goal shared almost equally by civilian and military leaders. When President Bush emphasized to leaders of the air offensive that limiting civilian casualties was "imperative," not only did they not question the point, they had already incorporated it into their plans. As the Gulf War Air Power Survey explains, "While presidential stress on limiting harm to innocent Iraqis undoubtedly arose from deep-rooted moral beliefs, it also reflected political realities. Both civilian and military leaders recognized that domestic and international support for military action against Saddam Hussein would disappear rapidly if large numbers of noncombatants were killed or maimed in coalition attacks."[51] While Bush's words would prompt Air Force leaders to resolve to "err on the side of caution," they were already well aware of the sensitivity of the issue of civilian casualties and its importance to the success of the coalition's cause.[52]

The restrictive rules for the air campaign were also consistent with the rhetorical stance, adopted by civilian and military leaders alike, that the U.S. quarrel was with Saddam Hussein, not the Iraqi people. This message was complemented by a consistent emphasis in press conferences on the precision with which the air war was being conducted and the

[49] See, e.g., John G. Heidenrich, "The Gulf War: How Many Iraqis Died?" *Foreign Policy* 90 (Spring 1993): 119; Kenneth P. Werrell, "Air War Victorious: The Gulf War vs. Vietnam," *Parameters* 22 no. 2 (Summer 1992): 46; Middle East Watch, *Needless Deaths in the Gulf War*, p. 19; and William M. Arkin, "How 'Smart' Was This War Really?" *MSNBC*, June 12, 1999, www.msnbc.com/news/279214.asp?cp1=1.

[50] Werrell, "Air War Victorous," p. 46.

[51] GWAPS, *Planning*, p. 91.

[52] Ibid. As the chief of the Air Force's International Law Division explained, "We want to fight the legal war, but we also want to fight the good international press war. That's one of the things Vietnam sensitized us to." Col. Robert Bridge, quoted in Steven Keeva, "Lawyers in the War Room," *ABA Journal* 77 (December 1991): 55.

limited harm done to noncombatants. As critics have noted, this emphasis, along with highly publicized video footage of precision-guided munitions (PGMs) scoring direct hits on their targets, created the false sense that the war was being fought almost exclusively with precision weapons. In truth, PGMs comprised only about 8 percent of all weapons used.[53] Still, this statistic is itself somewhat misleading since the vast majority of unguided "dumb" bombs were dropped not on strategic targets but on Iraqi forces in the field, far from densely populated areas. Targets in cities were indeed typically struck only with the most accurate weapons. The results were commented upon by several postwar visitors to Iraq, including BBC editor John Simpson: "The picture was the same everywhere really, that selected buildings had been damaged—fewer than 30 in Baghdad itself and very very many fewer than that in most of the other cities. There was a little bit of what they called collateral damage, say damage to other buildings and no doubt some people had been killed in those cities, but it wasn't very large."[54]

No matter how cleanly the air war was fought, however, it was almost impossible for results on the ground to live up to the antiseptic rhetoric of government officials. This was perhaps the first lesson of the fiasco at the Al Firdos bunker. There is no doubt that Al Firdos was seen as a public relations debacle for the United States. But there is also little doubt that, while tragic, the carnage at Al Firdos was no worse than hundreds or even thousands of similar tragedies played out in earlier wars. The difference, of course, was a dramatically strengthened bombing norm, and it is the Al Firdos episode that best illustrates the impact of this norm on late-twentieth-century warfare. First, Al Firdos demonstrated that the requirements imposed by the norm had in many cases become more stringent than those of international law. This, it will be recalled, was a complete reversal of the situation immediately prior to World War II, when the legal prohibition on bombing civilian populations was not supported by a strong norm. Although U.S. officials took pains to assert that the raid on the bunker had been lawful, the measures taken in the wake of the incident showed that this was largely beside the point. The political crisis arose from the fact that many civilians had died, not from the possibility that they had been killed unlawfully. It was the norm, not the law, that delimited the acceptable range of action.

[53] Arkin, "How 'Smart' Was This War Really?"
[54] Quoted in Philip M. Taylor, *War and the Media: Propaganda and Persuasion in the Gulf War* (New York: Manchester University Press, 1992), p. 219.

Second, the Al Firdos crisis was a *political* crisis rather than "merely" a moral one. While USAAF leaders during World War II may have suffered crises of conscience over American bombing late in the war, no significant political costs were involved. Al Firdos, by contrast, had real and tangible strategic consequences. U.S. officials saw it as a potential threat to the stability of the coalition and to international support for the war against Iraq.[55] While some also expressed concern that the bombing might turn domestic public opinion against the war, these fears were allayed by polls showing that a vast majority of Americans found no fault with U.S. actions.[56] The more significant concerns, instead, were possible repercussions in the international community.

Finally, the uniformity of reaction by military and civilian officials to the Al Firdos raid shows that by the time of the Gulf War the bombing norm was more deeply internalized by military organizations, at least in the United States, than it had been in earlier wars. Indeed, one of the most remarkable aspects of the incident is that the military seemed as sensitive to its political ramifications as the civilian leadership. While military authorities defended the legality of the raid, few failed to recognize that killing large numbers of civilians—even by accident—was a political land mine. The avoidance of noncombatant casualties was built into not only the targeting plans and rules of engagement for the air campaign but also the mind set and expectations of those charged with conducting it. It is a reflection of the influence of the bombing norm on modern warfare that, upon learning of the presence of civilians in the bunker, the first reaction of one senior air force official in Riyadh was not a legalistic defense of good intentions but a pithy "Boy, did we fuck up."[57]

KOSOVO

The 1999 NATO air campaign over the Federal Republic of Yugoslavia differed in important respects from the air war in the Persian Gulf. First, it was smaller in scale: it was fought over a smaller geographical area, involved fewer planes and pilots, dropped fewer tons of bombs,

---

[55] Atkinson, *Crusade*, p. 289.

[56] Of those surveyed in one poll, 79 percent blamed the Iraqi government for the incident, and just 13 percent thought that the United States should take greater steps to avoid hitting civilian areas in Iraq. John Mueller, *Policy and Opinion in the Gulf War* (Chicago: University of Chicago Press, 1994), pp. 317–18.

[57] Lt. Col. David Deptula, quoted in Atkinson, *Crusade*, p. 286.

flew fewer aircraft sorties, and flew them at a much less intense pace.[58] Second, whereas Operation Desert Storm served as the preliminary to a large-scale ground campaign, President Clinton explicitly ruled out the use of ground troops in Kosovo from the outset. What the two campaigns had in common, however, was the significance attached to avoiding collateral damage, especially civilian deaths, in the conduct of air operations. Although wartime press reports detailing the gruesome consequences of stray bombs, intelligence errors, and misidentified targets raised doubts about how successful these efforts were, postwar evidence suggests that the toll on the civilian population was indeed relatively limited. In an independent study, Human Rights Watch concluded that NATO bombing killed about five hundred civilians.[59] Although this was only about one-sixth the civilian death toll of Desert Storm, the number was roughly proportionate to Desert Storm in terms of deaths per bombing sortie—and actually double Desert Storm's figure for deaths per ton of bombs. (See Table 5–1.) This reflected several circumstances that made civilian casualties harder to avoid in Kosovo than in the Gulf War, including exceptionally bad weather, a more compact and densely populated theater of operations, less thorough preparation in developing an extensive target set, and, most problematic, mobile military targets that operated in close proximity to civilians, many of whom were refugees travelling the same roads as the troops who displaced them.[60]

As in the Gulf, the goal of avoiding civilian casualties affected the target selection process, operational details and rules of engagement, and the types of technologies used. Lawyers reviewed each proposed target, with many targets vetted by as many as nine people in different locations before being approved.[61] Potentially sensitive targets, includ-

[58] Arkin, "How 'Smart' Was This War Really?"; *PBS Frontline: War in Europe*, www.pbs.org/wgbh/pages/frontline/shows/kosovo/etc/facts.html.

[59] Yugoslav estimates of civilian deaths from NATO bombing ranged from 1,200 to 5,700. Human Rights Watch, *Civilian Deaths in the NATO Air Campaign*, www.hrw.org/reports/2000/nato.

[60] U.S. Department of Defense, *Report to Congress: Kosovo/Operation Allied Force After-Action Report* (Washington, D.C.: Office of the Secretary of Defense, 2000), p. 60; Arkin, "How 'Smart' Was This War Really?"; and Anthony H. Cordesman, *The Lessons and Non-Lessons of the Air and Missile Campaign in Kosovo* (Washington, D.C.: Center for Strategic and International Studies, 1999), p. 75. The extent of the problem caused by the proximity of displaced civilians to military targets is illustrated by the fact that five of the ten incidents with the greatest loss of civilian life involved attacks on convoys or transportation routes. Human Rights Watch, "Civilian Deaths in the NATO Air Campaign."

[61] Cordesman, *The Lessons and Non-Lessons of the Air and Missile Campaign in Kosovo*, pp. 74–75.

ing those in downtown Belgrade and those in which civilian casualties were deemed likely, were reviewed by officials in each of the nineteen NATO capitals, sometimes at very high levels.[62] Indeed, Lt. Gen. Michael Short, commander of NATO's Joint Force Air Component, commented that in the final days of the war, low likelihood of collateral damage "was the litmus [test] that we used to pick a target."[63] Beyond that, collateral damage concerns influenced what type of aircraft and what type of weapon was used against a target, as well as the angle of approach and the aim point.[64] Moreover, after several incidents in which civilian deaths led to criticism of its practices, NATO changed its rules of engagement to avoid similar problems. One example was the shift in late May from daylight attacks on bridges to nighttime attacks, when civilian traffic was figured to be lightest. Another was the tightening of the rules regarding the visual identification of mobile military targets in the wake of the disastrous bombing of Kosovar civilian convoys on the road between Djakovica and Decane on April 14.[65] In a third instance, President Clinton issued an executive order banning the use of cluster bombs by U.S. planes after civilians died in cluster bomb attacks in Nis on May 7.[66] Finally, the Kosovo campaign represented an advance over the Gulf War in terms of the technology of precision bombing. Newer guidance systems, including the more widespread use of global position system (GPS) technology, allowed for greater accuracy in adverse weather conditions. High-tech weapons also represented a larger proportion of the arsenal than they had in 1991; 35 percent of all weapons used in Yugoslavia were precision-guided munitions (compared to 8 percent in the Gulf), and attacks on bridges and targets in Belgrade used PGMs exclusively.[67] One correspondent in Belgrade reported that despite extensive attacks on targets within the city, "the high-tech nature of the war engendered a great deal of confidence that the residents were safe."[68]

Nevertheless, while in many ways the Kosovo campaign was another

---

[62] Human Rights Watch, *Civilian Deaths in the NATO Air Campaign.*

[63] John A. Tirpak, "Short's View of the Air Campaign," *Air Force Magazine* 82, no. 9 (September 1999), www.afa.org/magazine/watch/0999watch.html.

[64] Cordesman, *The Lessons and Non-Lessons of the Air and Missile Campaign in Kosovo*, p. 60.

[65] Human Rights Watch, *Civilian Deaths in the NATO Air Campaign.*

[66] Ibid.

[67] Ibid.

[68] Kerry Sanders, "Surreal War May Be Coming to an End," *MSNBC,* June 6, 1999, www.msnbc.com/news/276928.asp?cp1=1.

step forward for the bombing norm, it also demonstrated some of the limits of even a strong ethical norm when confronted with countervailing political and doctrinal pressures. For also apparent in Kosovo were tensions among conflicting goals that emerged more palpably than had been the case in the Gulf War. NATO's desire to avoid collateral damage was, in effect, in constant competition with both its goal of coercing Slobodan Milosevic and its strong interest in incurring as few casualties among its own airmen as possible—a goal expressed in military vernacular as "force protection." The result was different sets of constraints that sometimes worked at cross-purposes, leading to civilian losses that, while still relatively few, were greater than might have otherwise been the case. German General Klaus Naumann, chairman of the NATO Military Committee at the beginning of the war, explained that NATO had "three guiding principles: we had first of all to avoid if possible any of our own casualties and fatalities; secondly we were told to avoid collateral damage to the extent possible; and thirdly [to] bring it to a quick end. If you take these ingredients, it's very very difficult to find a proper solution to make this equation fly."[69] The emphasis upon force protection was, at least in part, a natural consequence of the perception that Western democracies have grown exceptionally sensitive to suffering casualties, and thus that combat losses would threaten the success of a military operation, especially one in which no vital interest was deemed to be at stake. This priority was manifested most notably in Kosovo in the decision to restrict NATO pilots to a minimum altitude of 15,000 feet, where they would be out of the range of small arms and hand-held antiaircraft fire. This entailed a sacrifice in precision in sorties that relied on visual identification of targets, which indeed was cited as a contributing factor in the civilian convoy bombings of April 14. As Short later acknowledged, "Under the limitations I had placed on the crew to stay above 15,000 feet . . . it was inevitable that we were going to drop a bad bomb."[70] After the convoy incident, Short amended the restrictions to allow forward control aircraft to fly as low as 5,000 feet; and strike aircraft, 8,000 feet.[71] In any event, efforts at force protection proved

---

[69] "Interviews: General Klaus Naumann," *PBS Frontline: War in Europe,* www.pbs.org /wgbh/pages/fron . . . shows/kosovo/interviews/naumann.html.
[70] "Interviews: General Michael C. Short," *PBS Frontline: War in Europe,* www.pbs.org /wgbh/pages/fron . . . shows/kosovo /interviews/short.html.
[71] Ibid.

remarkably successful: in over 38,000 sorties, NATO lost only two planes in combat, with no deaths.[72]

Another factor competing with the bombing norm in Kosovo was the doctrinal significance that many air forces continue to attach to degrading civilian morale as a means of winning wars. Paradoxically, although most military professionals have internalized the norm that civilians should not be *directly* harmed in air attacks, the notion that depriving a population of basic goods and services can be an effective source of pressure on its government remains an important part of strategic bombing doctrine. So while NATO commanders unfailingly expressed the belief that avoiding civilian casualties was a priority of the highest order, they also placed unrelenting pressure on their political superiors to allow them to "[bring] home the pain to Milosevic and his people."[73] Short reasoned: "If you wake up in the morning and you have no power to your house and no gas to your stove and the bridge you take to work is down and will be lying in the Danube for the next twenty years, I think you begin to ask, 'Hey, Slobo, what's this all about?' "[74] Consequently, when the air campaign intensified in late May, NATO increasingly targeted "dual-use" facilities such as television and radio stations, oil stocks and refineries, factories, and lines of communication, which apart from their potential military significance had an important impact upon civilian life in Yugoslavia.[75]

The awkwardness caused by the distinction between direct and indirect bombing effects was evident in the manner in which NATO approached the targeting of Yugoslavia's electrical grid. The implications of bombing electrical infrastructure had been one of the more contentious issues to emerge from the conduct of the air war in the Persian Gulf. While relatively few civilians were killed by the bombs that fell on Iraq, a much larger number—over one hundred thousand by some

---

[72] Cordesman, *The Lessons and Non-Lessons of the Air and Missile Campaign in Kosovo*, p. 24.

[73] NATO Supreme Allied Commander General Wesley Clark, quoted in John A. Tirpak, "The NATO Way of War," *Air Force Magazine* 82, no. 12 (December 1999), www.afa.org/magazine/watch/1299watch.html.

[74] Quoted in Gary Dempsey, "Destroying Serbia in Order to Save It," *CATO: Today's Commentary*, June 8, 1999, www.cato.org; shdailys/06–08–99.html.

[75] Human Rights Watch cited nine such attacks on "targets of questionable military legitimacy" as possible violations of international law, as well as criticizing NATO for the use of cluster bombs and the failure to take adequate precautions to discern the possible presence of civilians and to warn them of impending attack. Human Rights Watch, *Civilian Deaths in the NATO Air Campaign.*

estimates—eventually died as a consequence of the effects of coalition bombing, as the shutdown of the electrical grid led to the loss of water, sewer, and power services to Baghdad.[76] The debate that ensued in American military journals in the 1990s suggested that many strategists agreed with critics who saw these deaths as a serious black mark against the way the war was fought. A 1996 article in the journal of the U.S. Army War College argued that in the wake of the Gulf War, "the accepted view now is that the bombing of such targets [as the Iraqi electrical grid] has to be limited because of the certain effect on the frailest parts of a population, infants and the elderly. A good bet is that next time we will not be shutting off the lights."[77]

This bet looked like a winner for the first six weeks of the Kosovo campaign, as NATO planes conspicuously avoided striking Yugoslav electrical facilities. NATO commanders, however, pressed for permission to bomb the grid, seeing electricity as both a vitally important part of the Serb military machine and a lever which could be used to increase public discontentment with Milosevic.[78] Nevertheless, when NATO planes did eventually strike Belgrade's electrical grid in the first week of May, they did so with experimental weapons designed to short-circuit transformers without destroying them, thus potentially minimizing the long-term consequences of the power outages on the civilian population.[79] This compromise between ethical norms and doctrinal goals was threatened, however, by the lurking tension with the goal of force protection. Keeping the power out in Yugoslavia required repeated strikes against electrical stations, and such a predictable pattern of sorties against fixed targets was seen as posing an increasing threat to the safety of NATO pilots. Accordingly, U.S. Air Force officials lobbied for permission to strike the electrical grid with "hard" explosive munitions. As

[76] Harvey M. Sapolsky and Jeremy Shapiro, "Casualties, Technology, and America's Future Wars," *Parameters* 26, no. 2 (Summer 1996): 122. For a vivid description of some of the effects of the shutdown of the electrical grid on life in Baghdad, see Atkinson, *Crusade*, p. 282.

[77] Sapolsky and Shapiro, "Casualties, Technology, and America's Future Wars," p. 122. See also Thomas E. Griffith, Jr., "Strategic Air Attacks on Electrical Power: Balancing Political Consequences and Military Action," *Strategic Review* (Fall 1995): 38–46.

[78] Tirpak, "Short's View of the Air War."

[79] Bryan Bender, "U.S. 'Soft Bombs' Prove NATO's Point," *Jane's Defence Weekly*, May 10, 1999, www.janes.com/defence/features/kosovo/soft.html. When a NATO strike knocked out a major hydroelectric station in Belgrade on May 2, for example, power was restored to most of the capital within seven hours. "NATO Attack Darkens City and Areas of Serbia," *New York Times*, May 3, 1999, p. A13.

Short later expressed his position: "A soft kill is nothing more than a signal. . . . But if you're going to lose young people, you want to lose them having executed your best plan. And a soft kill—a demonstration of resolve—is not the best way to spend young people's lives."[80] NATO officials eventually acceded, and on May 24 alliance pilots destroyed critical components of the power grid serving Belgrade and central Serbia. In the sequence of decisions regarding the targeting of electrical facilities, in sum, we see the interplay among three norms that sometimes proved incompatible: the ethical norm against causing civilian casualties in bombing operations, the norm against incurring casualties to one's own forces, and the doctrinal norm that holds that making an enemy population miserable is an effective way to coerce its leaders. Much about the Kosovo campaign serves as a reminder, indeed, that even in limited wars fought for avowedly humanitarian purposes, ethical norms do not always unambiguously carry the day.

Nevertheless, the norm against bombing civilians played nothing less than a central role in the war over Yugoslavia. In fact, neither side's conduct of the war can be understood without it. NATO, of course, went to considerable lengths to avoid collateral damage and to portray the air campaign as humane and precise. Ironically, however, the norm may have been even more important to Serbia's wartime strategy. Apart from sporadic and ineffective antiaircraft fire, the Serbs avoided engaging NATO directly, opting instead for an indirect, asymmetrical strategy— one in which the bombing norm was an important weapon.[81] Knowing the attention that collateral damage would command in the media, the Serbian government exploited civilian bombing deaths to their fullest, shuttling foreign correspondents to bomb sites and in some cases manipulating scenes of carnage to heighten their impact upon reporters and television viewers.[82] The goal was not only to constrain NATO's conduct of the air war but also to stir up enough uneasiness within NATO

---

[80] "Interviews: General Michael C. Short." Not all military leaders agreed with the shift from "soft" to "hard" strikes on the electrical grid. See, e.g., "Interviews: General Charles Krulak," *PBS Frontline: War in Europe*, www.pbs.org/wgbh/pages/fron . . . shows/kosovo/interviews/krulak.html.

[81] Barry R. Posen, "The War for Kosovo: Serbia's Political-Military Strategy," *International Security* 24, no. 4 (Spring 2000): 51; and Daniel L. Byman and Matthew C. Waxman, "Kosovo and the Great Air Power Debate," *International Security* 24, no. 4 (Spring 2000): 33–34.

[82] Jim Maceda, "Battling the Serb Media Machine," *MSNBC*, April 11, 1999, www.msnbc.com/news/257880.asp?cp1=1; Cordesman, *Lessons and Non-Lessons from the Air and Missile Campaign in Kosovo*, p. 60. Cordesman reported that the Serbs "removed

countries to undermine the unity of the alliance. Nothwithstanding Milosevic's eventual capitulation on June 3, the strategy actually proved moderately successful on both counts, underscoring the extent to which the term "collateral damage" had become a fixture in the parlance of modern warfare.[83]

THE STATUS OF THE BOMBING NORM TODAY

The Gulf War and Kosovo are telling installments in a clear progression of the influence the bombing norm has had on the conduct of air warfare since World War II. This progression, however, has not been based on legal innovations, since international law on bombing has changed relatively little over that time, and then only as a reflection of evolving customary practice.[84] The essence of the change has instead been a more nebulous and gradual evolution in attitudes among states in the international community. Colonel Phillip Meilinger, former dean of the U.S. Air Force's School of Advanced Airpower Studies, remarks that "while legal efforts have generally fallen short, growing moral opinion emphasizes the protection of noncombatants."[85] This moral opinion, in turn, has both reflected and contributed to a fundamental change in the way strategic bombing has been conducted. As Table 5–1 illustrates, while bombing in some wars after World War II has been extensive, the relative number of civilian deaths has declined appreciably, reflecting a growing reluctance to put populated areas at risk. Eliot Cohen argues that "it is highly unlikely that advanced powers will again resort to the wholesale devastation of cities and towns, whether to shatter enemy morale or as a by-product of efforts to hit other target systems, such as railroad yards or factories."[86]

---

military vehicles and casualties from the scene of attacks to give the impression that they were strikes only against civilians, arranged corpses for dramatic effect, . . . altered the amount of civilian debris in the scene of such damage to improve the media effect, . . . [and] set bodies on fire before media coverage was permitted."

[83] Posen, "The War for Kosovo," pp. 66–69.

[84] Richard Wyman observed in 1984 that the rules proposed in 1923 by the Hague Commission of Jurists had become "the basis for all current regulation of air warfare." "The First Rules of Air Warfare," p. 101.

[85] Meilinger, "Winged Defense," p. 103.

[86] Eliot A. Cohen, "The Meaning and Future of Air Power," *Orbis* 39, no. 2 (Spring 1995): 200.

Table 5-1 Bomb Tonnage and Civilian Deaths in Selected Bombing Campaigns[87]

Target	Dates	Tonnage	Civilian Deaths	Deaths per Ton
Britain	1915–1918	< 300	1,413	4.71
Guernica	April 22, 1937	40.5	1,654	40.83
Britain	June–Dec. 1940	40,885	23,002	.56
Coventry	Nov. 14, 1940	533	568	1.06
Hamburg	July 24–30, 1943	5,128.12	42,600	8.03
Dresden	Feb. 13–15, 1945	7,100.5	25,000–60,000	3.52–8.45
Tokyo	Mar. 9–10, 1945	1,665	83,793	50.33
Hanoi/Haiphong	Dec. 18–29, 1972	20,000	1,623	.08
Iraq	Jan.–Feb. 1991	88,500*	approx. 3,000	.034
Yugoslavia	March–June 1999	6,303	488–527	.077–.084

*Includes tonnage dropped on Iraqi forces in the field.

Of course, one difference between the bombing campaigns in World War II and those since has been the stakes involved. All wars fought by major powers since 1945 have been, in some senses anyway, limited wars, and thus we should perhaps not be surprised that they have not been pursued as ferociously as that conflict. Nevertheless, just as the level of strategic necessity at various times during World War II fails to explain the pattern of strategic bombing in that war, neither is the trend toward more discriminate bombing since 1945 explained by the limited purposes for which more recent wars have been fought. While it may be natural to expect rules to be less stringent in World War II than in Kosovo, it is not clear why, judging from political and strategic exigencies alone, they would be any less stringent in the Korean War than in the Persian Gulf. Clearly, something other than the facile distinction between total war and limited war is at work here. I maintain that what is

[87] Parks, "Linebacker and the Law of War," p. 24; Kennett, *A History of Strategic Bombing*, p. 25; McElroy, *Morality and American Foreign Policy*, p. 163; Arkin, "How 'Smart' Was This War Really?"; "Facts & Figures," *PBS Frontline*; Human Rights Watch, *Civilian Deaths in the NATO Air Campaign*.

at work is that attitudes concerning the appropriate conduct of war have changed.

Several factors have contributed to this normative shift. Most fundamentally, of course, normative shifts reflect normative judgments, and the postwar invigoration of the bombing norm owes much to visceral moral reactions to the nightmare of World War II. Carl Kaysen writes, for example, that the dropping of the atomic bombs on Hiroshima and Nagasaki had an ironic effect: "Just when the vision of strategic air power as the supreme instrument of war became feasible in principle, it became impossible in practice. One reason, of course, was the likelihood of retaliatory response in kind. But an even deeper restraint was the wide abhorrence of the idea of unlimited destruction."[88] The atomic bombings, along with the conventional bombings of scores of other cities, actually delivered on Douhet's vision of urban destruction to which so many air power theorists had subscribed, but they exposed it as truly horrible. While unrestricted city bombing remained an awesomely destructive means of warfare, in the postwar world it seemed to offend, more than it had previously, people's "sense of what is right." This moral sense, as I have argued, provided the seed from which the bombing norm grew in the war's aftermath. Kaysen writes, "While the exigencies of World War II (as seen by the leading participants) eroded the moral constraints on the deliberate attack on noncombatants, the advent of the potential for limitless destruction appears to have restored them."[89]

Of course, if moral disapprobation alone were sufficient to establish a strong norm, then such a norm would have emerged in the 1920s and 1930s, when the prospect of apocalyptic bombing generated large and vocal disarmament movements in Britain and elsewhere. Along with revealing the horrors of bombing, however, World War II also revealed its limitations. The most ambitious claims of the interwar air advocates, including the moral argument that city bombing could make wars more humane, were exposed as false. The technological uncertainty of the interwar era was replaced by a hard and terrible knowledge of what bombing could and could not do. What it could do was level a city and kill scores of thousands of people in the space of a few minutes. What it could not do was make wars short and humane—or even win wars out-

---

[88] Carl Kaysen, "The Ultimate Bombing," *Technology Review* 98, no. 6 (Aug./Sept. 1995): 66.

[89] Ibid.

right. As Max Hastings writes of the Korean War, "Bombing could inflict a catastrophe upon a society without defeating it."[90] While the overall effectiveness of strategic bombing in World War II is still hotly debated, there is a consensus that its effect on enemy *civilian morale* had been dramatically oversold.[91] And in spite of enduring interest among air power advocates in the impact of bombing on morale, there has been little evidence in post–World War II experience that imposing even huge hardships on a civilian population is likely to contribute to victory in and of itself.[92] To the extent that this lesson is taken to heart, it diminishes the incentive to strike directly at civilians and therefore removes a potentially insuperable strategic obstacle to the establishment of a strong bombing norm.

The norm has also been aided by technological advances of two sorts. The first is what has been called "the CNN factor": the revolution in broadcast technology that has brought wars into living rooms halfway across the globe in real time. While those who died in Dresden, Coventry, and Tokyo were likely to remain abstract statistics to people in countries thousands of miles away, images of bodies being removed from the Al Firdos bunker were beamed into American homes the next morning. One effect has been to give faces to the victims of war and heighten sympathy for their suffering. Another, arguably just as important, has been to subject the conduct of military operations to far more intense scrutiny than in the past, thereby enhancing the incentives to fight wars cleanly and with a minimum of extraneous death and destruction. Both of these effects serve to reinforce the norm against bombing civilians.

The second crucial technological advance has been in the technology of bombing itself, specifically in the increasing precision that it has

---

[90] Hastings, *The Korean War*, p. 268.

[91] Indeed, both the U.S. and British Bombing Surveys reached this conclusion after World War II. Biddle, "British and American Approaches to Strategic Bombing," p. 126. See also Paskins and Dockrill, *The Ethics of War*, pp. 45–48; and Pape, *Bombing to Win*, chaps. 3, 4.

[92] This theme is treated extensively in Pape, *Bombing to Win*. Some airpower proponents have claimed, on the contrary, that Milosevic's capitulation in the Kosovo conflict owed much to the impact on morale of raids against dual-use infrastructure targets in Belgrade. See, e.g., interviews with Short and Clark at *PBS Frontline: War in Europe*. Others have questioned this interpretation, arguing that factors such as waning Russian support for the Serb cause and the prospect of a NATO ground invasion were likely far more important. See, e.g., interviews with Krulak and Ivo Daalder at *PBS Frontline: War in Europe*; Byman and Waxman, "Kosovo and the Great Air Power Debate"; and Posen, "The War for Kosovo."

allowed. After all, even if belligerents do not wish to bomb civilians, if they are incapable of missing them without forgoing bombing altogether it will be difficult for a strong norm to develop. Robert Tucker writes that "technology cannot make men bad, but it may surely give rise to circumstances in which it is increasingly difficult to be good."[93] This is an apt description of the state of affairs in the decades prior to World War II, when advances in technology made bombing dramatically more destructive without making it very precise. It also seems possible, however, that Tucker's dynamic might sometimes work in the opposite direction, making it easier to be good. This, I argue, is what has happened in the decades since World War II. It is surely no coincidence that the rise of the postwar bombing norm has been accompanied, *pari passu*, by an evolving technology that makes the accurate bombing of specific targets increasingly feasible. Clearly, as Tami Davis Biddle notes, the Gulf War was a watershed event in this regard:

> The most effective aerial bombing campaign in history was also the most discriminate. The coalition's focus on specific military targets, together with technology permitting unprecedented accuracy of weapon delivery, effectively precluded the kind of large-scale civilian fatalities that characterized the bombing campaigns of World War II. . . . These examples suggest at least the possibility of a broader trend with important ramifications for the law of aerial warfare. It may be that in future warfare, technology could produce a convergence between ethics and efficiency by permitting precise engagement of narrowly defined military targets. . . . If the most useful targets are also the most discriminate targets, and if technology makes discrimination possible, then the future may see behavior different than that which has characterized aerial warfare through the early part of this century.[94]

What Biddle describes as a future trend has in fact been at work for some time. Moreover, better technology has not only removed an obstacle to the growth of the bombing norm, it has become a contributing factor in its growth. In other words, by making it easier to "be good," as Tucker puts it, technology has also created *pressure* to be good by removing a possible excuse for being bad. Nor is this an extremely recent development. W. Hays Parks writes that several delegates to the 1974–77

---

[93] Quoted in Stanley Hoffman, *Duties beyond Borders* (Syracuse: Syracuse University Press, 1981), p. 47.

[94] Biddle, "Air Power," pp. 158–59.

Geneva Conference on the law of war "suggested that, with the advent of precision-guided munitions . . . the use of any other weapon which results in collateral damage or injury or death to civilians will constitute a war crime."[95] The proposal failed, but its logic is implicit in almost any consideration of strategic bombing in modern warfare. Belligerents in 1943 may have been excused for attacking a military target by razing the city in which it was located, but the United States would have been universally condemned had it done the same thing in Baghdad in 1991 or Belgrade in 1999. Modern technology, in effect, has considerably closed the gap between the "ought" and the "can," making the ought more compelling.

This raises the critical question of how a revitalized bombing norm relates to the distribution of power in the international system. While many states possess air forces, the difference in capabilities between a first-rate and a second-rate air force, as the Gulf War proved, can be vast. Few nations have state-of-the-art air power, primarily because it does not come cheap. Eliot Cohen writes, "Modern aircraft have become increasingly expensive, hence increasingly few in number: at $30 million or more apiece, the warplane is one of the most costly items a government can think of purchasing. The age of cheap manned aircraft is long since over."[96] While even equipment that is primitive by today's standards is immensely more accurate than that used in World War II, it cannot approach the precision of the sophisticated technology on display in Kosovo, especially when challenged by enemy fighters or antiaircraft artillery. A strong international bombing norm might serve to make the gap between the technological haves and have-nots even wider. If, for example, the United States bombs with precision because a) it ought to, and b) it can, and if this precedent further strengthens the understanding that this is the proper way to conduct aerial warfare, where does this leave states that rely on less sophisticated technology incapable of this degree of precision? Already at a material disadvantage, they are placed at a normative disadvantage as well, forced to choose between forgoing a potentially effective means of warfare or incurring the costs associated with violating an important international norm.

It follows from this that it is in the interests of states with advanced military capabilities to cultivate as exacting a norm against the bombing of civilians as they feel they are able to adhere to. Judged in this light, the

---

[95] Parks, "Conventional Aerial Bombing and the Law of War," p. 98.
[96] Cohen, "The Meaning and Future of Air Power," p. 193.

public emphasis placed on a "clean" air campaign by United States officials during recent conflicts takes on an added dimension. Not only did
the U.S. stance help to shield its actions from international criticism, it
also served to reinforce the idea that air war should be waged as discriminately as possible. For example, when an otherwise impotent Iraq
launched Scud missiles against targets in Saudi Arabia and Israel in an
attempt to fracture the coalition, it was criticized not only for its aggression against a neutral state (Israel) but also for the indiscriminate nature
of the Scud attacks. Lt. Gen. Charles Horner, the CENTCOM air component commander, condemned the Scud as "a lousy weapon, a terror
weapon."[97] Relative to the technology available to the coalition, this was
true. But given overwhelming coalition air superiority, it was one of the
only weapons Saddam Hussein had at his disposal, and he had a valid
strategic rationale for using it. Nevertheless, compared to the more precise coalition bombing, the Scud attacks stood out as wanton and reck-
less, reinforcing Saddam's status as an international pariah. With regard
to the consequences of the bombing norm for strong states, therefore,
the advance of technology has reversed the situation that prevailed in
the first half of the twentieth century, when better technology generally
meant more destructive capability, and normative restrictions on bombing worked to the detriment of the great powers. The bombing norm
may, therefore, be in the midst of a century-long transformation from a
weak convention-dependent norm with ambiguous implications for the
interests of strong states to a stronger power-maintenance norm that
reinforces their position in the international system. Ironically, the very
forces that thwarted efforts to keep the bombing genie in the bottle in
the early 1900s—great power interests and technological innovation—
may now point the way toward greater restraint in aerial warfare.

UNINTENDED EFFECTS AND CAVEATS

Of course, as both the Gulf War and Kosovo experiences show, there
are some ways in which the heightened bombing norm can lead to
undesirable consequences, even for the strong states that apparently
stand to benefit the most from it. First, a strict norm against the bombing of civilians will by definition allow states less flexibility in the conduct

---

[97] Quoted in David A. Fulghum, "Desert Storm Highlights Need for Rapid Tactical Intelligence," *Aviation Week and Space Technology*, February 11, 1991, p. 18.

of military operations. While this reduction of options will generally work to the advantage of militarily capable states who can devise more than one way of accomplishing an objective (including the use of precision bombing), circumstances may arise in which the only way to achieve desired goals is to risk running afoul of normative sensibilities. This problem may, moreover, be compounded when a belligerent uses the bombing norm strategically to handcuff a more powerful foe, as both Iraq and Serbia did when confronting the air power of the United States and its allies. This is not simply a strategic problem for strong states; it can be a humanitarian problem, as well, since it creates perverse incentives to accentuate the suffering of innocent people. Beyond seeking political gains from civilian deaths in Kosovo, for example, the Serbs were willing (as both the North Vietnamese and the Iraqis had been previously) to expose civilians to danger by using them as shields to protect military targets from attack—and in one particularly disturbing case, to massacre civilian survivors of a NATO bombing raid in order to increase the "body count" for propaganda purposes.[98] Such practices are troubling manifestations of the bombing norm indeed.

A second, and related, adverse effect is that heightened sensitivity to civilian casualties greatly decreases the margin for error in bombing operations, especially when combined with the presence of electronic media on the modern battlefield. After all, even the most sophisticated technology is far from infallible, especially amidst the extreme stress and confusion of wartime. Eliot Cohen comments that, precision technology notwithstanding, "As television makes military blunders and accidents ever more evident, airmen will find themselves trying to explain away civilian suffering that previous generations would have accepted as the regrettable but inevitable price of military action."[99] This is a particular danger if the sophistication of the available weapons leads officials to make inflated public claims about the precision with which bombing can be carried out. In the Gulf War, for example, the incessant public emphasis on avoiding civilian casualties only added to the negative impact of the Al Firdos bombing, when, as one commentator puts it,

[98] Human Rights Watch, *Civilian Deaths in the NATO Air Campaign*, especially Appendix A, "Incidents Involving Civilian Deaths in Operation Allied Force"; Human Rights Watch, "Kosovo Human Rights Flash #33: Civilians at Risk by Yugoslav Use of Civilian Property for Military Purposes," April 30, 1999, www.hrw.org/hrw/campaigns/kosovo98/flash5.shtml.

[99] Cohen, "The Meaning and Future of Air Power," p. 200.

"the images of charred bodies . . . spoiled the administration's effort to portray the war as bloodless."[100] Even if expectations remain more realistic, a heightened norm surely increases the operational requirements for the conduct of successful bombing campaigns, placing new demands on planning and intelligence as well as on the pilots themselves. Success, after all, begets expectations of more success, and the "friction" present in all military operations assures that some failure is inevitable. It is in this sense that Rick Atkinson writes about the Gulf War that "the Air Force fell victim to its own precision."[101] The ironic effect was that "public debate over civilian casualties escalated far out of proportion to physical reality."[102]

These dangers aside, a couple of caveats are in order before celebrating the humanitarian benefits of a revitalized bombing norm. First, while war, especially intrastate war, has been a common phenomenon in the last half-century, strategic bombing has been a relatively rare feature of these wars. Consequently, conclusions about the conduct of bombing since World War II must be drawn from a small set of cases. Moreover, these cases involve only a few nations, the most frequent being the United States. By the same token, however, this is not entirely inappropriate. Bombing has always been a mode of warfare predominantly limited to a relatively small number of powerful states. The cases from the post–World War II experience, in that sense, are not necessarily aberrations. Moreover, for some of the reasons discussed in Chapter 2, the practices of powerful states near the core of international society will tend to set a disproportionately strong precedent on the formation and definition of norms in the international system. Therefore, it is not necessary to dismiss apparently clear trends in the conduct of bombing simply because they are defined by only a few cases.

Second, it could be objected that the normative limits on bombing discussed here are in fact not universal but rather apply only to a few exceptional states—the United States and a handful of other Western democracies.[103] It could be argued, for example, that the Soviet air cam-

---

[100] Atkinson, *Crusade*, p. 287. Eliot Cohen argues that the "most dangerous legacy" of the Gulf War is "the fantasy of the near-bloodless use of force." Eliot A. Cohen, "The Mystique of U.S. Air Power," *Foreign Affairs* 73, no. 1 (Jan./Feb. 1994): 120.

[101] Atkinson, *Crusade*, p. 293.

[102] William M. Arkin, "Baghdad: The Urban Sanctuary in Desert Storm?" *Airpower Journal* 11, no. 1 (Spring 1997): 6.

[103] Certainly, evidence from the Kosovo experience suggests that the European member-states of NATO are at least as strongly committed to the bombing norm as the United

paign against Mujahedin rebels in the war in Afghanistan and the Russian air campaigns in Chechnya in 1994–1995 and 1999–2000, all of which resulted in extensive civilian casualties, show that the power of the bombing norm to constrain states is severely limited.[104] There is little doubt that these cases represent failures of the bombing norm. Moreover, it is possible that some norms might exert a stronger influence on some states than others. This is because international sanctions are only one means by which normative pressure can be brought to bear. Domestic public opinion may sometimes also play a role, as may the individual consciences of state officials.[105] As we have seen, this does not mean that norms exercise no influence on states in which these factors are less important.[106] Still, even international pressures can affect different states in different ways at different times, depending upon their status in international society. The effectiveness of the norm in the Soviet-Afghan War was probably diminished by the fact that the Soviets had already been roundly condemned by much of the international community for their continuing presence in Afghanistan, so they faced few additional costs for bombing aggressively in an attempt to deprive the Mujahedin of bases of support. The bombings in Chechnya—and similar attacks on villages by the governments of Sierra Leone and Sudan in civil wars in those countries—also raise the question of what effect the norm has in an internal, rather than an interstate, war.[107] The underlying moral rationale—preventing unnecessary civilian suffering—would remain the

States. See, e.g., "Interviews: General Michael C. Short"; "Interviews: General Wesley Clark"; and Posen, "The War for Kosovo," p. 51.

[104] On the bombing of Afghan villages and resulting civilian casualties, see Pape, *Bombing to Win*, p. 353; David C. Isby, *War in a Distant Country: Afghanistan: Invasion and Resistance* (London: Arms and Armour Press, 1989), pp. 56, 66; and Jeri Lauber and Barnett R. Rubin, *"A Nation is Dying": Afghanistan under the Soviets, 1979–87* (Evanston, Ill.: Northwestern University Press, 1988), pp. 10–17. On Chechnya, see Human Rights Watch, *"No Happiness Remains": Civilian Killings, Pillage, and Rape in Alkhan-Yurt, Chechnya*, www.hrw.org/reports/2000/russia_chechnya2/; "New Russian Attacks Batter Civilians in Chechnya," Human Rights Watch Press Release, November 10, 1999, www.hrw.org/hrw/press/1999/nov/chech1110.htm; "Chechnya: Civilian Casualties in Urus-Martan and Novy Sharoi," Human Rights Watch Press Release, November 9, 1999, www.hrw.org/hrw/press/1999/nov/chech1109.htm; and Benjamin S. Lambeth, "Russia's Air War in Chechnya," *Studies in Conflict and Terrorism* 19 (1996), 374.

[105] McElroy, *Morality and American Foreign Policy*, chap. 2.

[106] Chapters 2, 3, supra.

[107] "Sierra Leone Government Bombing Causes Civilian Deaths," Human Rights Watch Press Release, July 12, 2000, www.hrw.org/press/2000/07/s10711.htm; "Sudan," *Human Rights Watch World Report 1999*, www.hrw.org/hrw/worldreport99/africa/sudan.html.

same, but it would be applied in a different political context. NATO's intervention on behalf of Kosovo notwithstanding, the principle of sovereignty remains a powerful shield for states resisting scrutiny of the treatment of their own citizens.[108] While this surely would not insulate offending states from international criticism, it is likely to dampen the tangible political consequences of violating the norm.[109] In any case, troubling episodes in Afghanistan, Chechnya, and elsewhere provide reasons to temper optimism about bombing trends in recent decades.

Finally, it must be acknowledged that even very precise bombing can exact a terrible toll on a civilian population. Casualties aside, NATO bombing set Yugoslav society back many years, inflicting an estimated $30 billion in damage to the economy, driving the unemployment rate toward 50 percent, and forcing down annual per capita income to less than $1,000.[110] The bombing campaign in the Gulf War, while restrained in many ways, brought about a humanitarian catastrophe, thanks to the long-term effects of damage to electrical and industrial infrastructure. As one critic wrote, "With this kind of strategy in use, the traditional definition of collateral damage is inadequate to calculate the suffering that war imposes on civilians."[111] In some cases, recognition of this fact can itself help to refine the norm so that future air campaigns may be more likely to avoid incurring such effects. Still, as NATO attacks on electrical and other dual-use facilities in Yugoslavia shows, progress of this sort often follows a pattern of "two steps forward, one step back." Indeed, as long as strategists see the potential for deriving military gain from civilian suffering, however attenuated, the goal of protecting civilians from the effects of war will be forced to compete with the perceived requirements of military effectiveness.

Nevertheless, it cannot be denied that the normative standards for

---

[108] There is no such blind spot in international law; Protocol II to the Geneva Convention of 1949—to which Russia is a signatory—makes the standards for the protection of noncombatants in international wars applicable to internal armed conflicts, as well. Frederic L. Kirgis, "Russian Use of Force in Grozny," *ASIL Insight*, December 1999, www.asil.org/insigh39.htm.

[109] So, for example, while a State Department spokesman noted that the United States was "extremely concerned about the indiscriminate use of force" in Chechnya and warned of "damage to Russia's international reputation," he also expressed U.S. support for "Russia's right to defend its sovereignty and territorial integrity." Robyn Dixon, "Russia Bombs Cities, Convoys," *Los Angeles Times*, November 9, 1999. See also Ian Black, "Patten's Message to Russia," *The Guardian* (London), March 1, 2000, p. 17.

[110] Posen, "The War for Kosovo," p. 80; Dempsey, "Destroying Serbia in Order to Save It."

[111] George A. Lopez, "The Gulf War: Not So Clean," *Bulletin of the Atomic Scientists* (September 1991): 35.

strategic bombing have changed markedly since the Second World War, or that these standards have had an increasingly significant impact upon the way in which wars have been fought by major powers. Of course, no norm governing the use of force, any more than international law, can ever stray far from the fundamental reality that, in the words of one U.S. Army lawyer, "The business of the military in war is killing people and breaking things."[112] Nevertheless, military action has almost always been subject to rules, both formal and informal, and those rules—no less than purely strategic considerations—are crucial to understanding the manner in which force is ultimately used.

[112] Colonel Zane Finkelstein, quoted in Parks, "Linebacker and the Law of War," p. 26.

CHAPTER 6

The Limits of International Ethics

> Politics will, to the end of history, be an area where conscience
> and power meet, where the ethical and coercive factors of
> human life will interpenetrate and work out their tentative and
> uneasy compromises.
>
> Reinhold Neibuhr, *Moral Man and Immoral Society*

In the preceding chapters, I have shown how norms governing the use
of force can serve as meaningful constraints upon states in the international system. While norms against the bombing of noncombatants and
the assassination of foreign leaders have their foundations in moral principles, they derive much of their normative force, as well as their power
to command adherence, from understandings held in common
throughout international society. Because of the interest most states
have in the practices and institutions that constitute international society, as well as the prospect of sanctions for rule-breakers, norms affect
the policy calculus of states in concrete terms. In this way, ethical norms
mediate between abstract moral principles and state action through the
structure of the international system, thereby providing a link between
the disciplinary categories of international ethics and international relations theory, as described in Chapter 1.

It is possible, however, that this conclusion will prove unsatisfying to
some students of international ethics. While my analysis views interna-

tional norms as important sources of ethical restraint, it also remains grounded to a large extent in state power and the self-interested behavior of state actors. As such, it pays less attention to behavior based upon altruism and self-sacrifice, qualities that are more commonly associated with ethics. This chapter, then, addresses some possible objections to the account of ethical norms and structural ethics set forth so far. First, returning to the realist proposition that altruistic action is out of place in international politics, I seek to identify the source of obstacles to international altruism in the institutional position of national leaders. The fact that states must act through individuals morally accountable to a national constituency, I argue, has important implications for both international ethics and structural international relations theory. I then respond to possible objections that the view of international ethics expressed in this book retains too tenuous a connection to moral imperatives and altruistic motives—in short, that it is too watered-down to deserve the designation of "ethics" at all. Finally, I conclude with a few thoughts on the importance of the normative context of international politics and the challenges inherent in studying it.

THE "STATESMAN'S DUTY" AND THE ETHICS OF ALTRUISM

Perhaps the most fundamental distinction between international and interpersonal ethics is that the main actors in the international sphere are not autonomous individuals but collective bodies—primarily states. Although the notion of a state is a highly abstract and contested one, it is common for theorists, policy professionals, and casual observers of international politics alike to speak of states in anthropomorphic terms— states are said to "act," "react," "decide," even "think" and "feel" in a manner roughly congruous to individuals.[1] This anthropomorphism reflects a paradox. As Arnold Wolfers explains, "Because states are abstractions, or at best fictitious personalities, it is not the state that decides and acts but always individuals, though they be statesmen."[2] Precisely because these individuals *are* "statesmen," however, their decisions and actions are undertaken in a considerably different context.[3] First

[1] Indeed, rationalist theory explicitly relies on the assumption that states can be thought of in these terms.

[2] Arnold Wolfers, *Discord and Collaboration: Essays on International Politics* (Baltimore: Johns Hopkins University Press, 1962), p. 48.

[3] The term "statesman" is, of course, often considered anachronistic today, at least partly because of its gender-specificity. Nevertheless, it captures better than any alternative

The Limits of International Ethics

and foremost, in their role as statesmen they act not for themselves but
for others—the national constituency to which they owe an institutional
duty. In George Kennan's words, statesmen are agents, not principals,
and therefore are not perfectly free to act in accordance with their personal convictions if these might compromise the interests of the state.[4]
"No more than the attorney vis-à-vis the client," Kennan writes, "nor the
doctor vis-à-vis the patient, can government attempt to insert itself into
the consciences of those whose interests it represents."[5]

Indeed, it is common to find statesmen explaining policy decisions in
precisely these terms. We saw in Chapter 4 that Roosevelt, while apparently genuinely morally troubled by the prospect of bombing civilians in
the years prior to World War II, set aside these compunctions to become
a forceful advocate of city bombing upon the U.S. entry into the war.
Similarly, Secretary of War Henry Stimson explained in connection with
the decision to drop the atom bomb on Japan: "No man, *in our position
and subject to our responsibilities*, holding in his hand a weapon of such possibilities . . . could have failed to use it."[6] Also to the point is this recollection of former Secretary of State Dean Acheson:

> Nor did [morality] bear upon the decision of those called upon to
> advise the President in 1949 whether and with what degree of urgency
> to press the attempt to produce a thermonuclear weapon. A respected
> colleague advised me that it would be better that our nation and
> people should perish rather than be a party to a course so evil as pro-
> ducing that weapon. I told him that on the Day of Judgment his view
> might be confirmed and that he was free to go forth and preach the
> necessity for salvation. It was not, however, a view which I could enter-
> tain as a public servant.[7]

The point is stated most bluntly by German author Johannes Haller,
who is quoted by Reinhold Niebuhr in his study *Moral Man and Immoral
Society*: "No state has ever entered into a treaty for any other reason than

---

the relationship that is central to my argument in this chapter—one who not only acts on
behalf of the state but also somehow embodies the interests of the state in the international arena. I will therefore use the term in this chapter, while acknowledging its limitations and trying to ameliorate them through the use of gender-neutral pronouns.

[4] George F. Kennan, "Morality and Foreign Policy," *Foreign Affairs* 64, no. 2 (Winter
1985/1986):206.

[5] Ibid.

[6] Quoted in Walzer, *Just and Unjust Wars*, p. 267 (emphasis added).

[7] Quoted in Richard Wasserstrom, "On the Morality of War," in *War, Morality, and the
Military Profession*, p. 300.

self-interest. A statesman who has any other motive would deserve to be hung."[8]

Ethical Implications

It is easy to see how what I will call the "statesman's duty" problem makes altruism and self-sacrifice an unlikely model for relations between states. Even an extremely scrupulous statesman with a highly developed moral sense would find it difficult to commit his or her state to behave altruistically in the international arena, since to do so would entail a breach of the duty owed to the state—and the state's citizens—in whose name and on whose behalf the action was undertaken. As a result, even a world of states led by just and beneficent individuals would tend to be characterized by self-regarding behavior.[9] There are two ironies at work here. First, the self-interested behavior of states can actually be based upon personal self-sacrifice on the part of statesmen, to the extent that they are required to subordinate their own moral preferences to the interests of the state. In this sense, a statesman committing the state to sacrifice a measure of its welfare (whether in the form of security, wealth, reputation, or what have you) without receiving some benefit in return may paradoxically be seen as acting selfishly. Acheson's disdainful response to his colleague's moral qualms over the hydrogen bomb, for example, conveys a clear sense that he considered the colleague's stance to be self-indulgent, if not self-righteous.[10] Herbert Butterfield puts the matter this way: "If an individual consents to make self-sacrifice—even to face martyrdom before a foreign invader—it is not clear that he has a socially recognizable right to offer the same sacrifice on behalf of all his fellow-citizens or to impose such self-abnegation on the rest of his society."[11]

The second irony is that this institutional dynamic may sometimes

---

[8] Quoted in Reinhold Niebuhr, *Moral Man and Immoral Society: A Study in Ethics and Politics* (New York: Charles Scribner's Sons, 1932), p. 84.

[9] Although, it should be noted, it need not necessarily be characterized by conflict, as neorealists would assert. The question of whether self-interest inevitably leads to conflict rather than cooperation is of course exactly what is at stake here and will be dealt with in some detail below.

[10] Of course, others may find in Acheson's response itself no small measure of self-righteousness.

[11] Quoted in Jack Donnolly, "Twentieth-Century Realism," in *Traditions of International Ethics,* ed. Terry Nardin and David R. Mapel (Cambridge: Cambridge University Press, 1992), p. 105.

lead to selfish state behavior even in cases in which both the statesman *and* his or her constituents would prefer to behave altruistically. This is because the statesman's duty requires deference not simply to the collective moral judgment of the public at a given time but also, perhaps even more so, to the interests of the state itself as an autonomous (albeit abstract) entity. Certain constructions of state interests may, for example, be internalized in institutions and beyond the reach of the moral concerns of both statesman and constituency; or the statesman may be concerned that even a publicly popular beneficent action may be prejudicial to the interests of the state over time. In this way, the notion of state interests takes on a vitality of its own independent of public opinion and shapes the range of options available to the statesman in given circumstances.

As a result, the ethical landscape of statesmen (and therefore of states) is defined by a moral hierarchy of individuals based *primarily* not upon need, merit, or other characteristics that often determine interpersonal moral obligations, but upon national status, with preference given to those to whom an institutional duty is owed. In ethical terms, in other words, fellow citizens count more than foreigners to the statesman *in his or her role as statesman,* whether or not they do so in his or her capacity as a private individual. This preference, in turn, can make it difficult to act upon a priori moral imperatives premised upon the moral equality of individuals. Consider, for example, the principle of noncombatant immunity and the practice of strategic bombing. As Walzer repeatedly points out in *Just and Unjust Wars,* the essence of the principle is that noncombatants are to be protected *even if* this increases the risks to combatants or the burden on a belligerent state. In practice, however, the noncombatants at issue are usually citizens of another country (and an enemy country at that), while the soldiers in question are not only fellow countrymen but fellow countrymen who have, in a real sense, placed their lives at the disposal of the state. The unenviable but ineluctable question for a statesman under such circumstances then is, as Tami Davis Biddle puts it, "How does one weigh the lives of one's own soldiers against the lives of enemy civilians?"[12] Debates over the decision to drop the atomic bombs on Japan in 1945 often center upon just this question, with crucial importance being assigned to competing—and widely varying—estimates of the number of American troops that would have been

[12] Biddle, "Air Power," p. 156.

killed in a conventional invasion of Japan.[13] In terms of the strict application of noncombatant immunity, of course, this would be somewhat beside the point because, as Walzer argues, "the deliberate slaughter of innocent men and women cannot be justified simply because it saves the lives of other men and women."[14] But surely for a commander in chief it is never as easy as this, for the lives saved are not just any lives but lives entrusted to him or her under dire circumstances. We do not expect a leader in such a situation to be blind to national distinctions.

Of course, it does not follow that acts of true national altruism or self-sacrifice are impossible or unheard of, or that statesmen are not bound to consider ethical duties other than those to their national constituencies. Few would go as far, for example, as the World War II veteran who wrote in defense of the atomic bombings: "Not one American life was lost in an invasion. . . . Nothing else is of any consequence whatsoever."[15] Moreover, because statesmen are also autonomous human beings, they can never entirely shed the influence of their consciences; nor would most people wish them to. Still, the institutional situation of those who act on behalf of states provides an important constraint on action that tends to limit the ethical possibilities of international politics. Consequently, the problem of the statesman's duty illustrates the difficulty in assessing ethics in the international sphere according to a strict criterion of altruism or abnegation. Instead, actions are understood most reliably in terms of incentives and disincentives facing self-interested states. Whether the subject is foreign aid, motives for going to war, or norms restricting the use of force within war, states respond more readily to carrots and sticks than to more abstract formulations of moral duty. As I have repeatedly argued, however, this need not represent a dead end for international ethics, since state interests can be served through cooperative practices as well as through conflict. While the self-regarding nature of states may therefore make altruism and self-denial an unrealistic standard for ethical judgment in international politics, it is entirely compatible with a different ethical model—one premised upon shared stakes in an international society and characterized by an ethic of reciprocity and mutual restraint.

[13] See, e.g., Bernstein, "The Atomic Bombings Reconsidered"; and Paul Fussell, "Thank God for the Atom Bomb" and "An Exchange of Views," in Paul Fussell, *Thank God for the Atom Bomb and Other Essays* (New York: Summit Books, 1988).

[14] Walzer, *Just and Unjust Wars*, p. 262.

[15] Venlo Wolfsohn, "Letters," *Washington Post*, July 18, 1995, p. A20.

Theoretical Implications

The preceding analysis also has important implications for international relations theory. In one form or another, the statesman's duty problem has long been a central tenet of realist thought, and is often cited as one reason why ethical judgment is inappropriate to international politics.[16] In some versions of realism, and consistently in neorealism, however, the problem is conflated with what has been called "the anarchy problematic": Because states exist in an environment in which there is no supreme authority to enforce rights and settle disputes, they are forced to look out for themselves. As a result, as Robert Art and Kenneth Waltz argue, "States in anarchy cannot afford to be moral. The possibility of moral behavior rests upon the existence of an effective government that can deter and punish illegal actions. . . . The preconditions for morality are absent in international politics. Every state, as a consequence, has to be prepared to do what is necessary for its interests as it defines them. Anarchy is the realm where all can, and many do, play 'dirty pool.' "[17] While adherents of other varieties of realism are less stark in both their description of anarchy and its implications for international ethics, the passage from Art and Waltz provides a typical expression of the neorealist formulation of the problem: the structural fact of anarchy in the international system constrains states (or statesmen) in such a way as to make the pursuit of ethical goals difficult or impossible.[18]

Certainly, a nexus exists between the statesman's duty problem and the neorealist conception of anarchy as a structural constraint on international ethics. Both seek to explain why states adopt consistently self-serving foreign policies. A neorealist would in fact likely portray the

---

[16] See, e.g., Kennan, "Morality and Foreign Policy," pp. 205–7.

[17] Robert J. Art and Kenneth N. Waltz, "Technology, Strategy, and the Uses of Force," in *The Use of Force*, p. 6.

[18] More typical of traditional (pre-Waltzian) realism is the less drastic conclusion that anarchy makes ethical action more difficult, but not impossible, and frustrates attempts to judge foreign policy by the same moral criteria as interpersonal relations. The following 1951 passage by Georg Schwarzenberger is typical of this position: "The cleavage between individual morality and international morality corresponds to the difference between social relations in a community and those in a society bordering on anarchy." Quoted in Donnolly, "Twentieth-Century Realism," p. 95. This position is also central to Martin Wight's influential 1966 essay "Why Is There No International Theory?" in *Diplomatic Investigations* ed. Butterfield and Wight. For an extremely useful survey of realist and neorealist thought on international ethics, see Donnolly, "Twentieth-Century Realism."

institutional pressures upon statesmen to act in the interests of the state simply as internal manifestations of the anarchy problematic. Nevertheless, there are significant distinctions between the two ideas that are important to the theoretical debate over norms and ethics. These distinctions, in turn, reflect differences between the rationalist underpinnings of the neorealist project and a more interpretivist or constructivist approach.[19] As noted in Chapter 1, neorealist theory takes structural constraints to be rigid and unchanging, existing independent of and theoretically prior to interactions between actors in the system. Most fundamentally, then, while neorealism sees state egoism as a product of the anarchical structure of the international system, the statesman's duty approach would follow constructivism in suggesting that the causal dynamic may best be understood as running in the other direction. In other words, the anarchical structure of the international system, instead of simply constraining state actors, is itself a *product* of state action. Moreover, contrary to neorealist theory, anarchy is less a material fact than an intersubjective construction defined by practices and understandings based on the institutional duties of statesmen to their constituencies. While still viewing anarchy as part of the structure of the international system, this approach employs a far more fluid notion of structure than does neorealist theory in that it recognizes the importance of ideational constructs in shaping the environment in which agents such as states interact.

This has two implications for norms and international ethics. First, because the normative content of anarchy is defined by statesmen's understandings of their institutional circumstances rather than any immutable material fact, we should be skeptical of the neorealist claim that anarchy inevitably leads states into conflict with one another.[20] As Alexander Wendt puts it, "Anarchy as such is not the structural cause of anything."[21] While Wendt argues that state egoism itself is a construction, for our purposes here it is not necessary to transcend egoism in

---

[19] This section draws heavily upon the constructivist critique of "the anarchy problematic," as expressed most prominently by Alexander Wendt and David Dessler. See, e.g., Wendt, "The Agent-Structure Problem in International Relations Theory"; Wendt, "Anarchy Is What States Make of It"; and Dessler, "What's at Stake in the Agent-Structure Debate?"

[20] This key contention of neorealism has been the target of many broadsides from constructivist scholars. See especially Wendt's critiques in "Anarchy Is What States Make of It" and "Collective Identity Formation and the International State."

[21] Wendt, "Constructing International Politics," pp.77–78.

order to refute neorealism. We may consider, for example, Barry Buzan's argument that even the logic of self-interest can as easily lead to the creation of an international society—complete with rules, norms, and cooperative institutions—as to a dog-eat-dog world of Hobbesian realism.[22] Drawing on work in the English School tradition, Buzan identifies two views concerning the nature and origins of international society: the "civilizational" view, which emphasizes a sense of shared history and culture; and the "functional" view, which places less stock in cultural prerequisites than in the "consciously organizational" desires of states to derive the benefits of society.[23] While Buzan holds that international societies in fact exhibit characteristics of both views, he is especially interested in examining the implications of the functional view in order to demonstrate that, contrary to neorealism, states in anarchy can move beyond fundamental self-help measures such as the balance of power. Without denying that states under conditions of "immature anarchy" may constantly resort to force to ensure their security, he crafts a persuasive argument that such states would nevertheless find themselves pressured to develop some arrangements for the regulation of their dealings with one another. In fact, the same uncertainty and insecurity that drive conflict in anarchy will, according to Buzan, "virtually force the eventual development of at least a few basic elements of international society. . . . Units that have no choice but to interact with each other on a regular, long-term basis, and that begin to accept each other as essentially similar types of sociopolitical organization, will be hard put to avoid creating some mechanisms for dealing with each other peacefully."[24] Therefore, Buzan maintains, "The development of international society can be seen as a rational long-term response to the existence of an increasingly dense and interactive international system."[25] This argument is a valuable complement to a study of ethical norms because it shows how a common interest in rules and institutions need not stem from idealistic impulses but can instead be a perfectly plausible outcome from the starting assumptions of rational and egoistic states under anarchy.

The second implication of the constructivist logic inherent in the statesman's duty position rests on the recursive nature of the relationship between agents and structures. While structures such as anarchy do

---

[22] Buzan, "From International System to International Society."

[23] Buzan associates the "civilizational" view with the work of Martin Wight, while Hedley Bull is seen as the exemplar of the "functional" view.

[24] Buzan, "From International System to International Society," pp. 342–43.

[25] Ibid., p. 334.

in fact constrain state actors, both states and their environments are shaped and reshaped through mutual interaction. Moreover, as the case studies have shown, states are not always simply along for the ride: they can adopt policies, either alone or in concert with others, aimed at changing the environment in which they operate. In other words, as Gary Goertz points out, states "are not passive vis-à-vis their environment as many structural arguments imply."[26] This is significant in terms of ethics because it raises the possibility that states may seek to overcome structural obstacles to cooperation and ethical action through the building of institutions. As the institutionalist literature argues, institutions can create more stable and predictable patterns of interaction, permit states to pool resources to increase the benefits of cooperation, safeguard against defection and free-riding, and so on. By changing the incentives facing state actors, institutions can, in effect, *change the content and meaning of the statesman's duty to his or her constituents, which in turn can alter the normative significance of the structural "fact" of international anarchy.* Again, this is not a matter of getting beyond egoism; it is instead a matter of redirecting the avenues by which egoistic interests are pursued. Of course, the ability of states to change their environment is far from unlimited, a fact that institutionalists, including constructivist institutionalists, know as well as anyone. Norms are not easy to manipulate, and the complexity of the international system creates dynamics that can frustrate the intentions of actors.[27] Moreover, enhancing cooperation through institution-building is never as simple as merely replacing realism "with a more communitarian and peaceful discourse," as John Mearsheimer characterizes the constructivist project.[28] Nevertheless, it is impossible to ignore the fact that states regularly devote considerable resources to the establishment of practices and institutions aimed at increasing cooperation and safeguarding their security and well-being without resort to conflict. Arms control regimes and the confidence-building measures that they often incorporate are but one type of example.

[26] Goertz, *Contexts of International Politics*, p. 11.

[27] On the difficulty involved in manipulating norms, see Chapter 2, supra; and Kier and Mercer, "Setting Precedents in Anarchy." On the way in which complex systems create unintended results that can defeat purposive action, see Robert Jervis, *System Effects: Complexity in Political and Social Life* (Princeton: Princeton University Press, 1997).

[28] John J. Mearsheimer, "A Realist Reply," *International Security* 20, no. 1 (Summer 1995): 90.

Moreover, the benefits of institutions often derive as much from intangible and ideational structures as from the more concrete rules and regulatory bodies that they establish. For example, in defending the proposed Chemical Weapons Convention, Kenneth Adelman, former director of the U.S. Arms Control and Disarmament Agency, argues that objections that the treaty would be unverifiable miss the point. The important benefit, Adelman writes, "lies in the norm."[29] He reasons:

> All of us support domestic laws against swindling and murder, though many bad guys in society don't acknowledge or abide by them. The laws, however, help punish those (probably few) found and proven to be swindlers and murderers. *Above this, such laws establish or re-enforce norms of civilized behavior.* . . . Parkinson's most astute law says that the success of any policy is measured by the catastrophes that do not occur.[30]

Adelman points to the Non-Proliferation Treaty as an example of an agreement that fundamentally changed the way acquisition of nuclear weapons was viewed in the international community. As a result, the spread of such weapons dramatically slowed—despite the fact that the treaty was "blatantly lacking universal coverage, real verification provisions or tough enforcement."[31] That Adelman, a self-described arms control skeptic, would extol the benefits of a treaty on the basis of its normative precedent illustrates the value that statesmen attach to ideas and institutions in helping to ameliorate the uncertainty of the international system. In fact, institutions play such a fundamental role in contemporary international politics that they are often simply taken for granted. Mearsheimer, for example, in support of his much-discussed contention that post–Cold War Europe is likely to experience a renewal of major conflict, predicts that "proliferation in Europe will undermine the legitimacy of the 1968 Nuclear Non-Proliferation Treaty, and this could open the floodgates of proliferation worldwide."[32] His references to the treaty's "legitimacy" and its importance in stemming the spread of

[29] Kenneth L. Adelman, "The Chemical Weapons Fight (Cont'd)," *Washington Post,* March 13, 1997, p. A23.

[30] Ibid. (emphasis added).

[31] Ibid.

[32] John J. Mearsheimer, "Why We Will Soon Miss the Cold War," in *Conflict After the Cold War: Arguments on the Causes of War and Peace,* ed. Richard K. Betts (Boston: Allyn and Bacon, 1994), p. 53.

nuclear weapons show that Mearsheimer implicitly accepts the very institutionalist logic that he dismisses elsewhere. That an avowed neorealist such as Mearsheimer slips so easily into the language of institutionalism underscores the fact that norms and institutions, far from being fanciful utopian aspirations, are real—and important—features of the international system.

BUT IS IT ETHICS?

The foregoing analysis of ethical norms from a constructivist viewpoint, and its implications for the debate over institutionalism in international politics, clearly speaks to major issues in both international relations theory and international ethics. An objection remains to be addressed, however. Specifically, it could be objected that, after being distorted by the process of "geopolitical construction" and watered-down by being tied to reciprocity and convention, the norms described bear so little resemblance to the moral principles on which they are originally based that they should not be considered ethical norms at all. Instead, the objection goes, they are simply another type of instrumental norm aimed at serving state interests, not deserving of any special prescriptive significance merely because they are ostensibly connected to moral principles.

The problem with this objection is that it reprises the rationalist error of viewing ethics as an all-or-nothing proposition. As argued in Chapter 1, this position lacks coherence and severely handicaps the study of international ethics. Rather than revisit that argument here, I will limit myself to a simple appeal to common usage. This objection asks that we hold states to a moral standard that in our everyday judgments we do not even apply to individuals. Reserving the designation of "ethics" for only those actions free of any trace of self-interest imposes an unrealistic and unduly demanding criterion of moral assessment that would make Machiavellians of us all. While morality may be pure in the abstract, in application it is a social phenomenon, and social phenomena are complex. Moreover, norms are never devoid of power. The mere presence of power, however, like the mere presence of interest, is neither morally good nor bad. Therefore, the fact that ethical norms are geopolitically constructed by the processes of international politics should be considered morally neutral in and of itself. There is an inherent contradiction, moreover, between the common realist objection that morality is a luxury of the strong in international relations and the assumption that power and morality are somehow incompatible. If morality truly is a luxury of the strong, this should serve not as a denial of morality but rather as an endorsement of the moral possibilities of power. If the strong alone can afford to act morally, it is not a prima facie bad thing that the strong are often disproportionately influential in setting the normative agenda for international society.[33]

There are three more specific responses to any objection that my approach to ethical norms takes too broad a view of ethics. First, as I have argued, the norms in question are at their core based upon moral principles, would not exist but for this basis, and continue to reflect these principles no matter how imperfect or even perverse their effects may be in application. The raison d'être of the norms in question is to promote restraint in various means of the taking of human life, and much evidence exists that they often succeed in doing so. One would be hard-pressed to argue that there is no ethical difference between these norms and more purely instrumental norms in international politics. Does the prohibition of international assassination, for example, bear no closer relationship to morality than international shipping regulations? Do norms protecting noncombatants in war have the same moral status as World Trade Organization tariff schedules? As Jeffrey Legro observes, part of the significance of norms restricting the use of force resides in the fact that, whether they are obeyed or not, they raise the question of ethics in warfare at all. By identifying certain means of warfare as being subject to restraint, such norms provide a brake in a realm of endeavor where the use of unrestricted force, in Legro's words, would otherwise be "automatic."[34]

A second, closely related, response is that these norms do in fact give rise to judgments about moral praise and blame. Violations of restrictions on certain types of force can lead to condemnation of the transgressor that is of a fundamentally different nature than that for disregarding more mundane rules. Grievances over alleged violations of rules regulating trade, communications, property rights, and so on are regularly aired and sometimes adjudicated with little fanfare. On the other hand, transgressions involving illegitimate uses of force—such as war crimes in the former Yugoslavia or the use of chemical weapons by

---

[33] Nor is it necessarily a good thing. Neither power nor proximity to the core of international society necessarily means that a state is any more likely to behave morally or possess more profound moral sensibilities than other states.

[34] Legro, "Which Norms Matter?" p. 16.

Iraq—are viewed far more seriously, being universally perceived as involving issues of a different order altogether.

Third, the importance of reciprocity in some norm compliance, although it leads to what I have described as morally anomalous results, does not vitiate the ethical content of the norm or its effects. This is true whether the reciprocity is of a specific "tit-for-tat" kind or a more generalized "diffuse" kind.[35] Although, as Robert Keohane points out, specific reciprocity may be morally neutral in and of itself,[36] it can have morally beneficial effects when it maintains patterns of restraint or cooperation that serve a moral good. Moreover, it can create or reinforce a more diffuse sense of reciprocity that can serve as the basis for a system of ethics, much as I have argued that it forms part of the basis for an international society. Although Keohane takes a step in this direction in *After Hegemony*, his conclusions regarding the ethical significance of reciprocity are heavily qualified. Nevertheless, reciprocity has been the subject of a great deal of attention in the field of moral philosophy.[37] A central theme of much of this work is that reciprocity is ethically significant in its own right, as it creates a disposition toward morally right actions. This is a subtle view that recognizes the complexity of moral judgment and, as my argument suggests, is well-suited to an examination of the moral content of international relations. This outlook also complements the constructivist understanding of both norms and interests as the products of the interplay between ethical impulses on one hand and rational self-interest and power on the other.

CONCLUSIONS

It is my hope that this study of ethical norms in international politics has impressed upon the reader three important points. The first is that norms are complex; that they are hard to grasp by reference to any one or two variables alone. Consequently, an understanding of the role of norms in the international system requires a much more nuanced view of power, causation, and structure than is commonly posited by theories

[35] See Robert O. Keohane, "Reciprocity in International Relations," *International Organization* 40 (Winter 1986): 1–27.

[36] Ibid.

[37] See, e.g., Robert E. Goodin, *Motivating Political Morality* (Cambridge, Mass.: Blackwell, 1992), especially chapter 2; Allen Buchanan, "Justice as Reciprocity versus Subject-Centered Justice," *Philosophy and Public Affairs* 19, no. 3 (Summer 1990): 227–52; Ruth Anna Putnam, "Reciprocity and Virtue Ethics," *Ethics* 98 (January 1988): 379–89; and Lawrence C. Becker, *Reciprocity* (London: Routledge & Kegan Paul, 1986).

of international relations. Norms reflect many different influences, including some that are historically contingent. Therefore it is not surprising that theories focusing on only one or two variables, or neglecting historical contingencies in a search for universal laws, fail to comprehend them fully.

Second, norms—and the entire normative context of international politics—are important. Although often dismissed by international relations theorists, norms can have a substantial impact on state behavior, as they not only provide incentives and disincentives to certain types of action but also help constitute the ideational background for all states in international society. As Quentin Skinner argues:

> The explanation of political behavior depends upon the study of political ideas and principles and cannot meaningfully be conducted without reference to them. . . . [T]he problem facing an agent who wishes to legitimate what he is doing at the same time as gaining what he wants cannot simply be the instrumental problem of tailoring his normative language in order to fit his projects. It must in part be the problem of tailoring his projects in order to fit the available normative language.[38]

Understanding norms therefore allows us to understand aspects of international politics that would otherwise remain anomalous. To this extent, the complexity of norms reflects the complexity of international politics itself.

Finally, I hope that this study has shown that keeping ideas about power and interest in the international system separate and distinct from ideas about ethics and norms detracts from the ability to understand *either one* very well. E. H. Carr, the intellectual godfather of twentieth-century realism, wrote, "It is an unreal kind of realism which ignores the element of morality in any world order."[39] This is a particularly important insight in the context of the post–Cold War international order, where new debates have sprung up over the proper direction for foreign policy and the proper place of ethics in foreign policy, and where concepts like "the national interest" and "humanitarianism" no longer seem as clear-cut as they might have in the past. What is needed is a perspective on norms, and international politics in general, that sees

[38] Quoted in N. J. Rengger, "Serpents and Doves in Classical International Theory," *Millennium* 17, no. 2 (1988): 219.
[39] Carr, *The Twenty Years' Crisis*, p. 235.

ethics and power not as foils but as integral parts of the same structure—sometimes clashing, sometimes reinforcing one another. Adopting such a perspective allows us to see that ethical considerations are not extraneous anomalies, or poorer brothers to interests, but aspects of the structure of international society in the same way that more traditional constraints are. We are, finally, reminded that what Reinhold Niebuhr wrote in the 1930s about the "uneasy compromises" forged in the political realm when "conscience and power meet" is not merely some kind of quaint reflection on the challenges of doing good in the modern world, but in fact a central truth in international politics, and one that the study of norms bears out very well.[40]

[40] Niebuhr, *Moral Man and Immoral Society*, p. 4.

Bibliography

Aiken, Henry D., ed. *Hume's Moral and Political Philosophy.* New York: Hafner Press, 1948.

Anderson, Chris A. "Assassination, Lawful Homicide, and the Butcher of Baghdad." *Hamline Journal of Public Law and Policy* 13 (Summer 1992): 291–321.

Arkin, William M. "Baghdad: The Urban Sanctuary in Desert Storm?" *Airpower Journal* 11, no. 1 (Spring 1997): 4–20.

Art, Robert J., and Kenneth N. Waltz. "Technology, Strategy, and the Uses of Force." In *The Use of Force: International Politics and Foreign Policy,* 2d ed., ed. Robert J. Art and Kenneth N. Waltz. Lanham, Md.: University Press of America, 1983.

Atkinson, Rick. *Crusade: The Untold Story of the Persian Gulf War.* New York: Houghton Mifflin, 1993.

Avant, Deborah D. "The New Institutional Economics and Norms of Warfare." Paper presented at the annual meeting of the International Studies Association, 1994.

Ayala, Balthazar. *De Jure et Officiis Bellicis et Disciplina Militari Libri III.* 1582. Reprinted in *The Classics of International Law,* trans. John P. Bate. Washington: Carnegie Institution of Washington, 1912.

Baldwin, David. "Neoliberalism, Neorealism, and World Politics." In *Neorealism and Neoliberalism: The Contemporary Debate,* ed. David Baldwin. New York: Columbia University Press, 1993.

Barnett, Michael N. "The United Nations and Global Security: The Norm Is Mightier than the Sword." *Ethics and International Affairs* 9 (1995): 37–54.

Baxter, Richard R. "So-Called 'Unprivileged Belligerency': Spies, Guerrillas, and Saboteurs." *British Yearbook of International Law* 28 (1951): 323–45.

Becker, Lawrence C. *Reciprocity.* London: Routledge and Kegan Paul, 1986.

Beitz, Charles. "Bounded Morality: Justice and the State in World Politics." *International Organization* 33, no. 3 (Summer 1979): 405–24.

Ben-Yehuda, Nachman. *Political Assassinations by Jews: A Rhetorical Device for Justice.* Albany: State University of New York Press, 1993.

Beres, Louis Rene. "Assassinating Saddam: A Post-War View from International Law." *Denver Journal of International Law and Policy* 19, no. 3 (1991): 613–23.

——. "On Assassination as Anticipatory Self-Defense: Is It Permissible?" *University of Detroit Mercy Law Review* 70, no. 13 (1992): 13–35.

——. "The Permissibility of State-Sponsored Assassination during Peace and War." *Temple International and Comparative Law Journal* 5 (1991): 231–49.

Bernstein, Barton J. "The Atomic Bombings Reconsidered." *Foreign Affairs* 74, no. 1 (Jan./Feb. 1995): 135–52.

Best, Geoffrey. *Humanity in Warfare.* New York: Columbia University Press, 1980.

Bialer, Uri. "Elite Opinion and Defence Policy: Air Power Advocacy and British Rearmament during the 1930s." *British Journal of International Studies* 6 (April 1980): 32–51.

——. *The Shadow of the Bomber: The Fear of Air Attack and British Politics, 1932–1939.* London: Royal Historical Society, 1980.

Biddle, Tami Davis. "Air Power." In *The Laws of War: Constraints on Warfare in the Western World,* ed. Michael Howard, George J. Andreopoulos, and Mark R. Shulman. New Haven: Yale University Press, 1994.

——. "British and American Approaches to Strategic Bombing: Their Origins and Implementation in the World War II Combined Bomber Offensive." In *Airpower: Theory and Practice,* ed. John Gooch. London: Frank Cass, 1995.

Blair, Clay. *The Forgotten War: America in Korea, 1950–1953.* New York: Times Books, 1987.

Bornstein, Joseph. *The Politics of Murder.* New York: William Sloane Associates, 1950.

Bowyer-Bell, J. "Assassination in International Politics: Lord Moyne, Count Bernadotte, and the Lehi." *International Studies Quarterly* 16, no. 1 (1972): 59–82.

Boyle, Francis A. "International Law and the Use of Force: Beyond Regime Theory." In *Ideas and Ideals: Essays on Politics in Honor of Stanley Hoffmann,* ed. Linda B. Miller and Michael J. Smith. Boulder: Westview Press, 1993.

Brandenburg, Bert. "The Legality of Assassination as an Aspect of Foreign Policy." *Virginia Journal of International Law* 27, no. 3 (1987): 655–97.

Breckenridge, Scott D. *The CIA and the U.S. Intelligence System.* Boulder: Westview Press, 1986.

Brown, Chris. *International Relations Theory: New Normative Approaches.* New York: Columbia University Press, 1992.

Brown, Horatio F. *Studies in the History of Venice.* New York: E. P. Dutton, 1907.

Buchanan, Allen. "Justice as Reciprocity versus Subject-Centered Justice." *Philosophy and Public Affairs* 19, no. 3 (Summer 1990): 227–52.

Bibliography

Bull, Hedley. *The Anarchical Society.* New York: Columbia University Press, 1977.

Bull, Hedley, and Adam Watson, eds. *The Expansion of International Society.* Oxford: Clarendon Press, 1984.

Bush, George. *Public Papers of the Presidents of the United States: George Bush, 1991,* vol. 1. Washington, D.C. Government Printing Office, 1992.

Butterfield, Herbert, and Martin Wight, eds. *Diplomatic Investigations.* London: Allen and Unwin, 1966.

Buzan, Barry. "From International System to International Society: Structural Realism and Regime Theory Meet the English School." *International Organization* 47, no. 3 (Summer 1993): 327–52.

Byman, Daniel L., and Matthew C. Waxman. "Kosovo and the Great Air Power Debate." *International Security* 24, no. 4 (Spring 2000): 5–38.

Bynkershoek, Cornelius van. *Quaestionum Juris Publici Libri Duo.* 1737. Reprinted in *The Classics of International Law,* trans. Tenney Frank. Oxford: Clarendon Press, 1930.

Calhoun, Frederick S. *Power and Principle: Armed Intervention in Wilsonian Foreign Policy.* Kent, Ohio: Kent State University Press, 1993.

Carr, E. H. *The Twenty Years' Crisis, 1919–1939.* New York: Harper and Row, 1964.

Chase, Eric L. "Should We Kill Saddam?" *Newsweek,* February 18, 1991, pp. 16–17.

Churchill, Winston S. *Closing the Ring.* Cambridge: Houghton Mifflin, 1951.

——. *Triumph and Tragedy.* Cambridge: Houghton Mifflin, 1953.

Clinton, W. David. "The National Interest: Normative Foundations." *Review of Politics* 48, no. 4 (1986): 495–519.

Clodfelter, Mark. *The Limits of Air Power: The American Bombing of North Vietnam.* New York: Free Press, 1989.

——. "Pinpointing Devastation: American Air Campaign Planning before Pearl Harbor." *Journal of Military History* 58 (Jan. 1994): 75–101.

Cohen, Eliot A. "The Meaning and Future of Air Power." *Orbis* 39, no. 2 (Spring 1995): 189–200.

——. "The Mystique of U.S. Air Power." *Foreign Affairs* 73, no. 1 (Jan./Feb. 1994): 109–24.

Cohen, Sheldon M. *Arms and Judgment: Law, Morality, and the Conduct of War in the Twentieth Century.* Boulder: Westview Press, 1989.

Cordesman, Anthony H. *The Lessons and Non-Lessons of the Air and Missile Campaign in Kosovo.* Washington, D.C.: Center for Strategic and International Studies, 1999.

Cox, Robert W. "Social Forces, States, and World Orders: Beyond International Relations Theory." In *Neorealism and Its Critics,* ed. Robert O. Keohane. New York: Columbia University Press, 1986.

Crane, Conrad C. *American Airpower Strategy in Korea, 1950–1953.* Lawrence: University Press of Kansas, 2000.

——. "Evolution of U.S. Strategic Bombing of Urban Areas" *The Historian* 50 (November 1987): 14–39.

Crotty, William, ed., *Assassinations and the Political Order.* New York: Harper and Row, 1971.

Delos, J. T. "The Sociology of Modern War and the Theory of Just War." *Crosscurrents* 8 (1958): 248–66.

De Saussure, Hamilton. "The Laws of Air Warfare: Are There Any?" *Naval War College Review* 23 (Feb. 1971): 35–47.

Dessler, David. "What's at Stake in the Agent-Structure Debate?" *International Organization* 43 (Summer 1989): 441–73.

Donnolly, Jack. "Twentieth-Century Realism." In *Traditions of International Ethics,* ed. Terry Nardin and David R. Mapel. Cambridge: Cambridge University Press, 1992.

Douhet, Giulio. *The Command of the Air.* Trans. Dino Ferrari. New York: Coward-McCann, 1942.

Downing, Brian M. "Constitutionalism, Warfare, and Political Change in Early Modern Europe." *Theory and Society* 17, no. 1 (January 1988): 7–56.

Dzhirkvelov, Ilya. *Secret Servant: My Life with the KGB and the Soviet Elite.* New York: Harper and Row, 1987.

Evans, Tony, and Peter Wilson. "Regime Theory and the English School of International Relations: A Comparison." *Millennium* 21, no. 3 (1992): 329–52.

Finnemore, Martha. *National Interests in International Society.* Ithaca: Cornell University Press, 1996.

Finnemore, Martha, and Kathryn Sikkink, "International Norm Dynamics and Political Change." *International Organization* 52, no. 4 (Autumn 1998): 887–917.

Fitzgerald, Frances. *Fire in the Lake: The Vietnamese and the Americans in Vietnam.* New York: Vintage Books, 1972.

Ford, Franklin L. *Political Murder: From Tyrannicide to Terrorism.* Cambridge: Harvard University Press, 1985.

Forsberg, Kenneth. "Normative Principles and State Interests: Constructivism Illustrated." Paper presented at the meeting of the Northeast Political Science Association, Newark, N.J., November 3–5, 1995.

Fussell, Paul. "An Exchange of Views." In Paul Fussell, *Thank God for the Atom Bomb and Other Essays.* New York: Summit Books, 1988.

——. "Thank God for the Atom Bomb." In Paul Fussell, *Thank God for the Atom Bomb and Other Essays.* New York: Summit Books, 1988.

Futrell, Robert F. *The United States Air Force in Korea, 1950–1953.* Rev. ed. Washington, D.C. Government Printing Office, 1983.

Bibliography

Garrett, Jane. *The Triumphs of Providence: The Assassination Plot, 1696.* Cambridge: Cambridge University Press, 1980.

Garrett, Stephen A. *Conscience and Power: An Examination of Dirty Hands and Political Leadership.* New York: St. Martin's Press, 1996.

Gates, Robert M. *From the Shadows: The Ultimate Insider's Story of Five Presidents and How They Won the Cold War.* New York: Simon and Schuster, 1996.

Gentili, Alberico. *De Iure Belli Libri Tres.* 1612. Reprinted in *The Classics of International Law*, trans. John C. Rolfe. Oxford: Clarendon Press, 1933.

Gilderhus, Mark T. *Diplomacy and Revolution: U.S.–Mexican Relations under Wilson and Carranza.* Tucson: University of Arizona Press, 1977.

Goertz, Gary. *Contexts of International Politics.* Cambridge: Cambridge University Press, 1994.

Goertz, Gary, and Paul Diehl. "Toward a Theory of International Norms." *Journal of Conflict Resolution* 36 (1992): 634–66.

Goldstein, Judith, and Robert O. Keohane, "Ideas and Foreign Policy: A Framework for Analysis." In *Ideas and Foreign Policy*, ed. Judith Goldstein and Robert O. Keohane. Ithaca: Cornell University Press, 1993.

———, eds. *Ideas and Foreign Policy.* Ithaca: Cornell University Press, 1993.

Goodin, Robert E. *Motivating Political Morality.* Cambridge, Mass.: Blackwell, 1992.

Gordon, Michael R., and General Bernard E. Trainor. *The Generals' War: The Inside Story of the Conflict in the Gulf.* New York: Little, Brown, 1995.

Green, Donald P., and Ian Shapiro. *Pathologies of Rational Choice Theory: A Critique of Applications in Political Science.* New Haven: Yale University Press, 1994.

Greer, Thomas H. *The Development of Air Doctrine in the Army Air Arm, 1917–1941.* Washington, D.C.: Office of Air Force History, 1985.

Grieco, Joseph M. "Anarchy and the Limits of Cooperation: A Realist Critique of the Newest Liberal Institutionalism." In *Neorealism and Neoliberalism: The Contemporary Debate*, ed. David Baldwin. New York: Columbia University Press, 1993.

Griffith, Thomas E., Jr. "Strategic Air Attacks on Electrical Power: Balancing Political Consequences and Military Action." *Strategic Review* (Fall 1995): 38–46.

Grotius, Hugo. *De Jure Belli ac Pacis Libri Tres.* 1625. Reprinted in *The Classics of International Law*, trans. Francis W. Kelsey. Oxford: Clarendon Press, 1925.

Gulf War Air Power Survey. *Volume I: Planning.* Washington, D.C.: Government Printing Office, 1993.

———. *Volume II: Operations.* Washington, D.C.: Government Printing Office, 1993.

Haines, Herbert. "History and Assassination." In *Transactions of the Royal Historical Society*, 285–302. London: Royal Historical Society, 1889.

Hampson, Françoise J. "Means and Methods of Warfare in the Conflict in the Gulf." In *The Gulf War 1990–91 in International and English Law,* ed. Peter Rowe. New York: Routledge, 1993.

Hartigan, Kevin. "Matching Humanitarian Norms with Cold, Hard Interests: The Making of Refugee Policies in Mexico and Honduras, 1980–1989." *International Organization* 46, no. 3 (Summer 1992): 709–30.

Hastings, Max. *Bomber Command.* New York: Dial Press, 1979.

——. *The Korean War.* New York: Touchstone, 1987.

Heaps, Willard A. *Assassination: A Special Kind of Murder.* New York: Meredith Press, 1969.

Heidenrich, John G. "The Gulf War: How Many Iraqis Died?" *Foreign Policy* 90 (Spring 1993): 108–25.

Heimsath, C. H. "Indo-American Relations: Effects of the Korean Conflict." *Journal of International Affairs* 6 (Spring 1952): 151–62.

Henkin, Louis. *How Nations Behave.* New York: Council on Foreign Relations, 1979.

Hersh, Seymour M. "Target Qaddafi." *New York Times Magazine,* February 22, 1987.

Herz, Martin F., and Leslie Rider. *Prestige Press and the Christmas Bombing, 1972: Images and Reality in Vietnam.* Washington: Ethics and Public Policy Center, 1980.

Hoffmann, Stanley. *Duties Beyond Borders.* Syracuse: Syracuse University Press, 1981.

Hopkins, George E. "Bombing and the American Conscience during World War II." *The Historian* 28, no. 3 (1966): 451–73.

Howard, Michael. "Temperamenta Belli: Can War Be Controlled?" In *Restraints on War: Studies in the Limitation of Armed Conflict,* ed. Michael Howard. Oxford: Oxford University Press, 1979.

Howard, Michael, George J. Andreopoulos, and Mark R. Shulman, eds., *The Laws of War: Constraints on Warfare in the Western World.* New Haven: Yale University Press, 1994.

Hull, William I. *The Two Hague Conferences.* Boston: Atheneum Press, 1908.

Human Rights Watch. *Civilian Deaths in the NATO Air Campaign,* www.hrw.org/reports/2000/nato

——. *"No Happiness Remains": Civilian Killings, Pillage, and Rape in Alkhan-Yurt, Chechnya.* www.hrw.org/reports/2000/russia_chechnya2/

——. *World Report 1999,* www.hrw.org/hrw/worldreport99/africa/sudan.html

Hurrell, Andrew. "International Society and the Study of Regimes: A Reflective Approach." In *Regime Theory and International Relations,* ed. Volker Rittberger. Oxford: Oxford University Press, 1993.

Isby, David C. *War in a Distant Country: Afghanistan: Invasion and Resistance.* London: Arms and Armour Press, 1989.

Jackson, Robert H. "Martin Wight, International Theory, and the Good Life." *Millennium* 19 (Summer 1990): 261–72.

Jepperson, Ron, Alexander Wendt, and Peter Katzenstein. "Norms, Identity, and Culture in National Security." In *The Culture of National Security: Norms and Identity in World Politics*, ed. Peter J. Katzenstein. New York: Columbia University Press, 1996.

Jervis, Robert. *System Effects: Complexity in Political and Social Life*. Princeton: Princeton University Press, 1997.

Johnson, Boyd M., III. "Executive Order 12,333: The Permissibility of an American Assassination of a Foreign Leader." *Cornell International Law Journal* 25 (1992): 401–35.

Johnson, James Turner. *Just War Tradition and the Restraint of War*. Princeton: Princeton University Press, 1981.

Karnow, Stanley. *Vietnam: A History*. Rev. ed. New York: Viking Penguin, 1991.

Katzenstein, Peter J. "Introduction: Alternative Perspectives on National Security." In *The Culture of National Security: Norms and Identity in World Politics*, ed. Peter J. Katzenstein. New York: Columbia University Press, 1996.

Kaysen, Carl. "The Ultimate Bombing." *Technology Review* 98, no. 6 (Aug./Sept. 1995): 66–67.

Keegan, John. *A History of Warfare*. London: Hutchinson, 1993.

Keeva, Steven. "Lawyers in the War Room." *ABA Journal* 77 (December 1991): 52–59.

Kegley, Charles, Jr. "The Neoidealist Moment in International Studies?: Realist Myths and the New International Realities." *International Studies Quarterly* 37 (June 1993): 131–46.

Kelly, Joseph B. "Comments: Assassination in War Time." *Military Law Review* 30 (October 1965): 101–11.

Kennan, George F. "Morality and Foreign Policy." *Foreign Affairs* 64 (Winter 1985/1986): 205–18.

Kennett, Lee. *A History of Strategic Bombing*. New York: Charles Scribner's Sons, 1982.

Keohane, Robert O. *After Hegemony: Cooperation and Discord in the World Political Economy*. Princeton: Princeton University Press, 1984.

———. "Reciprocity in International Relations." *International Organization* 40 (Winter 1986): 1–27.

———. "International Institutions: Two Approaches." *International Studies Quarterly* 32, no. 4 (December 1988): 379–96.

———. *International Institutions and State Power*. Boulder: Westview Press, 1989.

Khong, Yuen Foong. "Structural Constraints and Decision-Making: The Case of Britain in the 1930s." In *Ideas and Ideals: Essays on Politics in Honor of Stanley Hoffman*, ed. Linda B. Miller and Michael J. Smith. Boulder: Westview Press, 1993.

Kier, Elizabeth, and Jonathan Mercer. "Setting Precedents in Anarchy: Military Intervention and Weapons of Mass Destruction." *International Security* (Spring 1996): 77–106.

Kirgis, Frederic L., "Russian Use of Force in Grozny." *ASIL Insight*, December 1999. www.asil.org/insigh39.htm

Klotz, Audie. *Norms in International Relations: The Struggle against Apartheid.* Ithaca: Cornell University Press, 1995.

Knightley, Phillip. *The Second Oldest Profession: Spies and Spying in the Twentieth Century.* New York: W. W. Norton, 1987.

Knott, Stephen F. *Secret and Sanctioned: Covert Operations and the American Presidency.* New York: Oxford University Press, 1996.

Kowert, Paul, and Jeffrey W. Legro. "Norms, Identities, and their Limits: A Theoretical Reprise." In *The Culture of National Security: Norms and Identity in World Politics,* ed. Peter J. Katzenstein. New York: Columbia University Press, 1996.

Krasner, Stephen D. "Structural Causes and Regime Consequences: Regimes as Intervening Variables." In *International Regimes,* ed. Stephen D. Krasner. Boston: M.I.T. Press, 1983.

——. "Westphalia and All That." In *Ideas and Foreign Policy: Beliefs, Institutions, and Political Change,* ed. Judith Goldstein and Robert O. Keohane. Ithaca: Cornell University Press, 1993.

Kratochwil, Friedrich, and John G. Ruggie. "International Organization: The State of the Art on the Art of the State." *International Organization* 40, no. 4 (1986): 753–75.

Kuehl, Daniel T. "Air Power vs. Electricity: Electric Power as a Target for Strategic Air Operations." In *Airpower: Theory and Practice,* ed. John Gooch. London: Frank Cass, 1995.

Lambeth, Benjamin S. "Russia's Air War in Chechnya." *Studies in Conflict and Terrorism* 19 (1996): 365–88.

Lauber, Jeri, and Barnett R. Rubin. *"A Nation Is Dying": Afghanistan under the Soviets, 1979–87.* Evanston, Ill: Northwestern University Press, 1988.

Lawrence, Thomas J. *The Principles of International Law.* 7th ed. Boston: D. C. Heath and Company, 1923.

Legro, Jeffrey W. *Cooperation under Fire: Anglo-German Restraint during World War II.* Ithaca: Cornell University Press, 1995.

——. "Which Norms Matter? Revisiting the 'Failure' of Internationalism in World War II." Paper presented at the annual conference of the American Political Science Association, Chicago, August 31–September 3, 1995.

Leiden, Carl. "Supplement F: Assassination in the Middle East." In James F. Kirkham, Sheldon G. Levy, and William J. Crotty, *Assassination and Political Violence: A Report to the National Commission on the Causes and Prevention of Violence,* Washington, D.C.: Government Printing Office, 1969.

Bibliography

Lewy, Guenter. *America in Vietnam.* Oxford: Oxford University Press, 1978.

Linklater, Andrew. "The Problem of Community in International Relations." *Alternatives* 15 (Spring 1990): 135–53.

Lipson, Charles. "International Cooperation in Economic and Security Affairs." *World Politics* 37 (October 1984): 1–23.

Lipson, Michael. "Nonlinearity, Constructivism, and International Relations; or, Changing the Rules by Playing the Game." Paper presented at the annual conference of the American Political Science Association, Chicago, August 31–September 3, 1995.

Lopez, George A. "The Gulf War: Not So Clean." *Bulletin of the Atomic Scientists* (September 1991): 30–35.

Lumsdaine, David H. *Moral Vision in International Politics: The Foreign Aid Regime, 1949–1989.* Princeton: Princeton University Press, 1993.

MacIsaac, David. "Voices from the Central Blue: Theorists of Air Power." In *Makers of Modern Strategy,* ed. Peter Paret. Princeton: Princeton University Press, 1986.

Manning, C. A. W. *The Nature of International Society.* London: Macmillan and the London School of Economics, 1975.

March, James G., and Johan P. Olsen. *Rediscovering Institutions: The Organizational Basis of Politics.* New York: Free Press, 1989.

Marshall, Alan. *Intelligence and Espionage in the Reign of Charles II, 1660–1685.* Cambridge: Cambridge University Press, 1994.

Mavrodes, George. "Conventions and the Morality of War." *Philosophy and Public Affairs* 4 (Winter 1975): 117–31.

McDougal, Myres S., and Florentino P. Feliciano. *The International Law of War: Transnational Coercion and World Public Order.* New Haven: New Haven Press, 1962.

McElroy, Robert W. *Morality and American Foreign Policy: The Role of Ethics in International Affairs.* Princeton: Princeton University Press, 1992.

Mearsheimer, John J. "The False Promise of International Institutions." *International Security* 19, no. 3 (Winter 1995): 5–49.

——. "A Realist Reply." *International Security* 20, no. 1 (Summer 1995): 82–93.

——. "Why We Will Soon Miss the Cold War." In *Conflict after the Cold War: Arguments on Causes of War and Peace,* ed. Richard K. Betts. Boston: Allyn and Bacon, 1994.

Meilinger, Phillip S. "Winged Defense: Airwar, the Law, and Morality." *Armed Forces and Society* 20, no. 1 (Fall 1993): 103–23.

Melman, Yossi. "Why the Plot to Kill Hussein Failed." *Los Angeles Times,* July 21, 1991, pp. M1–2.

Meron, Theodor. *Henry's Wars and Shakespeare's Laws: Perspectives on the Law of War in the Later Middle Ages.* Oxford: Clarendon Press, 1993.

Messerschmidt, Manfred. "Strategic Air War and International Law." In *The*

Conduct of the Air War in the Second World War: An International Comparison, ed. Horst Boog. New York: St. Martin's Press, 1992.

Middle East Watch. *Needless Deaths in the Gulf War: Civilian Casualties during the Air Campaign and Violations of the Laws of War.* Washington, D.C.: Human Rights Watch, 1991.

Morgenthau, Hans J. *Politics among Nations.* 1948. New York: McGraw-Hill, 1967.

Mueller, John E. *Policy and Opinion in the Gulf War.* Chicago: University of Chicago Press, 1994.

———. *Retreat from Doomsday: The Obsolescence of Major War.* New York: Basic Books, 1990.

Murray, Williamson. "British and German Air Doctrine between the Wars." *Air University Review* 31 (March/April 1980): 39–58.

———. "The Influence of Pre-War Anglo-American Doctrine on the Air Campaigns of the Second World War." In *The Conduct of the Air War in the Second World War: An International Comparison,* ed. Horst Boog. New York: St. Martin's Press, 1992.

Myers, Robert J. "The Virtue of Moral Restraint." *International Journal* 43 (Spring 1988): 320–35.

Nadelmann, Ethan. "Global Prohibition Regimes: The Evolution of Norms in International Society." *International Organization* 44, no. 4 (Autumn 1990): 479–526.

Nardin, Terry. "The Moral Basis of the Law of War." *Journal of International Affairs* 37 (Winter 1984): 295–309.

Newman, David, and Tyll Van Geel. "Executive Order 12,333: The Risks of a Clear Declaration of Intent." *Harvard Journal of Law and Public Policy* 12, no. 2 (Spring 1989): 433–47.

Newman, David, and Bruce Bueno de Mesquita. "Repeal Order 12333, Legalize 007." *New York Times,* January 26, 1989, p. A23.

Niebuhr, Reinhold. *Moral Man and Immoral Society: A Study in Ethics and Politics.* New York: Charles Scribner's Sons, 1932.

Nolan, Cathal J. *Principled Diplomacy: Security and Rights in U.S. Foreign Policy.* Westport, Conn.: Greenwood Press, 1993.

O'Brien, William V. "The Meaning of 'Military Necessity' in International Law." *World Polity* 1 (1957): 109–76.

Overy, Richard. *The Air War, 1939–1945.* New York: Stein and Day, 1980.

———. *Why the Allies Won.* London: Jonathan Cape, 1995.

Pape, Robert A. *Bombing to Win: Air Power and Coercion in War.* Ithaca: Cornell University Press, 1996.

Parker, Geoffrey. "Early Modern Europe." In *The Laws of War: Constraints on Warfare in the Western World,* ed. Howard, Andreopoulos, and Shulman. New Haven: Yale University Press, 1994.

———. *The Grand Strategy of Philip II.* New Haven: Yale University Press, 1998.

Parks, W. Hays. "Conventional Aerial Bombing and the Law of War." *Proceedings of the U.S. Naval Institute* 108, no. 5 (May 1982): 98–117.

———. "Linebacker and the Law of War." *Air University Review* 34, no. 2 (Jan./Feb. 1983): 2–30.

———. "Memorandum of Law: Executive Order 12333 and Assassination." *The Army Lawyer* (December 1989): 4–9.

———. "Rolling Thunder and the Law of War." *Air University Review* 33, no. 2 (Jan./Feb. 1982): 2–21.

Paskins, Barrie, and Michael Dockrill. *The Ethics of War.* Minneapolis: University of Minnesota Press, 1979.

Peters, Ralph. "A Revolution in Military Ethics?" *Parameters* 26, no. 2 (Summer 1996): 102–8.

Pierce, Albert C. "Just War Principles and Economic Sanctions." *Ethics and International Affairs* 10 (1996): 99–113.

Posen, Barry R. "The War for Kosovo: Serbia's Political-Military Strategy." *International Security* 24, no. 4 (Spring 2000): 39–84.

Price, Richard. *The Chemical Weapons Taboo.* Ithaca: Cornell University Press, 1997.

———. "A Genealogy of the Chemical Weapons Taboo." *International Organization* 49, no. 1 (Winter 1995): 73–103.

Price, Richard, and Nina Tannenwald. "Norms and Deterrence: The Nuclear and Chemical Weapons Taboos." In *The Culture of National Security: Norms, Identities, and World Politics,* ed. Peter J. Katzenstein. New York: Columbia University Press, 1996.

The Proceedings of the Hague Peace Conferences: The Conference of 1907. Vol. 3. New York: Oxford University Press, 1920.

Putnam, Ruth Anna. "Reciprocity and Virtue Ethics." *Ethics* 98 (January 1988): 379–89.

Quester, George. "Strategic Bombing in the 1930s and 1940s." In *The Use of Force: International Politics and Foreign Policy,* ed. Robert Art and Kenneth Waltz. 2d ed. Lanham, Md.: University Press of America, 1983.

Rapoport, David C. *Assassination and Terrorism.* Toronto: Canadian Broadcasting Corp., 1971.

Reisman, W. Michael, and Chris T. Antoniou, eds. *The Laws of War: A Comprehensive Collection of Primary Documents on International Laws Governing Armed Conflict.* New York: Vintage Books, 1994.

Rengger, N. J. "Serpents and Doves in Classical International Theory." *Millennium* 17, no. 2 (1988): 215–25.

Roberts, Adam. "The Laws of War in the 1990–91 Gulf Conflict." *International Security* 18, no. 3 (Winter 1994): 134–81.

Ross, Bruce. "The Case for Targeting Leadership in War." *Naval War College Review* 46, no. 1 (Winter 1993).

Rothenberg, Gunther. "Maurice of Nassau, Gustavus Adolphus, Raimondo

Montecuccoli, and the 'Military Revolution' of the Seventeenth Century." In *Makers of Modern Strategy*, ed. Peter Paret. Princeton: Princeton University Press, 1986.

Rousseau, Jean-Jacques. *On The Social Contract.* Ed. Roger D. Masters. Trans. Judith R. Masters. New York: St. Martin's Press, 1978.

Royse, M. W. *Aerial Bombardment and the International Regulation of Warfare.* New York: Vinal, 1928.

Ruggie, John Gerard. "Continuity and Transformation in the World Polity: Toward a Neorealist Synthesis." In *Neorealism and Its Critics*, ed. Robert Keohane. New York: Columbia University Press, 1986.

Sanders, David. "International Relations: Neo-realism and Neo-liberalism." In *A New Handbook of Political Science*, ed. Robert E. Goodin and Hans-Dieter Klingemann. New York: Oxford University Press, 1996.

Sapolsky, Harvey M., and Jeremy Shapiro. "Casualties, Technology, and America's Future Wars." *Parameters* 26, no. 2 (Summer 1996): 119–27.

Schmitt, Michael N. "State-Sponsored Assassination in International and Domestic Law." *Yale Journal of International Law* 17 (1992): 609–85.

Schnabel, James F., and Robert J. Watson, *The History of the Joint Chiefs of Staff, Vol. 3: The Korean War.* Wilmington, Del.: Michael Glazer, 1979.

Schwartz, Stephen. "Intellectuals and Assassins—Annals of Stalin's Killerati." *New York Times Book Review,* January 24, 1988.

Scott, James B. *The Hague Peace Conferences: American Instructions and Reports.* New York: Oxford University Press, 1916.

Select Senate Committee to Study Governmental Operations with Respect to Intelligence Activities. *Alleged Assassination Plots Involving Foreign Leaders.* Washington, D.C.: Government Printing Office, 1975.

Sherman, William T. *Memoirs of General William T. Sherman,* Volume 2. New York: D. Appleton, 1875.

Sherry, Michael S. *The Rise of American Air Power: The Creation of Armageddon.* New Haven: Yale University Press, 1987.

Sifakis, Carl. *Encyclopedia of Assassinations.* New York: Facts on File, 1991.

Smith, Malcolm. *British Air Strategy between the Wars.* Oxford: Clarendon Press, 1984.

Smith, Michael J. *Realist Thought from Weber to Kissinger.* Baton Rouge: Louisiana State University Press, 1986.

Smith, Steve. "The Forty Years' Detour: The Resurgence of Normative Theory in International Relations." *Millennium* 21, no. 3 (1992): 489–506.

Sofaer, Abraham D. "Thinking Past the Moment." *U.S. News and World Report,* February 18, 1991, p. 28.

Spaight, J. M. *Aircraft in War.* London: Macmillan, 1914.

——. "The Chaotic State of the International Law Governing Bombardment." *Royal Air Force Quarterly* 9, no. 1 (January 1938): 24–32.

——. *War Rights on Land.* London: Macmillan, 1911.

Bibliography

Stephanopoulos, George. "Why We Should Kill Saddam." *Newsweek*, December 1, 1997, p. 34.

Stowell, Ellery C. "Comment: Military Reprisals and the Sanctions of the Laws of War." *American Journal of International Law* 36 (1942): 643–50.

Taylor, Philip M. *War and the Media: Propaganda and Persuasion in the Gulf War.* New York: Manchester University Press, 1992.

Taylor, Telford. "Just and Unjust Wars." In *War, Morality, and the Military Profession,* ed. Malham Wakin. Boulder: Westview Press, 1979.

Thomson, Janice A. "Norms in International Relations: A Conceptual Analysis." *International Journal of Group Tensions* 23 (1993): 67–83.

Tilly, Charles. "Reflections on the History of European State-Making." In *The Formation of National States in Western Europe,* ed. Charles Tilly. Princeton: Princeton University Press, 1975.

Tirpak, John A. "The NATO Way of War." *Air Force Magazine* 82, no. 12 (December 1999). www.afa.org/magazine/watch/1299watch.html

———. "Short's View of the Air Campaign." *Air Force Magazine* 82, no. 9 (September 1999), www.afa.org/magazine/watch/0999watch.html

Tocqueville, Alexis de. *Democracy in America.* New York: Vintage Classics, 1990.

Toulmin, Stephen. *Cosmopolis: The Hidden Agenda of Modernity.* New York: Free Press, 1990.

Turner, Robert F. "Deterring Humanitarian Law Violations: Strengthening Enforcement." Paper presented at the Center for Law and National Security, Charlottesville, Virginia, November 4–5, 1994.

———. "Killing Saddam: Would It Be a Crime?" *Washington Post*, October 7, 1990, pp. D1–2.

U.S. Department of Defense. *Conduct of the Persian Gulf War: Final Report to Congress.* Washington, D.C.: Office of the Secretary of Defense, 1992.

———. *Report to Congress: Kosovo/Operation Allied Force After-Action Report.* Washington, D.C.: Office of the Secretary of Defense, 2000.

van Creveld, Martin L. "The Persian Gulf Crisis of 1990–91 and the Future of Morally Constrained War." *Parameters* 22, no. 2 (Summer 1992): 21–40.

———. *Supplying War: Logistics from Wallenstein to Patton.* Cambridge: Cambridge University Press, 1979.

———. *The Transformation of War.* New York: Free Press, 1991.

Vattel, Emmerich de. *Le droit des gens: ou, Principes de la loi naturelle, appliques a la conduite et aux affaires des nations et des souverains.* 1758. Reprinted in *The Classics of International Law,* trans. Charles G. Fenwick. Washington, D.C.: Carnegie Institution of Washington, 1916.

Verrier, Anthony. *Assassination in Algiers: Churchill, Roosevelt, de Gaulle, and the Murder of Admiral Darlan.* New York: W. W. Norton, 1990.

Vitoria, Francisco de. *De Jure Belli.* 1532. Reprinted in *The Classics of Interna-*

tional Law, trans. John P. Bate, Washington, D.C.: Carnegie Institution of Washington, 1917.

Waltz, Kenneth. *Theory of International Politics.* Reading, Mass.: Addison-Wesley Publishing Company, 1979.

Walzer, Michael. *Just and Unjust Wars.* Rev. ed. New York: Basic Books, 1992.

Wasserstrom, Richard. "On the Morality of War." In *War, Morality, and the Military Profession,* ed. Malham Wakin. Boulder: Westview Press, 1979.

Watson, Adam. *The Evolution of International Society.* London: Routledge and Kegan Paul, 1992.

Watt, D. C. "Restraints on War in the Air before 1945." In *Restraints on War: Studies in the Limitation of Armed Conflict,* ed. Michael Howard. New York: Oxford University Press, 1979.

Webster, Charles, and Noble Frankland, *The Strategic Air Offensive against Germany, 1939–1944.* Vol. 4. London: Her Majesty's Stationery Office, 1961.

Welch, David A. *Justice and the Genesis of War.* Cambridge: Cambridge University Press, 1993.

Wendt, Alexander. "The Agent-Structure Problem in International Relations Theory." *International Organization* 41, no. 3 (Summer 1987): 335–70.

———. "Anarchy Is What States Make of It: The Social Construction of Power Politics." *International Organization* 46, no. 2 (Spring 1992): 391–425.

———. "Collective Identity Formation and the International State." *American Political Science Review* 88, no. 2 (June 1994): 384–96.

———. "Constructing International Politics." *International Security* 20, no. 1 (Summer 1995): 71–81.

Werrell, Kenneth P. "Air War Victorious: The Gulf War vs. Vietnam." *Parameters* 22, no. 2 (Summer 1992): 41–54.

Wight, Martin. *Systems of States.* Leicester: Leicester University Press, 1977.

———. "Western Values in International Relations." In *Diplomatic Investigations,* ed. Herbert Butterfield and Martin Wight. London: Allen and Unwin, 1966.

———. "Why Is There No International Theory?" In *Diplomatic Investigations,* ed. Herbert Butterfield and Martin Wight. London: Allen and Unwin, 1966.

Willenz, Eric. *German Press Reaction to the Air War in Korea.* Santa Monica: RAND Corp., 1951.

Williams, Paul W. "Legitimate Targets in Aerial Bombardment." *American Journal of International Law* 23, no. 3 (July 1929): 570–81.

Woodward, Bob. *The Commanders* New York: Simon and Schuster, 1991.

Wolfers, Arnold. *Discord and Collaboration: Essays on International Politics.* Baltimore: Johns Hopkins University Press, 1962.

Bibliography

Wright, Peter. *Spycatcher: The Candid Autobiography of a Senior Intelligence Officer.* New York: Viking, 1987.

Wyman, Richard H. "The First Rules of Air Warfare." *Air Force Review* 35, no. 3 (March/April 1984): 94–102.

Zengel, Patricia. "Assassination and the Law of Armed Conflict." *Mercer Law Review* 43 (1991): 615–44.

Zouche, Richard. *Iuris et Iudicii Fecialis, sive, Iuris Inter Gentes, et Quaestionnum de Eodem Explicatio.* 1650. Reprinted in *The Classics of International Law,* trans. J. L. Brierly. Washington: Carnegie Institution of Washington, D.C., 1911.

Index

Cornell Studies in Security Affairs

A SERIES EDITED BY

ROBERT J. ART
ROBERT JERVIS
STEPHEN M. WALT